TO BEIJING AND BEYOND

TO BEIJING AND BEYOND

Pittsburgh and the United Nations

Fourth World Conference on Women

Edited by Janice Auth

UNIVERSITY OF PITTSBURGH PRESS

Published by the University of Pittsburgh Press, Pittsburgh, Pa. 15261

Copyright © 1998, University of Pittsburgh Press

Manufactured in the United States of America

Printed on acid-free paper

10   9   8   7   6   5   4   3   2   1

Joan Chittister's essay in part 7 is from Joan Chittister, "Fourth UN Conference on Women, Part II," in *Beyond Beijing* (Kansas City, Mo.: Sheed &
Ward, 1996), pp. 165–69. Reprinted with the permission of Sheed & Ward,
115 E. Armour Blvd., Kansas City, MO 64111. To order call: 1-800-333-7373.
Reprinted with the permission of Sheed and Ward.

Library of Congress Cataloging-in-Publication Data
To Beijing and Beyond : Pittsburgh and the United Nations
    Fourth World Conference on Women / Janice Auth, editor.
        p.   cm.
    Includes index.
    ISBN 0-8229-5653-5 (pbk. : alk. paper)
    1. World Conference on Women (4th : 1995 : Peking,
China)   2. Women—Social conditions—Congresses—
Attendance.   3. Women—International cooperation—
Congresses—Attendance.   4. Feminists—Pennsylvania—
Pittsburgh.   I. Auth, Janice, 1945– .   II. World
Conference on Women (4th : 1995 : Peking, China)
HQ1106.B43   1998
305.42—dc21   97-45366
                                          CIP

A CIP catalog record for this book is available from the British Library.

FOR MY DAUGHTERS

Caring asks doing. It is a long baptism into the seas of
humankind, my daughter. Better immersion than to live
untouched. . . . Yet how will you sustain? . . . Why is it
like it is? . . . And why do I have to care?

—Tillie Olsen, *Tell Me a Riddle*

The world of humanity is possessed of two wings—One is
women and the other men. Not until both wings are equally
developed can the bird fly.

—This quotation from the writings of the Baha'i Faith represented the spirit of the conference and forum for me. I
  heard this sentiment expressed again and again in a variety
  of ways. UN Secretary-General Boutros Boutros-Ghali said,
  "Equality, peace and development must reach every
  woman on earth. When the rights and hopes of women in
  all these fields are advanced, so will all human society
  come to benefit." Hillary Clinton said, "It is no longer acceptable to discuss women's rights as separate from human
  rights." Dr. Nafis Sadik, executive director of the UN Population Fund, in a statement after the conference, said: "Like
  Cairo, the Beijing Conference set some new benchmarks.
  . . . *Most important, the connection is made between advancement for individual women and progress for the whole
  society*" (italics mine).

Contents

Preface

The idea for this book began in 1995 when I was attending the nongovernmental forum of the UN Fourth World Conference on Women in Beijing. As I talked with my friends and fellow travelers from Pittsburgh, I realized each of us was having a unique and unforgettable experience. As we gathered at the beginning or end of each day, we shared stories about what had happened to each of us in the course of that day or the preceding one. The range and variety of the stories were such that I knew I wanted to collect them and make them available to others when we all returned home. It is my hope this book will serve as a souvenir for those who attended and a guidebook for those who did not.

But even more than that, I have compiled this book as a record of a historical event. Forty-three individuals from the Pittsburgh area attended either the conference or the forum or both. The forty-three included college presidents, psychologists, writers, students, teachers, retirees, social workers, homemakers, ministers, and entrepreneurs, and reflected Pittsburgh's ethnic, racial, religious, and economic diversity. Fourteen of them were passengers on the Women's International League for Peace and Freedom Peace Train. All are, or have been, associated with a variety of nongovernmental organizations that exist to improve social conditions for women and therefore for all people. They went to Beijing for different reasons, under different auspices, with different issues to address, but a common thread unites them: each is deeply rooted in Pittsburgh and deeply committed to improving the quality of life here and everywhere. Their presence at this international event has created another connection between Pittsburgh and the rest of the world.

The anecdotes, reports, impressions, and narratives in this book vary greatly in length, style, content, and intent. They have been edited only for clarity, accuracy, and to avoid repetition. It is my hope that as you read, you will learn not only about the events and the issues but also about the people—your friends, neighbors, coworkers, and family members—whose words are recorded here. Their words are truly a kaleidoscope, literally a "beautiful shape."

The book also documents the remarkable initiative, energy, and vision of those who began the work of Pittsburgh/Beijing '95 and Beyond (PBB). PBB, a sort of umbrella organization, was created to plan for Pittsburgh participation in the Fourth World Conference on Women, but it quickly became a vital link between information about the conference and the myriad of grassroots organizations in this area that were interested in acquiring this information. PBB has been described as a conduit for information from the Beijing conference to the local area. The word *conduit* can be associated with both water and electricity. Beijing was yet another call for the transformation of society through the recognition and valuation of women. But it was more than that. This conference, unlike the previous three UN conferences on women, moved further. *Women and men must work together* was a theme often repeated. *When the lives of women improve, everyone stands to benefit,* was another articulation of that theme. In that sense, what happened in Beijing is, like water, essential for the growth of all humanity. But Beijing was also a celebration of the diversity, resourcefulness, and tenacity of the human spirit, and in that sense it was electric. PBB has been the conduit for both the "water" and the "electricity" of the UN Fourth World Conference on Women. PBB has helped Pittsburgh stand out among cities for the work done here toward making a global conference relevant to a local community. This book is an attempt to record that effort and to further the PBB initiative by continuing to be a conduit for the rivers of information and sparks of inspiration that are a result of what began in Beijing.

Water and electricity both imply change. Water brings forth new life, reinvigorates and freshens, provides relief, and effects cures. Electricity illumines, activates, empowers. Both help us to move forward. The water and electricity of this conference are only as good as their ability to bring about change where change is needed.

Thank you to all who listened and continue to listen to the messages of Beijing. Gertrude Mongella, secretary-general of the conference, expressed the hope that her mother, back in her village in Tanzania, would hear about what happened, not only from her own daughter but from other sources as well. In a small way, this book is meant to fulfill that hope.

Acknowledgments

I would like to express my deepest gratitude to everyone who contributed written material, whether long or short, grand or humble, personal or general, profound or amusing, academic or anecdotal. I value all of it and I thank you for your generosity of mind and spirit. Your contributions are the heart and soul of this book.

Thanks also to everyone who contributed ideas, photographs, suggestions, and inspiration, and everyone who said, "How's the book coming along?" Your love, support, and interest kept me going.

Special thanks to Teresa Wilson for connecting me with the University of Pittsburgh Press and to Cynthia Miller and everyone at the press for their guidance and encouragement.

And, most important, thank you to my family for believing in me and for helping me to take pride in my work.

Acronyms

AAUW	American Association of University Women
ACCD	Allegheny Conference on Community Development
ACWF	All China Women's Federation
CEDAW	Convention on the Elimination of all forms of Discrimination Against Women
CNN	Cable News Network
CPA	Center for Policy Alternatives
CPAPD	Chinese Peoples' Association for Peace and Disarmament
CSW	Commission on the Status of Women
CTB	Comprehensive Test Ban
DAWN	Development Alternatives with Women for a New Era
ECOSOC	Economic and Social Council
ECW	Episcopal Church Women
GA	General Assembly
GNP	gross national product
ICC	International Criminal Court
ICW	International Council on Women
IWY	International Women's Year (1975)
NECWB	National Education Center for Women in Business
NGO	nongovernmental organization
NOW	National Organization for Women
PBB	Pittsburgh/Beijing '95 and Beyond
PLEN	Public Leadership Education Network
SBA	Small Business Administration
STAR	Strategies, Training, and Advocacy for Reconciliation
UNAP	United Nations Association of Pittsburgh
UNESCO	United Nations Education, Scientific and Cultural Organization
UNIFEM	United Nations Development Fund for Women

USAID	United States Agency for International Development
WARC	World Association of Reformed Churches
WEDO	Women's Environment and Development Organization
WFA	World Federalist Association
WFAP	World Federalist Association of Pittsburgh
WHO	World Health Organization
WILPF	Women's International League for Peace and Freedom
YWCA	Young Women's Christian Association

TO BEIJING AND BEYOND

Introduction

Many people from Pittsburgh attend international conferences. There is nothing unique about the fact that forty-three Pittsburghers attended the United Nations Fourth World Conference on Women except that this was the largest gathering of women anywhere, ever. To be a part of this global event was to be a part of the entire world. To then return home and convey some of this experience to this region was to make a powerful connection between Pittsburgh and the rest of the world. To be present in Beijing or to hear about what happened there was to examine one's own life and experiences in the context of shared human aspirations and obstacles all over the world. This conference declared that all people, despite their differences, deserve a universal form of human rights. Beijing was an affirmation of the oneness of humanity, a testimonial to the idea that we can all be conduits of information and inspiration from one to another because we are all inextricably connected by our commonalities, even as we are distinct and unique.

> Pittsburgh and its history are the capsule history of America, the saga of its cities. It is the familiar story: fighting for the land, clearing the wilderness, working, toiling, struggling, putting down roots, inventing, producing, consuming, despoiling, then rebuilding, regenerating and renewing. (Stefan Lorant, *Pittsburgh: The Story of an American City*)

Pittsburgh is an American city—a conglomerate of ethnic groups, religious organizations, and diverse neighborhoods that have evolved out of centuries of toil and triumph. The area owes many of its place-names—Allegheny, Monongahela, Ohio, Aliquippa, Youghiogheny—to its early inhabitants, the indigenous peoples who made up the vast Iroquois league of nations as far back as 1390. The Iroquois nation was distinctive for two reasons: its Great Binding Law, which influenced the authors of the constitution of the United States of America, and its recognition and valuation of its women, who were given the responsibility and privilege of choosing the leaders of the confederation. Into this egalitarian society came French trappers and traders, the first to tell the outside world of the riches and possibilities of this region. George Washington later encouraged the British to construct a fort at the forks of "la belle riviere" as the French had named the Ohio. The ensuing battles resulted in a fort named after William Pitt instead of the Marquis Duquesne.

Pittsburgh is a city that has learned to use its resources to adapt to changing conditions. In the early 1800s, when competition from other burgeoning cities threatened an economy based on commerce, the city turned to manufacturing, taking advantage of the abundance of local timber, coal, and iron ore, as well as the facility of water transportation.

At the start of the twentieth century, European immigrants, fleeing persecution, war, famine, and lack of opportunity, flocked to the region, lured by the promise of work in the coal mines. Situated at a critical juncture of three great rivers, Pittsburgh was, for many, synonymous with opportunity, a chance to look ahead, a chance to begin anew. Immigrant labor eventually built the steel empire and the neighborhoods that would become the heart and soul of the city.

More than halfway through the twentieth century, the city itself became a metaphor for the lives of those immigrants, whose grandchildren were now beginning to feel the effects of a nascent global economy. After the decline and eventual collapse of the steel industry, Pittsburgh looked ahead, assessed its potential, and once again began anew. The skies cleared, and out of the smoke and smog emerged a model of a "renaissance city" with a new vision and a new direction.

In the past twenty years, Pittsburgh, with its world-renowned hospitals and organ transplant center, has reached out into the international community. Its universities attract many students and faculty from abroad, and recent immigrations have broadened the ethnic base to include Cambodian, Russian, and Tibetan populations. The tourism industry is growing, with six hundred nonstop flights each day in and out of the Pittsburgh International Airport; the business community includes more than 220 foreign companies. The goal of the recently formed Pittsburgh Regional Alliance is to market the city to the rest of the world. There seems to be no doubt Pittsburgh wants to connect with the world at large, to be a part of the global structure, the international market of ideas as well as products. Now, in the last few remaining years of the twentieth century, the face of Pittsburgh is every color, every shape; the voice of Pittsburgh is every language.

But apart from its prehistory, which was influenced by Iroquois women, Pittsburgh has been very much shaped and steered by *men*. One can hardly think of Pittsburgh without thinking of Andrew Carnegie and Andrew Mellon, Henry Clay Frick or Henry John Heinz. Men built the industries of the city, and men, with the exception of Mayor Sophie Masloff from 1988 to 1994, have ruled the city. Although a number of strong, influential women such as Rachel Carson, Jane Grey Swisshelm, Sara Soffel, and others have left their mark here, women, by and large, have been, and continue to be, the area's most underutilized and unrecognized resource. Notwithstanding the fact that it is even difficult to gather specific and accurate information about the status of women's health, employment, and education in this region, the behind-the-scenes contribution of women to the growth of Pittsburgh is not even being discussed.

In 1984 William Genge, then chairman of Ketchum Communications, said, "Pittsburgh is going through an identity crisis, and its new role is not yet clearly perceived or defined." Pittsburgh's new role may well be to once again assess its strengths and resources, and to define that new identity, as an American city of the twenty-first century, by bringing women to the table and incorporating women's thinking fully into the life of the city. This will bring to fruition the process that began with the Iroquois, who balanced their society not by treating men and women exactly alike but by recognizing and valuing equally the unique contribution each can make to a community. Looking at photographs of the men in a history book about Pittsburgh, one is starkly reminded of the old saying, "Behind every successful man there is a woman." Undoubtedly she was back there, but she can't be seen by the camera. She has been the invisible support of successful and powerful men everywhere. The next step for Pittsburgh, as well as for the entire world, is to put women into the picture. Once again, at the start of this new century, this city is challenged to adapt, to regenerate, and to renew—to move forward.

i TIME FOR A CHANGE

Understanding the universe of gender relations, which vary enormously from culture to culture, is no easy task. But it must be done. And it must be done by having men and women sitting as equals at the table. . . . No society can realize its potential while repressing the talents of half its people. Isn't it time for a change?

> —*James Gustave Speth, Administrator,*
> *United Nations Development Program*

For millennia women have dedicated themselves almost exclusively to the task of nurturing, protecting and caring for the young and the old, striving for the conditions of peace that favor life as a whole. It is time to apply in the arena of the world the wisdom and experience that women have gained.

> —*Daw Aung San Suu Kyi, Nobel Peace Laureate,*
> *keynote speaker, opening plenary*

A History of United Nations Women's Conferences

Janice Auth

The struggle for women's rights as part of the agenda of the United Nations began in 1947 with the establishment of its Commission on the Status of Women (CSW), a legacy of the energetic presence of Eleanor Roosevelt.*

By proclamation of the UN General Assembly (GA), 1975 was designated as International Women's Year (IWY). The first intergovernmental conference on women was held in Mexico City from June 16 through July 2, 1975. Most of the delegates to this first conference were men, and the number of nongovernmental organizations (NGOs) represented was very small. The themes of this IWY world conference were equality, development, and peace. Two documents emerged from the deliberations of the two thousand government delegates: *Declaration of Mexico on the Equality of Women and their Contribution to Development and Peace* and *World Plan of Action for the Implementation of the Objectives of International Women's Year*. In October 1975 the United Nations declared 1976–85 a Decade for Women.

The second conference, held in Copenhagen, Denmark, July 14–29, 1980, marked the midpoint in this decade. The World Conference of the UN Decade for Women: Equality, Development, and Peace added three subthemes to the agenda: education, employment, and health. The goal of this conference was to assess progress made since the first world conference and to outline actions to be taken during the second half of the Decade for Women. The document adopted at this conference was the *Program of Action*.

From July 15 to July 26, 1985, the UN convened a final Decade for Women World Conference in Nairobi. With equality, development, and

*Dorothy Ann Kelly, *Cross Currents*, spring 1996. This article was adapted from '95 Preview, an occasional bulletin of the International Women's Tribune Center, 777 United Nations Plaza, New York, N.Y. 10017.

peace as the primary themes and education, employment, and health as the subthemes, the delegates attending the world conference to review and appraise the achievement of the UN Decade for Women adopted the *Forward-Looking Strategies for the Advancement of Women to the Year 2000*, which, it was hoped, would renew commitments to furthering women's issues.

The proposal to have an International Women's Year was first put before the UN General Assembly by a women's nongovernmental organization, the Women's International Democratic Federation. And NGOs have been at the forefront of activities throughout the IWY and the Decade for Women that followed.

June 16 to July 2, 1975, in Mexico City, six thousand women (and a few men) participated in the IWY tribune, the parallel nongovernmental meeting organized by an NGO planning committee. The three themes of IWY—equality, development, and peace—served as the focal point for daily plenary sessions. In addition, workshops were held—one hundred planned by the committee, one hundred spontaneous—covering a multitude of issues ranging from rural women's small businesses to the training of women astronauts. In keeping with its original intentions, the IWY tribune did not issue any declarations. It did, however, open up new possibilities for action and gave birth to new programs and organizations.

From July 14 to July 28, 1980, in Copenhagen, concurrent to the convening of the UN world conference, ten thousand women and again some men attended a parallel NGO forum. The forum's themes were the same as those of the world conference, but participants also discussed countless other issues, such as female sexual slavery, wages for housework, feminism, appropriate technology, women's studies, and much more. As with the 1975 IWY tribune, the NGO forum did not issue declarations but did contribute to a growing international women's movement and to the development of new networks worldwide.

From July 10 to July 19, 1985, the parallel meeting to the UN world conference in Nairobi, Forum 85, was held at the University of Nairobi. An estimated fifteen thousand people took part in plenary sessions, workshops (this time more than fourteen hundred), demonstrations, exhibitions, and discussion groups that included such special events as tech and tools, an international film and video festival, a peace tent, and a crafts bazaar. Issues at Forum 85 included those on the agenda at the UN world conference plus many more, such as women, law, and development; lesbian rights and research issues; and women in arts and music. Forum 85 did not issue formal declarations but did provide the stimulus for dozens of new organizations and networks, and it gave an international platform for feminist perspectives and women's approaches to a variety of issues.

The goal of the UN Fourth World Conference on Women and the NGO forum was to "bring together women and men to challenge, create, and transform global structures and processes at all levels through the empowerment and celebration of women."

This fourth in the series of UN conferences on women was the largest gathering ever held under the auspices of the United Nations. The total number of people registered for the official conference was 16,921, including delegates, NGO representatives, and media representatives. Action for equality, development, and peace was the theme of the conference held in Beijing September 4–15, 1995. Delegates from 189 countries adopted the Platform for Action (see "Bringing Beijing Home" in part VI and "A Summary of the Platform for Action" in appendix D).

Look at the world through women's eyes was the theme of the NGO forum that met in Huairou, China, August 30–September 8, 1995. An estimated 40,000 people participated in more than three thousand workshops, demonstrations, cultural presentations, plenary sessions, and informal discussion groups. It was a place of learning, lobbying, networking, and celebrating.

The four UN conferences on women and the attendant nongovernmental organization gatherings have kept alive over the past twenty years a continuously evolving awareness of the condition of the world's women. Each succeeding event has unfolded upon the recommendations and actions of the previous ones. Beijing was the culmination of that process of unfoldment so far. But Beijing was also a beginning:

Securing the equality of women and men, in law and in fact, is the great political project of the twentieth century. A crucial role in the realization of that project has been entrusted to the United Nations. . . . We are meeting to take that great enterprise forward into the twenty-first century and beyond: to consolidate the legal advance, to build on the political understandings, and to commit ourselves to action. (UN Secretary-General Boutros Boutros-Ghali)

The Significance of the UN World Women's Conferences

Margaret E. Galey

The advancement of women worldwide is one of the great success stories of the United Nations.[1] That success has resulted from the efforts by the UN Commission on the Status of Women and the four world women's conferences in fostering international collaboration and agreement among governments on a range of international measures to advance women's status. In addition, the four UN world women's conferences—the World Conference on International Women's Year (1975), the World Conference of the UN Decade for Women (1980), the World Conference to Review and Appraise the UN Decade for Women (1985), and the Fourth World Conference (1995)—have also provided the occasion for convening unofficial parallel nongovernmental organization (NGO) forums. These NGO forums facilitate individual and group contacts across geographic boundaries and spur new international networks and NGOs. Local communities like Pittsburgh have become involved in these international conferences mainly through their participation in the NGO forums. But in Beijing, local community groups were permitted to send a representative to the official meeting. Thus members of the Pittsburgh/Beijing '95 and Beyond project were able to participate in the transnational event—the NGO forum—as well as the conference of governments.

In considering the significance of these conferences, recall that sovereign states are no longer the sole actors in international relations. They share the world stage with an increasing number of international institutions as well as NGOs. The increasingly complex relations between and among these entities cause scholars to distinguish intergovernmental from transnational relations. The latter—contacts, coalitions, and interactions across geographic boundaries not controlled by the central foreign policy organs of government—have spurred the growth of international networks and NGOs such as multinational corporations, global religious societies, international foundations, and women's international associations. Nongovernmental organizations also influence official governmental and intergovernmental activity and are influenced by it. Reciprocal influence characterizes relations between and among transnational organizations and governments in contemporary world politics.[2]

Also recall that prior to the UN's establishment in 1945, the women's movement was primarily a transnational phenomenon and had not yet become a priority for intergovernmental attention. Starting with the era of the French Revolution, private associations of women began to form. By the middle of the nineteenth century, associations of women suffragists, temperance workers, teachers, college graduates, nurses, peace workers, social workers, and labor officials formed national, then international associations. The leaders of these associations convened international meetings and congresses in capital cities of North America and Western Europe to develop common agendas and strategies to influence governments and international institutions to improve women's condition. For instance, in 1919 in Paris, the French National Women's Suffrage Alliance sponsored a gathering of representatives of women's organizations to develop goals and strategies to influence the Paris Peace Conference. Representatives met with the Big Four and persuaded them to incorporate into the League of Nations covenant a reference to women in relation to the International Labor Organization and the League Secretariat. Another example is important: American women suffragists, after winning the vote in 1920, traveled to Latin America to help Latin women organize to seek their political rights. Latin and American women later pressed for the creation of the Inter-American Commission on Women within the Pan American Union. Subsequently, Latin members of the Commission worked to influence the San Francisco Conference to incorporate the phrase "without distinction as to race, sex, nationality or religion" as part of the human rights provisions in the UN Charter. Then at the UN's first session in 1946, these same Latin women joined with women leaders from Denmark and France to influence government representatives in the Economic and Social Council (ECOSOC) to establish first the subcommission and a year later the Commission on the Status of Women.[3] This intergovernmental commission, with its initial membership of fifteen women appointed by governments, would be the focal point for women within the United Nations, their efforts to advance their situation, the source of initiative for the world conferences, and a main vehicle for implementing conference decisions.

I. Significance of the Conferences: Governments and Intergovernmental Relations

The involvement of governments in the advancement of women, including in the world women's conferences, has come about through decisions by governments in international intergovernmental organizations, notably the United Nations and its Commission on the Status of Women (CSW). The commission is an intergovernmental body whose members are appointed by governments. Its aims, amended in 1947, have been to prepare recommendations for ECOSOC on promoting women's rights in political, economic, civil, social, and educational fields with the aim of implementing the principle that men and women should have equal rights.[4] Since 1946, CSW's contribution to the advancement of women worldwide has included the preparation of four conventions that articulate women's international human rights. One addresses political rights of women; a second, the nationality of married women; and a third, the consent to marriage and the registration of marriages. The fourth is the comprehensive Convention on the Elimination of All Forms of Discrimination Against Women (CEDAW). The UN's Commission on the Status of Women has also prepared principles on equal parental rights and duties and made recommendations on inheritance, property ownership, traditional practices, equal pay, pension and retirement plans, and education at all levels. They have encouraged the UN specialized agencies to advance women's issues. For example, they urged the World Health Organization (WHO) through ECOSOC to end the practice of female circumcision in the early 1950s; the International Labor Organization (ILO) to establish standards on equal employment opportunities for women; and the UN Education, Scientific, and Cultural Organization (UNESCO) to improve access of women and girls to education. In cooperation with the specialized agencies, CSW members also prepared a long-term program for the advancement of women in development, which the UN

General Assembly endorsed in 1970. This became the basis for CSW's recommendations concerning women and development.[5]

In the early 1970s, the General Assembly began sponsoring global conferences of governments on the human environment (1972), food (1974), and population (1974). As a result of this intergovernmental activity, governments began to recognize that women were not only child bearers but also initial and principal educators of children, major producers and preparers of food, and custodians for the household and the health and well-being of the family. This perception of women's role led governments to begin to recognize the salience of women's issues.

The Commission on the Status of Women hastened to secure this new recognition and offered two proposals. One called on UN members to commemorate International Women's Year (IWY) in 1975. It was introduced by the Finnish member of CSW upon the urging of an NGO, the Women's International League for Peace and Freedom (WILPF). The other, proposed by the U.S. member, called for a world conference of governments to commemorate the International Women's Year. UN member governments in CSW, ECOSOC, and the General Assembly agreed to both proposals.

The first historic UN women's conference, the World Conference of International Women's Year (IWY), held in Mexico City in June 1975, highlighted the year-long commemoration of IWY. Delegations from 133 governments attended it and approved a world plan of action and recommended, among other measures, the UN Decade for the Advancement of Women as well as a second world conference in 1980. In Copenhagen, 143 government delegations attended the Conference of the Mid-Decade for Women, endorsed the controversial Program of Action, and recommended a third conference in 1985. The third world conference, held in Nairobi, Kenya, with 149 government delegations, approved the major conference document, *Forward Looking Strategies for the Advancement of Women to the Year 2000*. The fourth conference was postponed from 1990 to 1995 in order for CSW to gain ECOSOC approval for annual commission sessions starting in 1988. These were judged essential to manage an expanding program. In 1995 in Beijing, China, delegations from 189 governments gathered to discuss and approve the Beijing Declaration and Platform of Action.[6] This, the largest conference ever sponsored by the United Nations, then observing its fiftieth anniversary, symbolized the steady expansion of the international women's movement.

Whether called the plan of action or program or platform of action, each major document resulting from each world women's conference has identified a set of goals (equality, development, and peace), strategies to achieve those goals, and recommended action to be undertaken by governments, international institutions, NGOs, and individuals to advance women's status. In these respects, the action plans reflect international public policies negotiated and endorsed by an increasing number of UN member governments. The adoption and subsequent reaffirmation of successive plans with similar, if not identical goals and action recommendations helps legitimate the advancement of women on the agendas of the UN and its specialized agencies and programs and all of its member governments.

But there are several related points of significance. One concerns preparations for a world conference. Each government must develop a national report describing policies and laws that support the advancement of women within its society and progress made since the previous report. In addition, governments also develop official positions on the principal themes, recommended actions, and issues within the draft conference document to be discussed at the conference itself. In developing national positions, the government agency authorized to act as lead agency may have to resolve differing, even conflicting views within the bureaucracy if the government is intended to speak with one voice internationally. Preparing national positions for the conference as well as the government's participation in the conference is likely to sensitize government personnel to the issues under discussion and raise consciousness about those issues, a matter discussed below.

Another point of significance concerns the government delegation. Each government is invited by the UN secretary-general to send a delegation to the conference. In contrast to other UN conferences, the World Women's Conferences have encouraged governments to appoint women to serve as representatives whether as heads or members of government delegations. Most women heads of delegations have been appointed by male presidents or prime ministers since only twenty-four women have been elected head of state since 1900. A few of these women, however, have led their government's delegation to these world conferences. Examples include Benazir Bhutto, Indira Gandhi, and Gro Bruntland. Several daughters of presidents, such as Maureen Reagan, or wives of presidents or prime ministers, such as Hillary Clinton, Jihan Sadat, and Leah Rabin have headed their government delegations. Delegation heads appoint members from government ministries of education, social affairs, foreign affairs, health and welfare, and if they exist, special offices or bureaus on women and children's affairs and from parliament and key NGOs.

A related point of significance concerns women representing governments. As members of national delegations, women participate in intergovernmental political processes of the world conferences within the framework of a conference agenda, rules of procedure, and organized committee meetings and plenary sessions as well as any government instructions for particular positions on issues before the conference. Delegation heads report to the conference on progress in their countries, discuss and articulate national positions and policies on women's status, and negotiate differences on positions to achieve commonly agreed upon recommendations for action in the conference document. Such participation helps raise awareness of the process of world politics and women's issues. Women engage in diplomacy and world politics, professional fields traditionally restricted to men. This is not to say that women are replacing men as diplomats or international negotiators, but their numbers are increasing. The advent of women officials in world politics has been a significant effect of the conferences.

Finally, brief discussion of the major conference goals, concepts, and themes can help to illustrate another significant aspect of the world conferences, namely the development of women's issues and their linkage with issues on the larger agenda by governments.

Equality

One of the chief aims of CSW—equality—was also a principal theme and goal of International Women's Year and each of the world conferences. From 1946, the notion expanded to cover virtually all spheres of activity. CSW's charge to make recommendations to promote women's rights with the aim of implementing the principle that men and women have equal rights resulted in innumerable recommendations and several conventions. Notably, after preparing conventions on political rights, then consent to marriage, then nationality of married women, and principles of parental rights and duties, CSW members undertook the preparation of the first comprehensive treaty on women's rights, the Convention on the Elimination of All Forms of Discrimination Against Women. Initiated within CSW, endorsed by the 1975 conference, and approved in 1979 by the GA, this convention incorporated provisions of earlier conventions and important resolutions into an international treaty that for the first time defines and prohibits sex discrimination in political, economic, social, civil, and cultural spheres of activity. By October 1997, 161 governments had ratified the convention. A significant exception remains the United States government.

A particularly heinous inequality addressed by the first conference in 1975 was the practice of apartheid. Delegates called for a study of the effects of apartheid on women and children. The report prepared by the secretariat was discussed by CSW and forwarded to the 1980 conference, which underscored the double burden for black women living under apartheid and led to resolutions urging its elimination.

Economic equality, already defined by CSW in terms of access to employment opportunities, equal remuneration, age of retirement, and pensions, was expanded by the women's conferences to include women's need for access to financial credit and bank loans. The conferences also acknowledged women's participation in the informal work sector, their role as food producers and household workers, and their contribution to the gross national product. As major UN collections of data failed to include information on women's work, delegates endorsed the collection of such information for future compendiums and as a basis for policy development.

Besides expanding the concept of women's equality per se, the conferences offered delegates the opportunity to begin linking women's issues with issues on the larger political agenda. One example was women's linking the call for eliminating apartheid in South Africa with imposing sanctions against South Africa, a position that not all governments agreed upon, but one which gained broad conference support in Copenhagen and Nairobi.

Development

A second major goal of IWY as well as the conferences has been to promote women's access to economic and social development. Concepts of development began to enter into CSW discussions in 1963 when the GA invited CSW to prepare a long-term program for the advancement of women. This program, which addressed women's role in employment, education, community development, civic participation, and family planning, was approved by the GA in 1970. Subsequently, development became a key theme of the IWY and the women's conferences, at which delegates discussed the need for women to be integrated into development. The latter meant equal access to planning and implementing development projects, whether in agriculture, industrial, or service sectors or in educational, health, and family planning services. Women's roles as agricultural workers and food producers was also acknowledged. At each of the conferences, delegates identified special groups of disadvantaged women deserving particular consideration: rural women, migrant women, youth, the disabled and handicapped, and the aging and recommended action to alleviate their plight. By 1980 governments determined the feminization of poverty to be a major trend characterizing women's conditions and offered proposals to end it. Important statistical information needed to chart women's contributions to economic and social development has been gathered and published by the UN secretariat in a number of excellent compendiums, including *Women's Role in Development* and *The World's Women 1995: Trends and Statistics.*[7]

Peace

Peace, a primary goal of the United Nations as well as the women's conferences, has evolved in the last thirty years from the notion of war prevention, arms control, and disarmament to conflict resolution, violence prevention, and the security and dignity of the person. Women delegates have contributed to expanding the concept of peace and linked their concerns with traditional and newer definitions of the term.

Several examples are illustrative. First, the Soviet Union initiated in 1978 the "struggling women" declaration, which extolled women's role in the struggle for peace and in promoting arms control and disarmament. The GA approved it in 1982. Second, at the 1975, 1980, and 1985 conferences, delegates linked women's interest in peace with calls for ending civil strife and war in the Middle East, then South Africa and Central America, and still later, the former Yugoslavia. Women's concepts of peace and security have also been linked with humanitarian assistance and intervention. For instance, CSW prepared the Declaration on the Protection of Women and Children in Armed Conflict. Discussing this at the conferences, delegates have called attention not only to the need to provide protection to women and children but to the fact that the women and children as a result of such conflict constitute the overwhelming number of refugees. Delegates in turn have urged improved treatment of such refugees in camps and increasing voluntary support for the UN Office of the High Commissioner for Refugees to provide it.

Third, at the 1980 conference, delegates endorsed a study on violence against women. The resulting report was sent to the 1985 conference for discussion. The conference recommended the preparation of a declaration which was undertaken by CSW in consultation with the Committee on the Elimination of All Forms of Discrimination Against Women (CEDAW) and approved by the GA in 1993.[8] Besides addressing a widespread and increasingly acknowledged problem women faced throughout the world, this declaration also illustrated an important way in which women delegates have expanded their concern for peace by defining the security of the person to be part of it. Women have also aimed to advance human dignity by seeking to outlaw female circumcision or female genital mutilation (FGM). As early as the 1950s, CSW had recommended that the World Health Organization take steps to end this practice. Regarding the issue as cultural, not medical, WHO for many years dismissed the request. The Commission on Human Rights then took up the matter and appointed a special rapporteur to study and report action on the subject. This report, available to the 1985 conference, led delegates to call for eliminating the practice. Global publicity and ongoing pressure led the WHO executive council in 1993 to approve a resolution outlawing its practice.[9]

Two additional examples of ways that women have helped expand the traditional concept of peace are their efforts to have rape defined as a war crime and to ban land mines. Thanks largely to women's voices at the 1993 UN Human Rights Conference, delegates agreed to define rape to be a war crime. The 1995 Beijing Conference affirmed this link and condemned rape. The conference also linked women's efforts to achieve peace to the political problem of eliminating the millions of land mines in the former and existing war zones.

The international intergovernmental UN world women's conferences have been significant for several reasons. They have offered opportunities for women to become informed about national, foreign, and global issues and their linkages with other issues on the larger global agenda. They have meant that governments themselves have had to develop policies and positions on a range of issues addressed by the conferences and to prepare reports to communicate progress made in promoting the advancement of women within their national societies.

II. Significance of the Conference for Transnational Relations

Transnational organizations have played a vital role in advancing women's status. Before the UN was established, the women's movement was primarily a transnational phenomena. Several transnational women's organizations existed, having evolved from earlier local and national organizations. They included the International Council of Women (ICW), the International Alliance of Women, the International Federation of Business and Professional Women, the Countrywomen of the World, the International Young Women's Christian Association, the World Women's Temperance Union, the International Federation of University Women, and the International Association of Nurses. After CSW was established in 1946, these organizations sought accreditation to CSW meetings under UN charter article 71 and ECOSOC rules of procedure. They offered important suggestions orally or in writing, provided support for CSW resolutions submitted to ECOSOC and the GA, and helped to implement resolutions adopted by CSW by publicizing them within their increasingly large worldwide memberships.

When the UN General Assembly began sponsoring global conferences in the 1970s, these organizations gained official accreditation to attend and to address points of interest in the respective conference documents. Until the early 1990s, only organizations with regional and international membership were permitted to be accredited. Starting with the Rio Conference on Environment and Development in 1992, the conference's secretary-general welcomed and authorized national and local organizations to be accredited to the conference. This practice continued and at the Beijing conference in 1995, enabled representatives of local and national NGOs, such as the Pittsburgh/Beijing '95 and Beyond project, to attend the government conference as well as the NGO forum.

As for NGO forums, when the GA decided to convene the first world women's conference in Mexico City in 1975, it was clear that an organized effort would be necessary to enable thousands of interested individuals and groups not affiliated with the UN to join and participate in the conference. A planning committee for the *Mexico City Tribune*, the unofficial NGO forum, organized the parallel forum in Mexico City. This unofficial conference attracted eight thousand women and men. The NGO forum in Copenhagen registered about twelve thousand participants, and twenty thousand gathered for the week-long NGO forum in Nairobi in 1985. Beijing was the largest conference ever held by the UN. Some forty thousand attended the NGO forum. The increasing numbers of individuals from local, national, regional and international associations who attended the NGO forums participated in organized seminars, workshops, and meetings. They made contacts, interacted with those from other countries and cultures, and built networks of interest and new associations.

The 1975 NGO forum resulted in the establishment of the International Tribune Center and publication of a newsletter, the *Tribune*, circulated to all registered participants. Later, the center published manuals on a range of subjects from sewing and gardening to organizing community groups to help women and girls gain awareness of their role in society. At the NGO forums, new transnational organizations formed such as the International Women's Rights Action Watch, women's projects within existing human rights groups such as Human Rights Watch and in professional societies such as the International Studies Association and the American Society of International Law.

The exponential increase in the number and types of women's NGOs throughout the world in the last two decades is attributable to the four women's conferences. The new NGOs represent every hue in the ideological rainbow: religious, radical, conservative, grassroots, and elite; local, national, regional, and international. Some provide welfare or development services; others aim to organize women; still others conduct research on women's lives or work, or advocate social or political change. These groups represent a new breed different from the older, well-established women's NGOs that had held consultative status with the UN for decades. Among the new breed is Development Alternatives with Women for a New Era (DAWN), a network of scholars from the developing countries established before the Nairobi conference. The International Women's Tribune Center that grew out of the Mexico City conference was an important, earlier networking effort. In the late 1980s, Bella Abzug masterminded Women's Environment and Development Organization (WEDO).

Thanks to their experience at the 1975, 1980, and 1985 women's conferences, leaders and members of large numbers of transnational associations worked to influence the major conference document for the Fourth World Conference in Beijing, China. They also sought to influence other UN–sponsored conferences of governments, such as the 1992 World Environment Conference in Rio, the 1993 World Conference on Human Rights in Vienna, the 1994 Population Conference in Cairo, and the 1995 Social Development Conference in Copenhagen. To this end, they expended their own efforts and held conference preparatory sessions and a daily NGO women's caucus with assistance from WEDO. At Rio, Cairo, and Vienna, the women's caucus met every morning to review negotiations of the previous day and establish advocacy priorities and develop strategies to influence delegates at the government conferences. Each afternoon, the women's caucus shifted its site to the official conference to coordinate efforts between the NGOs and members of the press.

Women's NGOs also worked to organize global campaigns, build coalitions, and prepare policy documents including proposed resolutions, treaties, protocols, and conventions.[10] Already, they have encouraged governments to ratify the various conventions, especially the Convention on the Elimination of Discrimination Against Women.

III. Consciousness-Raising at Individual and Group Levels

Implicit in this discussion of the significance of the conferences for intergovernmental and transnational relations has been the effect on individuals and groups who participate in them. Individual participation in intergovernmental and transnational relations may offer consciousness-raising, a learning experience, and/or attitude change. The women's conferences are said to be important consciousness-raising events. Participation in transnational relations is said to promote attitude change. But what does this mean? Whose consciousness is raised, about what, and to what end? What attitudes are changed?

Consciousness-raising may occur at an individual as well as a collective level. For individuals, personal awareness may increase through participation in activities intended to raise consciousness about one or more of the issues women face, whether literacy, education, health, family planning, or employment. The critical element, however, is participation in activities that increase awareness or consciousness, about the nature or cause of the problem that is detrimental to women.[11] There is also organizational consciousness, that is, the awareness of the problem by the group and an identification with other women as objects of injustice or discrimination. Collective consciousness-raising is reflected in activities that increase the capacity of women to work together to achieve common goals based on a mutually shared understanding of the problem.[12]

The UN women's conferences and NGO forums have facilitated individual and collective consciousness-raising for several categories of conference participants:

1. The official participants—members of government delegations, accredited representatives of NGOs, including media representatives and secretariat staff.

2. The thousands of unofficial participants—leaders and members of

NGOs as well as interested individuals from an increasing number of UN member states who attend workshops, speakouts, seminars, and briefings at the NGO forums.

3. Those who participate indirectly by providing backup in home government departments where they receive and analyze reporting cables from their conference delegation and send cables with instructions on policy and voting or suggestions about strategy and tactics.

4. The "attentive publics" who participate by reading and discussing press accounts, scrutinizing media coverage of the conferences, and working in their local communities.

All of these participants may experience consciousness-raising. But it is the conference-goers whose awareness of cultural, religious, linguistic, economic, social and political differences and similarities is heightened by participation who are likely to gain increased consciousness. Such increased consciousness also includes awareness of world politics, which inevitably intrudes into conference deliberations, and the UN functions and procedures. Naturally, the extent and effect of individual and collective consciousness-raising will vary from individual to individual and group to group. Yet such consciousness-raising can contribute to attitude change and, in turn, promote social change and transform social structures to eliminate discriminatory laws and practices and promote equality. Historic examples offer perspective on the importance of the UN conferences as consciousness-raising as well as empowering events. Two hundred years ago, amid the French Revolution, Mary Wollstonecraft, a writer with extraordinary consciousness of women's conditions authored the *Vindication of the Rights of Women* to help define women's conditions and raise the consciousness of other women.[13] But women were not yet organized to identify common problems or to mobilize resources to transform the social order. Generally, they joined with men to transform the corrupt French monarchy into a representative government that granted male citizens their rights. Roughly one hundred years later, in the 1880s, Elizabeth Cady Stanton, who had organized the first women's conference in Seneca Falls, New York, in 1848, created with the help of her associates the National Women's Suffrage Association and later the International Council of Women, with constituent chapters in numerous foreign states, in the hopes of influencing governments to improve women's lots. Despite their achievements, the ICW and other similar associations were circumscribed in their efforts by available resources, the need for legitimacy, and competing priorities of governments. Not until the CSW initiated and the GA approved the call for International Women's Year and a world conference structure was a global intergovernmental and transnational process developed to define common issues and establish common strategies aimed at transforming the social order and the condition of women in national societies around the world. Intergovernmental institutions have been essential to this process as have transnational associations of women and the reciprocal relations between them. But the intergovernmental and transnational processes have enabled a critical mass of women to gain greater awareness and understanding of issues and strategies to mobilize energy and resources to influence social change whether in law, policy, custom, or culture to improve their situation.

Historic and contemporary transnational women's organizations have contributed to international pluralism. By forming new networks and associations, they have continued to contribute to pluralism and to aggregate interest within the international women's movement. No single transnational women's organization has become or sought to become an all-embracing, powerful, universal women's organization with the stature of an autonomous or quasi-autonomous actor in world politics. The Women's International Democratic Federation may have approximated this stature within the pre-1991 U.S.S.R and Eastern Europe. However, its cohesiveness appears to have dissipated with the crumbling of the former Soviet Union and the growth of new women's organizations in the newly independent states.

Transnational women's associations and networks have helped to promote women's advancement within national societies. But apart from advancing women's status, the women's movement reflects diverse interests that spell fragmentation and multiplicity of goals rather than singleness of purpose. Nonetheless, women's organizations are likely to remain a force for governments and international institutions to reckon with for many years to come. The women's conferences have helped to legitimate existing associations and to develop new ones. Groups such as those noted here that are sensitive to women's issues and understand local power structures are in a position to hold governments accountable to the principles, goals, and action recommendations they pledged to achieve when they endorsed these international public policies and reform documents at the conferences.

Significance of the Women's Conferences: Implementation

The major conference documents endorsed by the conference of governments are to be implemented. Each contains a set of goals, strategies, and action recommended to governments, international institutions, transnational organizations, and individuals. The UN Commission on the Status of Women has been an important focal point within the U.S. system for promoting international implementation and monitoring progress in advancing women's status. Transnational associations affiliated with CSW are also important to the process of implementing internationally agreed upon goals and recommendations. But national governments at home must act to implement recommendations agreed upon at the conferences, and national memberships of transnational associations can hold them accountable to implementing those recommendations.

The U.S. government provides a useful example. Within its federal government, the U.S. delegation to the Beijing conference made a series of commitments. Following the conference, the President's Interagency Council on Women publicized the Beijing Platform of Action along with the U.S. commitments. Among these, the U.S. delegation endorsed U.S. ratification of the Convention on the Elimination of All Forms of Discrimination Against Women. On September 28, 1996, the Interagency Council sponsored a nationwide teleconference in which U.S. delegation members reported on progress made since Beijing and plans for future efforts. In May 1997, the Interagency Council prepared and published *America's Commitment,* a description of federal programs benefitting women and new initiatives intended to follow-up the UN Fourth World Conference on Women.[14] The President's Inter-Agency Council continues to be the principal governmental council to promote national implementation of the Beijing Platform of Action. To further implement the Beijing Platform of Action within a bilateral context, the Department of State, in cooperation with the U.S. Ambassador to Vienna, Austria, sponsored Vital Voices: Women in Democracy in July 1997. One hundred and fifty women from the newly independent states of Eastern and Central Europe, along with 150 from Western democracies, assembled to discuss common concerns in politics, business, and law and the role women can play in helping to promote democracy.[15]

In terms of NGOs, the National Women's Conference Committee convened a twentieth-anniversary commemoration of the 1977 Houston Conference in Washington, D.C., in November 1997. Representatives of national societies of major transnational associations attended to discuss progress achieved since 1977 and action still to be taken.[16]

At the state government levels, implementation is not well publicized, although almost forty of the fifty states have commissions on women. In the state government of Pennsylvania, a Commission on the Status of Women initially established in the early 1970s has most recently been inactive. Governor Ridge signed an executive order reestablishing the Commission in June 1997. A reestablished Commission could help implement relevant recommendations from the Beijing Platform of Action along with the U.S. commitments relevant to the state. A progress report on Pennsylvania's activities in the area of women's advancement would be a useful step forward.

Within western Pennsylvania, the executive committee of the Pittsburgh/Beijing '95 and Beyond project prepared and circulated to interested persons a follow-up statement of activities organized within the critical areas of concern of the Beijing Platform. The project leaders and members participated in the nationally televised teleconference on September 28, 1996, sponsored by the U.S. Delegation and Inter-Agency Committee. The more than forty women from the Pittsburgh area who attended the international conference of governments and the NGO Forum have gained increased consciousness about the issues and the goals, strategies and recommended action needed to advance women's status in the region. Ideally, they will be in a position to monitor whether and to what extent law, policies, and customs need to be altered to promote equality, development, and peace within the region.

The governmental and unofficial, transnational associations of women that have been so tremendously significant to the advancement of women internationally are also important at national, state, and local levels. Energized with new awareness of internationally agreed upon goals, strategies, and recommended actions from Beijing, the Pittsburgh/ Beijing '95 and Beyond project can itself contribute to implementing international action plans at home.

Notes

1. *The United Nations and the Advancement of Women,* Blue Book Series (New York: United Nations, 1995); Anne Winslow, ed., *Women, Politics and the United Nations* (Westport, Conn.: Greenwood, 1995); Hilka Pietilla and Jean Vickers, *Making Women Matter,* rev. ed. (Atlantic Highlands, N.J.: Zed Books, Ltd., 1994).

2. Robert O. Keohane and Joseph S. Nye Jr., eds., *Transnational Relations and World Politics* (Cambridge: Harvard University Press, 1971), ix–xi; xvii.

3. Margaret E. Galey, "Forerunners in Women's Quest for Partnership," in *Women, Politics and the United Nations,* 1–10.

4. UN, ECOSOC, Res. 48(4), March 29, 1947.

5. *The United Nations and the Advancement of Women,* 8–26; 37–64.

6. *The World Plan of Action,* approved by the UN World Conference on IWY in Mexico City, appears in *Report of the World Conference on International Women's Year* (New York: United Nations, 1975). The *World Program of Action,* approved by the UN World Conference of the UN Decade for Women held in Copenhagen, appears in *Report of the World Conference of the UN Decade for Women* (New York: United Nations, 1980). *Forward-Looking Strategies for the Advancement of Women to the Year 2000,* approved by the World Conference to Review and Appraise the UN Decade for Women held in Nairobi, Kenya, appears in the *Report of the World Conference* (New York: United Nations, 1985). The *Platform of Action,* approved by the Fourth World Women's Conference, held in Beijing, China, appears in *Report of the World Conference* (New York: United Nations, 1995).

7. *The World's Women 1995: Trends and Statistics* (New York: United Nations, 1995). *The World Survey of the Role of Women in Development* (New York: United Nations, 1994). See also *The United Nations and the Advancement of Women,* 26–37, and *Women in Politics and Decision-making in the Late Twentieth Century: A United Nations Study* (Boston: Martinus Nijhoff, 1992).

8. UNGA Res. 48/104 of 20 December 1993. See Document 107 in *Advancement of Women,* 459–62. The Committee on the Elimination of Discrimination Against Women was established following the entry into force of the Convention on the Elimination of Discrimination Against Women by Articles 17 through 22 of the Convention. The committee consists of expert members who review the reports of states parties to the convention and make recommendations to improve domestic law and practice concerning the status of women. The text of the convention is found in Document 69 in *Advancement of Women,* 234–40.

9. M. Galey, "Women Find A Place," in Winslow, *Women, Politics and the UN,* 19.

10. Marty Chen, "Engendering World Conferences: The International Women's

Movement and the UN," in *NGOs, the UN and Global Governance,* ed. Thomas G. Weiss and Leon Gordenker (Boulder, Colo.: Lynn Reinner, 1996), 139–55.

11. Margaret Schuler, *Empowerment and the Law* (Washington, D.C.: OEF International, 1986), 29.

12. Ibid.

13. Mary Wollstonecraft, *Vindication of the Rights of Women* (London: Penguin, 1988).

14. *America's Commitment: Federal Programs Benefitting Women and New Initiatives as Follow-up to the UN Fourth World Conference on Women* (Washington, D.C.: President's Interagency Council on Women, 1997).

15. Swanee Hunt, "Women's Vital Voices," *Foreign Affairs* (July/August 1997): 2–7.

16. *Building on Beijing: United States NGOs Shape Women's National Action Agenda* (Muscatine, Iowa: Stanley Foundation, 1977).

PITTSBURGH/ BEIJING '95 AND BEYOND

Nairobi was all about the problems of women. Beijing was about the power, the potential of women.

—*Maureen Reagan*

A Brief History
Regina Birchem, Carol Campbell, and Teresa Wilson

Early in 1984, in preparation for the UN Third World Conference on Women to be held in Nairobi, Kenya, the next year, Carol Campbell initiated the Beyond Nairobi Conference for Women in southwestern Pennsylvania, a forward-looking strategy session to mark the close of the UN Decade for Women. Even though Bella Abzug appeared as the keynote speaker for the event held at the downtown YWCA, there did not exist, at that time, the collective will in the Pittsburgh community to address recommendations of the Nairobi conference document at the local level.

A decade later, in January 1994, Ms. Campbell, as president of the United Nations Association of Pittsburgh, and Teresa Wilson, vice president of international programming for Pennsylvania Peace Links, convened about a dozen internationally minded women to determine the local interest level in the UN Fourth World Conference on Women and accompanying NGO forum to be held in Beijing in August–September 1995. The energy and interest of this ad hoc group were such that they adopted the name Pittsburgh/Beijing '95 and Beyond (PBB) to express their goal of making the global conference meaningful and of lasting importance locally. An executive committee (Carol Campbell, Margaret Galey, Mary Rusinow, Clarke Thomas, and Teresa Wilson) with considerable knowledge concerning women's issues and UN conferences initiated plans for Pittsburgh's participation in the conference. "Participation in the conference" included not only attending the UN conference and associated events but also promoting the conference themes—equality, development, and peace—and the subthemes—health, education and employment—in Pittsburgh and southwestern Pennsylvania.

A series of meetings began, involving at first ten, then twenty, then ever-increasing numbers of interested participants. Out of these meetings, a mailing list of more than four hundred women, representing themselves and many and diverse local organizations, was generated. Newsletters regarding the conference were produced and distributed.

A task force, convened by Sohini Sinha and Adelaide Smith, organized a forum of events from March 24 to April 7, 1995. The six committees that formed around the themes and subthemes of the conference
held a variety of activities scheduled around International Women's Day,
March 8. These activities included radio interviews, a Chinese festival for
women's health at Magee-Womens Hospital, a women-in-transition art
exhibit and panel discussion, a peace workshop at LaRoche College, a
theater performance based on the work of Zora Neale Hurston, a sympo-
sium featuring keynote speaker Anna Quindlen, an interfaith dialogue at
the Pittsburgh Islamic Center, and workshops and lectures on employment, equality, and education.

A major effort was put forth from the very beginning to engage young
women and members of the academic community in the preparations for
and follow-up to the Beijing conference. The University of Pittsburgh
Graduate School of Public and International Affairs generously donated
space and equipment as a resource center and office. Chatham College
and Carlow College offered meeting space and program support. Regina
Birchem was hired as a part-time coordinator.

Many organizations and individuals contributed to the success of
PBB. Initial funding was provided by the Heinz philanthropies and
prominent local political leaders. Later grants came from the Pittsburgh
Foundation and the Jewish Health Care Foundation. Magee-Womens
Hospital gave generous assistance in printing brochures and newsletters.
The World Federalist Association of Pittsburgh contributed time and
money to the effort. Numerous others made the work and mission of PBB
a priority within their own organizations.

PBB became an umbrella organization for women representing campus organizations; women's studies programs; community groups related
to health, housing, domestic violence, and other crises; peace and political organizations; religious groups and churches; colleges, universities,
and other educational institutions; and women's employment and volunteer groups.

Several individuals participated in the regional pre-Beijing conference
in Wilmington, Delaware, and some also attended the UN preparatory
committee meetings in New York City and in China. More than forty

people from Pittsburgh communities attended the conference and forum in Beijing. PBB acquired NGO status for participation at the conference. This status enabled PBB to have two women, Mary Rusinow and Carol Campbell, accredited to attend the official government meetings as observers and to participate in NGO caucuses. Scholarships totaling more than $11,500 were raised through PBB and Pennsylvania Peace Links to send four women who might not otherwise have been able to attend (Sohini Sinha, Andrea Blinn, Linda Hunt, and Adelle Williams). Fourteen people participated in the Peace Train, a month-long journey from Helsinki to Beijing organized by the Women's International League for Peace and Freedom, based in Geneva, Switzerland. On their return from Beijing, participants described their rich experiences through more than four hundred talks and presentations in the Pittsburgh community during 1995 and 1996.

The Beijing conference produced a Platform for Action. The goal of PBB was to move from local needs (Pittsburgh) to global needs (Beijing '95) and then to implement the recommendations of the platform here in our home communities—and beyond. This was to be accomplished by providing local organizations with information about the platform and by assisting them to coordinate their efforts to implement it.

A new steering committee (Brenda Kagle, Suzanne Polen, Roseann Rife, and Louise Wilde) was formed early in 1996 to guide the "beyond" work of PBB. This included reporting to the foundations that had provided grants, organizing a daylong conference around the national teleconference on September 28, 1996, creating and distributing a final brochure, and organizing records and materials to be turned over to the archives at Carnegie Library in Oakland, Pennsylvania, and the Hillman Library at the University of Pittsburgh.

PBB played a unique role in the community by providing expertise and knowledge of the official UN and U.S. documents relating to the Beijing conference, an office and resource center with documents and contacts, a speakers' bureau on the Beijing events and documents, a liaison between Pittsburgh and government agencies such as the White House Interagency Council on Women, and a diverse membership with extensive knowledge of the Pittsburgh community.

The work of PBB came to an end in November 1996, but the task of "bringing Beijing home" continues. Three organizations, Pennsylvania Peace Links, the World Federalist Association of Pittsburgh, and the U.S. Committee for UNIFEM/Western Pennsylvania chapter, have agreed to field further inquiries. Other local organizations and institutions must work together, and with governments, to make the goals and aspirations of women expressed in the Beijing Platform for Action, the major document agreed upon at the conference, a reality locally and around the world.

Funding Pittsburgh/Beijing '95 and Beyond

Clarke Thomas

I became involved in the Pittsburgh/Beijing '95 and Beyond project as program chair for the United Nations Association of Pittsburgh. We saw participation in the Beijing conference as an important way to exemplify the role of the United Nations in its fiftieth anniversary year beyond General Assembly and Security Council debates, which capture so much of the world's attention.

As it turned out, on committees and in planning sessions, I was often the only man present—a refreshing switch on the usual minority representation in the general run of affairs. Because efficient, highly capable women were present, this particular male felt no need to assert himself in these meetings.

An early goal of PBB was to select several women, through an application process, and to provide financial assistance for them to attend the conference. Other than participating in selecting scholarship recipients, my main role was in helping raise money for the project and for scholarships. This effort proved to be more difficult than expected.

A basic problem was that the Beijing project didn't fit the usual parameters of foundation-grant policy. Foundations like to have applications statistically based, with money spent either locally through some established organization or to some local benefit. These obviously are desirable objectives.

But the Beijing project was something different. It was unusual in being a grassroots effort, coming simultaneously from women activists in many organizations but not specifically from their organizations as such. And they saw it not only as participation in an international effort on behalf of women in many lands but also as a possible springboard for action in Pittsburgh to meet what they considered inhibiting situations for women. (It turned out in Beijing that the Pittsburgh women found the same scenario had occurred elsewhere—a spontaneous grassroots interest, with a hope that attendance at Beijing could promote women's causes internationally and help ignite action back home in their own communities.)

It proved difficult to translate these hopes and dreams into language that fit foundation criteria. We were told there was a lack of statistics; yet it proved difficult to obtain funding for requisite surveys by academic experts. It was suggested that we should show that women were "speaking with one voice" on the issue—an impossibility when women, as with any other group, are split among themselves on so many differing agendas.

In fairness to both sides, it could be said that the foundations found themselves unable to provide money that didn't meet criteria that an amorphous group like this couldn't provide.

Fortunately, timely help came from two sources within the larger community. One was a $2,500 scholarship, provided by a prominent woman civic leader; the other was from the Heinz philanthropies, which provided two $2,500 scholarships, thanks to Executive Director Frank Tugwell.

This generosity was in addition to some ongoing support that had come both from within the women's community itself and from numerous broadly based civic organizations. Pennsylvania Peace Links provided one $4,000 scholarship to a woman of color to participate in the Peace Train from Helsinki to Beijing, joining thirteen others from the Pittsburgh area. A private source provided another $2,500. In addition, donations and in-kind support came from many individuals and organizations for operations, as well as for scholarships.

Looking back on the Beijing conference, it is not clear that governments, which seemed quite willing to endorse the Platform for Action at the conference, are following through on their commitments. Apparently, monitoring the governments to see that they fulfill their promises is being left to the formal women's groups and to the many grassroots organizations whose presence in the NGO component of the Beijing conference made it so memorable for thousands of women.

This effort in Pittsburgh was taken up under an altered rubric—Pittsburgh/Beijing and Beyond—involving not only the nearly fifty women who went to Beijing but many other organizations that have put the Beijing Platform for Action on their agendas. Funding for coordinating this effort was provided by the Pittsburgh Foundation ($5,000) and the Jewish Health Care Foundation ($2,000).

Editor's note: Funding for the "beyond" work of Pittsburgh/Beijing and Beyond was also provided by the many organizations who contributed honoraria on behalf of women who, upon returning from Beijing, made presentations to those organizations (see "Conversations After Beijing" in appendix B).

Other funding sources included Three Rivers Community Fund; U.S. Department of Labor, Women's Bureau Region III; the Equitable Foundation; many generous private contributors; and the University Center for International Studies, University of Pittsburgh, which provided office space.

iii THE PEACE TRAIN

Women's International League

for Peace and Freedom,

August 7–29, 1995

In 1994 Barbara Lochbihler, secretary-general of the Women's International League for Peace and Freedom (WILPF), came to Pittsburgh to describe her dream of a Peace Train that would begin in Helsinki, Finland, where the Eightieth Congress of WILPF would be held in early August 1995. This journey would terminate in Beijing, China, at the NGO forum, which would overlap the official governmental United Nations Fourth World Conference on Women in September. In the year following Barbara's visit, an ad hoc group of more than four hundred peace activists and individuals from many grassroots organizations, colleges, and health and cultural institutions was formed (see part II). From this group, fourteen made the decision to travel on the Peace Train.

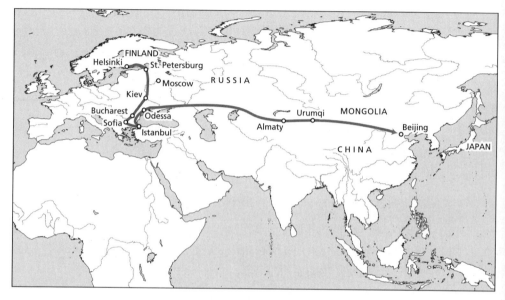

The Peace Train route.

The Women's International League
for Peace and Freedom

Regina Birchem

Jane Addams, the social worker, suffragist, and Nobel Peace Prize winner, was the founder of the Women's International League for Peace and Freedom. In one of her books, *The Long Road of Women's Memory*, published in 1916, she included an essay entitled "Women's Memory—Challenging War." The essay reflects on a conversation she had with two German women who had lost their sons in the war in Europe. The German women saw the war as a tragic setback in social progress and in programs of health, education, and culture.

Addams wrote:

> This may be a call to women to defend those at the bottom of society who, irrespective of the victory or defeat of any army, are ever oppressed and overburdened. The suffering mothers of the disinherited feel the stirring of the old impulse to protect and cherish their unfortunate children, and women's haunting memories instinctively challenge war as the implacable enemy of their age-long undertaking.

In her book *Peace and Bread in Time of War*, Addams describes the reaction of many, who worked with the immigrants and in settlement communities in Chicago and elsewhere, to the outbreak of the European war. It was a reversal of all they were trying to achieve in social arrangements among people of a wide variety of ethnic backgrounds living together peaceably and with dignity in urban communities. The Carnegie Endowment sponsored several lecturers who spoke at colleges throughout the country. The lectures were on the history of the peace movement and on proposals for rational negotiation as an alternative to war. Jane Addams herself gave twelve such lectures.

Several organizations were formed during the first months of the war. The membership included many well-known suffragists, a sort of who's who of women of the time, from both sides of the conflict. A two-day convention called by Carrie Chapman Catt and Jane Addams brought three thousand U.S. women together and became the beginning of the Women's Peace Party. They proposed a plan for continuous mediation among the warring countries. Music and theater were used to promote their program. For example, the Carnegie Endowment for International Peace gave five thousand dollars to finance the Little Theater Company of Chicago's production of Gilbert Murray's version of *The Trojan Women* by Euripides.

In March 1915 Dutch, Belgian, and British women issued an invitation for an International Congress of Women to be held at the Hague, the Netherlands, April 28 to May 1. Many of the women were members of the International Suffrage Conference. In those days without email or fax machines, without having the right to vote, without transatlantic jet flights, and in a time of war, the women quickly organized the conference.

Forty-seven women from the United States paid their own expenses, trusted in the usefulness of the venture, and set sail for Holland in mid-April on a Dutch cargo ship upon which they were almost the only passengers. They used the ship's salon for daily conferences and discussions on the history of the peace movement and the task confronting them.

When they arrived within sight of the cliffs of Dover, they were not allowed to go further for three days. Immediately, they telegraphed everyone they knew in England and Washington to exert pressure to be allowed to continue the journey. Meanwhile, they were ridiculed by the press as "peacettes" and were accused of lowering the morale of the soldiers. Eventually they were allowed to continue their journey. They arrived in Rotterdam two hours before the start of the congress.

British women faced more daunting problems. The North Sea was closed to traffic the very day eighty-seven British women were about to depart for the Hague. They waited in protest at the British port during the entire congress for a boat or "flying machine." Two British women already on the Continent represented Britain at the conference.

More than a thousand women came to the congress from twelve countries. They were all suffragists and believed in the peaceful resolution of conflict. They were prominent women in the international suffragists movement who rejected the idea that war was inevitable. They proclaimed that the war was not their war and they were going to work together to end it.

A committee consisting of two women from each country was formed and called the Women's International Committee for Permanent Peace with headquarters in the Netherlands. Four years later it became the Women's International League for Peace and Freedom.

The women were committed to creating international relations such that war would become impossible, to working for the equality of women, and to educating coming generations so these goals would be realized.

> The League is made up of people who believe that we are not obliged to choose between violence and passive acceptance of unjust conditions for ourselves and others; who believe, on the contrary, that courage, determination, moral power, generous indignation, active goodwill can achieve their ends without violence. We believe that experience condemns force as a self-defeating weapon although men are still so disposed to use it in education, in dealing with crime, in affecting or preventing social changes, and above all in carrying out national policies. We believe that new methods, free from violence, must be worked out for ending abuses and for undoing wrongs, as well as for achieving positive ends. (Jane Addams, *Bread and Peace in Time of War,* 1922)

What keeps the members of the league together across oceans and national and cultural boundaries is the international congresses held every three years. Women from all the countries in which we have sections—now more than forty—participate. The 1995 congress, WILPF's eightieth year, was held in Helsinki, Finland. The theme of this congress was building a sustainable and secure world society. At its conclusion, on August 7, the WILPF Peace Train departed for Beijing.

Banners Are Statements

Mary Leigh Touvell

After the formation of the Pittsburgh/Beijing '95 and Beyond coalition, Mary Rusinow designed the logo for PBB with the help of Hongfen Zhang who wrote the Chinese letters spelling *Pittsburgh*. Hongfen Zhang is the wife of a Heinz Fellow at the University of Pittsburgh. This logo and the UN nongovernmental organizations' logo of the eight dancing women was used on tote bags for promotion of the UN Fourth World Conference on Women and the corresponding NGO forum in China.

Mary Leigh Touvell and Bertha Hayes with the PBB banner.

Those persons going to Beijing from Pittsburgh wished to recognize each other in the crowds so scarves were made using the PBB logo printed in black on gold cloth—what else but our city's sports colors!

Banners were requested for use on the Peace Train as it traveled from Helsinki to Beijing. Ideas were bantered about and I volunteered the construction of our statement using the PBB logo and the NGO logo. "Pittsburgh to the forum and conference in Beijing to learn and share, returning to work in our community for equality, development, and peace as active dancing people."

Our banner was hung at the Eightieth Congress of the Women's International League for Peace and Freedom in Helsinki, displayed in the window of the traveling Russian train, carried at each city stopover, and captured on foreign news cameras until it finally reached the Peace Tent in Huairou, China.

Signatures on the banner are those of the Peace Train travelers.

Lessons from the Peace Train

Miki Rakay

On August 7, 1995, 224 women and 9 men from forty-two countries left Helsinki by train for St. Petersburg, Russia. The next day they boarded their uniquely routed sixteen-car train for Kiev, Ukraine; Bucharest, Romania; Sofia, Bulgaria; Istanbul, Turkey; Odessa, Ukraine; Almaty, Kazakhstan; Urumqi, China; and Beijing.

The travelers were culturally, politically, economically, and philosophically diverse—and any other "-ally" one can think of. The common link was the intensity of their desire for peace and social justice, many bonding in warm personal comradeship. The ages spanned eighteen to eighty-six, predominantly Western in background and middle-aged. There were 110 from the United States, including a determined few with serious physical disabilities. About twenty young women from many countries participated in a rolling school (led by two university professors), which was held daily in one of the two conference cars. These dynamic women developed great solidarity through process, discussion, and interchange. Issues of sexism, ageism, nationalism, and racism engaged their perceptions. These issues percolated to the surface and climaxed in a full train meeting held on the grass in a Saratov park adjacent to the railroad station. The question, Is the peace train a community? elicited a bell curve of responses from yes! to no!

On the train, at the seven scheduled overnight stops and the two unscheduled daytime stopovers in Saratov and Voronezh, Russia, multiple workshops and seminars were scheduled. Small informal discussions never ceased from early morn to late at night, through meals in the three dining cars, on bus trips to hotels and to prearranged regional meetings. Impromptu gatherings included the traditional wedding, without the far-away groom, of a Sudanese woman from Cairo, dressed in veils, hands painted with henna.

The Peace Train was met at each stop, prearranged by WILPF, by coalitions of women's groups who had organized series of discussions on peace, disarmament, conflict resolution, worsening economic situations, increasing joblessness and the resulting hardships, and violence.

The French resumption of nuclear testing in the Pacific drew passionate protest from the Helsinki WILPF Congress and throughout the trip, especially in the Chernobyl area where the impact of that disaster is still being felt. Contempt for the indigenous people in the affected area has resulted in catastrophic effects on the health of women and children. The issues of environment, nuclear energy, and nuclear testing were constants at all the stops.

We had varying degrees of significant interchange with the local inhabitants we met at each stop. Often we were the listeners with few questions. The views we heard ran the gamut from the intransigence of some still-entrenched Communist Party members (sometimes under euphemisms for the party name) longing for the old days of security with good social benefits, to the hope and support and perceptions of new freedoms with an as-yet-unrealized free market economy. In Russia the existence of a Mafia control filters through all walks of life.

In Bucharest we discussed the impact of the Bosnian war on the 4 million Romanians who live in the former Yugoslavia and on the economy and trade relations between the two countries. The embargo has stopped navigation on the Danube River. This, combined with the ravaged economy of the post-Ceaușescu regime, the rise of the sex industry, the increase of tuberculosis, the link between power and violence, and the lack of jobs, job security, and child care, exposes the enormous fragility of life in Romania. As one of the women said, "We're thirsting for our experience in these times of transition." The sad tales of increased criminality, nationalism, domestic violence, and the concomitant decrease in women's rights continued at our stop in Sofia, Bulgaria.

In Sofia, following an overview of the Bosnian War and its effect on women, two young Serbian women from Belgrade gave a fervent presentation of the struggle for life during war and their devotion to and participation in the Women in Black. One day a week, dressed in black, they stand silently in the main square in protest of the war. Their range of services includes material support for refugees. Other meetings dealt with violence against women and minorities. Zena Borisova, a Roma, recited a litany of laws and customs discriminating against her people.

Istanbul, population 7 million, eight bus hours and a border crossing away, vibrated and surged with people, energy, bustle, traffic, noise, pollution, ancient ruins, mosques, enterprises, new buildings, and crowded old buildings. In this multifaceted society, women are caught between two worlds: religion and secularization. Turkey constitutionally separates government and religion. Morcati, or the Purple Roof, shelters for abused women hosted some of us in their administrative offices, down a steep dingy alley off a main street. Until 1926 *shari'a*, the Islamic legal code, prevailed. Now the Swiss civil code is the law. Laws of property and inheritance do not discriminate between men and women, but in practice laws, as well as customs, favor men in all matters.

At the large meeting in the evening, a vibrant, powerful group of women gave the history of the Turkish Women's Movement. The feminist movement is responsible for removing the "curtain of silence" around violence issues. After meetings with the Turkish women, WILPF Peace Train participants made specific demands of the Turkish government to end military attacks on Kurdish people. The Peace Train also urged all arms-supplying countries to stop the arms trade with Turkey, one of the largest importers of weapons in Europe. A plea was issued to President Tansu Ciller, the acclaimed woman president of Turkey, whom we gathered has disappointed many feminists.

Almaty, Kazakhstan, the largest of five Central Asian countries and formerly part of the Soviet Union, lies between the Russian and Chinese nuclear testing sites of Semipalatinsk and Lop Nor. Meetings were sponsored by Women of the Orient for Nuclear-Free World and Ecological Security, Unions of Victims of Nuclear Tests, and Semipalatinsk the names hauntingly echoing the concerns.

Urumqi, which was to have been the Peace Train's first overnight stop in China, is remembered as the stop we did not make. On August 17, in Odessa, we learned that the Chinese government, in coordination with the Russian, Ukrainian, and Kazakhstan governments, would not permit the Peace Train to cross the Kazakh-China border until August 26, and we would not be able to stay overnight in Urumqi. A valiant effort on the part of a hastily formed ad hoc committee, with embassy and governmental connections, protested this delay to no avail. The reason for the change has been the topic of many discussions; officially, there was no explanation. We crossed the border on the evening of August 26 at Alanshankou, a remote border station. This somewhat surrealistic event occurred at the far western edge of Xinjiang Province where, surrounded by uniformed men and a few women, we dragged our belongings off the Russian train, scrambled down a steep bank where the train had stopped, were herded into small buses and driven to the Chinese station, waited in long lines through an inconsistent security system, and several hours later, were led onto our new train.

The train left at midnight. We rumbled through Urumqi, with a brief platform stop at 9:00 A.M. on August 27. From the moving train, the pollution, industrialization, and Soviet-style concrete buildings gave way on the outskirts to the mud houses and courtyards I remembered from my visit there in 1983. The roads leading out of the city were lively with truck traffic. Time had not enhanced Urumqi.

On August 29, late in the evening, we emerged from the train onto the Beijing platform, to the strains of *Auld Lang Syne* and the helpful greetings of dozens of youthful volunteers. We were taken by bus to the Workers' Stadium where, amid organized confusion, we obtained official identification and then were bused to our various hotels. Bused is the operative word. Herds of buses took us to the Asian Games Stadium the next day to attend the NGO forum opening ceremonies, a colorful extravaganza of great preparation and cost. And buses would now be our main form of transportation to and from Huairou where, in the midst of tents, dust, mud, a melange of hastily built or not yet completed buildings, milling crowds in richly varied native dress, hundreds of scattered workshops, irksome toilet accommodations, and limited technology, we would make history.

I am often asked whether I would go again.

In a heartbeat!

Helsinki to Beijing

Molly Rush

Thanks largely to the generosity of the Thomas Merton Center support-ers, Shirley Gleditsch and I took off for New York and Helsinki at the end of July 1995, ready for adventure.*

We were mostly women, coming from forty-two countries. The train route had never been attempted before. Hotels and buses had to be se-cured in the cities where we would stop overnight. We would use three trains, along with a bus to Istanbul. The shipping company that was to take us across the Black Sea went bankrupt. The Russian train would twice need to change wheels to accommodate the different gauges of track. Plans had to be coordinated for meetings and workshops with women in each city. In some, the very idea of nongovernmental organiza-tions was a new one.

Despite all this, despite our frustration with Chinese officials, with travel agents, and even with WILPF over issues of communication and decision making, despite sore throats and coughs that raged through the train, I would not trade a minute of this truly once-in-a-lifetime experi-ence.

Since we've come home, those of us on the train, as well as the others from Pittsburgh who traveled directly to the conference and forum, have learned that each of us had different experiences and perceptions. What I have to say is just one view of an incredibly rich and important experi-ence that tens of thousands of women and men found in and on the way to Beijing.

Helsinki, August 6, Hiroshima Day: The peace groups in Helsinki held a candlelight vigil near one of Helsinki's beautiful fingers of water. Hundreds were there for the music, dance, speeches (some in Finnish), and lantern-floating ceremony. Of major concern was the just-announced French nuclear testing, which broke the moratorium in the West. I

*A version of this article first appeared in the November 1995 issue of the *New People,* the newsletter of the Thomas Merton Center.

thought of plans for the Pittsburgh vigil and felt very connected with the worldwide outpouring against the bomb. Next day we boarded the train.

St. Petersburg is a city full of the past grandeur of prerevolutionary Russia's emperors. The Hermitage collection includes an all-gold clock made for Catherine the Great. The clock, which chimed in public for the first time in years, features creatures that move, including an owl, a rooster, a squirrel, and a full-size peacock that spreads its tail and nods. Buildings and churches are being restored, but economic problems abound. Our Peace Train delegation met with the acting mayor and with women, among them a World War II veteran and one of a group of mothers of soldiers who fiercely criticized the war in Chechnya. At the station, we boarded our Russian Peace Train, sixteen cars long, with sleeping compartments, three cars for dining, and two for meetings. Our "wagon" was kept in order by Nadia, from Moscow.

Kiev, Ukraine, is described as a park with a city rather than a city with parks. It is dominated by a huge statue of Mother Ukraine, which may be replaced by a memorial to Chernobyl victims, we were told. Local women cooked for us an incredible six-course meal, served in the Parliament. We had paid for the ingredients. The next morning, we met with top officials, including the minister of defense, who told us there is not a plot of ground in Ukraine that has not been contaminated by the Chernobyl disaster, with drastic effects on health, especially children's. Western-U.S. promises to help pay for cleanup have not been kept.

Bucharest, Romania, was reached only after we were awakened for our passports by Moldovian security at 4 A.M. and after a layover to have the wheels changed on our train to fit a different gauge rail, an amazing process in which each car was lifted up separately. Corn, wheat, sunflowers, and wildflowers abounded as we rolled through the countryside of a nation devastated by cruel tyranny until 1989. Beggars were everywhere. Young unionists and human rights activists hosted an excellent workshop on women and work.

Many visited Ceaușescu's marble and gold palace, including Sister Joan Chittister, who was enraged at the monstrousness of what she saw. Silvia Kerim, a journalist I met on the street, pointed out graffiti on a wall, "Hitler, Stalin, Ceaușescu," left from the 1989 revolution, and a wooden cross commemorating a sixteen-year-old girl who was killed. "I could not have talked to you then," Silvia told me. She was happy to be able to buy bread, cheese, fruits, and vegetables in the market. "Even the melons ripen earlier," she said.

Sofia, Bulgaria, is in a terrible economic condition. But worse, unlike Bucharest, there seemed little hope. In one workshop, women spoke of wanting to return to the Communist past, when people's lives were better. Our hotel porter, who brightened on hearing we were going to Istanbul, remembered better days when she'd been able to travel. Now she has no apartment, no car, no hope. We took a cab downtown to a spot where the Sheraton Hotel abuts a courtyard with an ancient church standing amid two-thousand-year-old Roman ruins. Talk about juxtaposition! Before that, Shirley and I happened on a restaurant with a nice courtyard where a wonderful meal, including wine and a piece of an amazing chocolate torte, totaled about twelve dollars. Next: Turkey by bus.

Istanbul featured a very sophisticated talk on the history of the women's movement there and visits to a women's shelter and a women's library. I awoke in our hotel at 5 A.M. to the haunting sound of the Muslim call to prayer. We took a jammed tram to Hagia Sophia, an ancient Christian church that is being restored. It has a number of more recent Muslim additions. We visited a beautiful mosque, removing our shoes to enter. And, of course, the huge bazaar in this bustling city of 6 or 7 million people was a must. Children selling postcards and toys followed us down the streets. Streets were filled with women dressed in chador; we saw flowers, parks, and hundreds of shops; 1970s rock music blared from loudspeakers in sidewalk cafes. Such a contrast to the austere former Soviet bloc where Camel and Coke ads dominated the scenery.

Our buses took us back across the border, to where we thought our train was waiting. Oops! We had to go on to the next town before we could get back home to our train, welcomed with smiles by our Russian staff, now our friends.

Odessa, Ukraine, is a Black Sea resort. A ship from the Sixth Fleet was moored at the eclectic dock, but try to cash a traveler's check! We walked for endless blocks to the hotel where my guidebook had directed us, only to be told, "Sorry." After fifteen minutes of conferring, we were directed to a bank, another long walk on streets with names in Cyrillic letters. Finally, we found a small, modern building with only a round reception booth. Yes, we do cash them, but the money box is now locked up. We were crestfallen. We explained that we were out of cash and about to leave for Beijing. "Please wait," we were told. Refreshed with bottled water on a tray, we were led to a new white car. We took off, with us in the back, two young men in the front. We arrived back at the dock, where they had called ahead to a place that would cash my check. With a hundred dollars in my pocket, we found a cabbie who, when asked, "How much?" mumbled, "Money, money, money is not my motto." He dropped us off near the train station, next to a statue in the park. "Photograph Lenin!" he barked, taking off before we could pay him.

At this point we were informed by WILPF that the Chinese had canceled our scheduled stop in Urumqi and delayed our entry into China by two days. So we had a long, zigzag ride through Russia, with two unscheduled stops of a few hours each.

Voronezh, Russia, was once a closed city. It's big, over a million people. It was more than 90 percent destroyed during World War II and was rebuilt in a style in keeping with its past. We stumbled across a huge war memorial in a park. There we met Victor and Borodin. Ukrainian-born Victor, a former English teacher, told us about the city, translating for his friend and for some young Russian men we met as we drank the local beer in an outdoor cafe. Again, the story was one of economic decay. Victor was now a hotel porter, translating for guests, including U.S. astronauts visiting this city that once produced liquid rocket fuel.

Saratov, Russia, is on the beautiful, wide Volga River, a once-elegant city with some beautiful buildings, some old, some of the Soviet era with heroic mosaics. We took a long walk to the dock, where Mary Rusinow of Pittsburgh had negotiated a ride for about eighteen of us on an old tub for about three dollars a person, a bargain indeed. We rode back to the huge train station on a tram. At our stop, the conductor waved me off without collecting the fare. "God bless you," he said, on hearing we were heading for Beijing. But first came a two-day ride through Russia and Kazakhstan.

Almaty, Kazakhstan, surrounded by mountains, is a large, modern city. There we attended a workshop on ecology and art with speakers from Semipalatinsk, the site of seven hundred Russian nuclear bomb tests, including aboveground tests. "Under Stalin, no one asked about the effects," we were told. If you protested, you were removed from your job. The 1953 H-bomb explosion there still affects the people. The area is contaminated with radioactivity. Many have died or are suffering from cancer, radiation diseases, and malformations.

On February 28, 1989, the first powerful antinuclear crusade moved into action. Over 4 million signatures were collected. Soon all of Kazakhstan was involved in the antinuclear movement. The movement's president told us, "Get ready for peace; struggle for peace." (Instead of "If you want peace, get ready for war.") There were demonstrations, media campaigns, hunger strikes. Coal miners, shepherds, metallurgists—all demanded an end to the tests. In 1991 the test site was shut down. The movement's emblem depicts a Shoshone Indian from Nevada and an indigenous Kazakhi sharing a peace pipe. Now, members want to stop French and Chinese testing.

A new group, Women of the Orient for a Nuclear-Free World and a Safe Environment organized a march to the Chinese border. According to the latest medical data, 80-plus percent of young women have lost their breast milk; 70 to 90 percent have anemia; 30 to 40 percent of young children do not reach one year of age. They have also found an increase in malformed animals. I presented both groups with a poster depicting the words of Richard McSorley, S.J.: "It's a sin to build a nuclear weapon."

Beijing at Last: Pollution clung to the tops of tall buildings, hiding the city's beauty the first day after our arrival. We'd been met the night before by our young Chinese escorts, the only ones permitted to greet us at the rail station. The city had been cleared of dirt, homeless people, and prostitutes. Factories had been closed and auto traffic reduced by half. Banners greeted arrivals for the NGO forum. The opening ceremonies at the Olympic Stadium were awesome, with thousands of costumed dancers, acrobats, a symphony orchestra, and a Chinese opera. Twenty thousand doves of peace were released.

The next morning we took a special bus from our modern hotel to the

Changing the wheels on the Peace Train between Russia and China. (Photo by Miki Rakay)

Huairou forum site. Shirley Gleditsch and I somehow squeezed our way into the packed auditorium for the opening plenary session featuring Nobelist Daw Aung San Suu Kyi on video from Burma and Winona LaDuke. As Suu spoke of human rights and "taking the toys [weapons] from the men" and Winona called for an end to all nuclear testing, I glanced to my left where two Chinese women, professors, were listening. Later I asked them if they liked the talks. They said they did. Before we parted, one woman hesitantly asked about Henry David Thoreau. "Yes, I know of him," I said. "Is there civil . . ." She hesitated. "Disobedience?" I asked. "Yes, is there civil disobedience in the U.S. today?" I assured her that indeed there is as she hurried off into the crowd.

All the women—those from six African nations demonstrating against domestic violence in Huairou, the Romanian women working for labor

Traditional bread of Ukraine at the train platform in Odessa. (Photo by Molly Rush)

and human rights in Bucharest, the mothers pushing baby carriages in Voronezh, the women leading the Kazakhstan antinuclear movement, the welfare moms here in Pittsburgh—all are doing unremunerated work to build a better future.

Now the governments of the world have signed a document promising to give public recognition and value to women's work, paid and unpaid. On my return, I read about a thirty-eight-year-old Thai widow, Sawieng Singsathit, who was working seventeen hours a day for sixty cents an hour making clothes in a Los Angeles sweatshop. It is up to you and me to see that the promises made in Beijing are kept.

Power

Sohini Sinha

The idea of power was not one I thought to study while I was in graduate school. It was not a topic of international relations courses or in our informal student debates. Not until my adventure on the WILPF Peace Train did I seriously consider the definition and concept of power and its effect on history and everyday life.

Of the passengers on the Peace Train, nine were men. These nine men faced sexism and lived in a hostile environment for the duration of the twenty-two-day trip. They were not really allowed to participate in meetings on the train. For example, during a discussion group meeting, if a man raised his hand to ask a question or to make a comment, more often than not he was not called on by the facilitator to participate—he was excluded from the group. There were times when the men would come into the dining car and not know whom they could sit next to; who was a friend and who wasn't. This situation was, for me, the impetus to life-altering discoveries. I started to wonder why, if women are nurturing and empowering, did this hostile atmosphere exist on the Peace Train. No one ever said we had to be hostile toward the men nor was it written anywhere, so why was it occurring on this women-dominated train? I discovered that many of the women on the train did not believe men should be involved in women's issues. To me this notion is a fruitless one. I believe women's issues are ultimately human issues, and women and men have to work together to improve the status of women and of humankind as a whole. As a youth, I am actively working to interest other youth in the idea of partnership, young women and men working together.

My next and most important discovery had to do with the concept and definition of power. After a long and frustrating day in meetings about "the men," I began to analyze the situation surrounding the men and the hostility they were facing. As I started on my analysis I began to see the similarity between their situation and that of black South Africans under the regime of apartheid, the similarity between their situation and that of women in many corporate settings. As the list of similarities between the situation of the men and that of various minority groups in the world began to grow, I began to look for the common thread between the Peace Train and the world as a whole. The first thing I looked at was decision-making bodies and structures. I concluded that the decision-making structure on the train was different from the decision-making structures in the world. Next I looked at leadership composition. That certainly was different because in the world the majority of decision-making bodies are led by men, and on the train it was led by women. Finally, I thought to examine power. As I began this examination of power, I concluded that it is defined, in the international system, as oppression and domination of those considered to be powerless. This definition of power was in operation on the train, and it was there unconsciously. We did not decide as a train that we were going to oppress and dominate the men. We did it automatically. I then began to realize that this definition of power exists, unconsciously, in every aspect of our lives. It is what makes the world go round. For example, it can be found in corporate decision-making strategies; the World Bank and International Monetary Fund use it when they make their lending decisions; it operates within some family structures. I have come to the conclusion that before discrimination, such as the sexism I witnessed on the train, can be eliminated, we must redefine *power*. I believe redefining power is going to take conscious effort at first, but in time a new definition will be as pervasive as the current one. I am grappling with how to word the new definition of power so it will be accepted by all people, no matter where they are from in the world, and to this end I have been discussing my idea on redefining power in all my post-Beijing talks.

I believe we each need to alter the definition of power for ourselves, and as we live our lives from the new definition, it will then affect all of society. I have defined power, for myself, as the "empowerment of others." And I believe the empowerment of others begins when each and every person on the globe has food, shelter, clothing, and access to education. This definition works for me because if I empower others, if I see others as equal to myself, there is no room for discrimination against them. I have found that I have had to make a conscious effort to maintain this definition of power in my life, but the more I practice it, the more it becomes the natural thing to do.

Anna Marie
Adelaide Smith

Anna Marie lived in the compartment next to ours. A German woman in her early sixties, she had a sweet round face and gentle smile. English was her second language, so she would sometimes express frustration at her lack of ease when speaking to us.

The last night on the Russian train, everyone in our wagon felt a need to celebrate and acknowledge our time together. Anna Marie came into our compartment to toast the Peace Train. She was wearing a handsome necklace with a peace dove. When we commented on it, she told us she had had it for thirty years. And then she talked about her childhood and her family.

Her father had been a lawyer and was involved in left-wing politics in Germany. In 1936 he was arrested. Because of his legal skills, he was able to defend himself and obtain his release. Later, he was drafted and sent to Poland as a medic. While there, he was captured by the British and sent to a POW camp in Austria. He escaped and made his way back to Germany. For over a year and a half, his family did not hear from him, and they did not know if he was dead or alive.

In 1947 her mother developed cancer. She had an operation, but she needed medicine following the surgery. The cost of the medicine was a kilo of butter, which the family could not afford. Her mother died. When she was twelve and her sister was fourteen, they had to identify their mother's body.

Because of the war, Anna Marie's parents had been able to spend very little time together. After the war, her mother's illness and death were a cruel blow.

She ended her story with these words: "Plenty of reasons to work for peace."

The Great Adventure
Helsinki to Beijing
Lois Goldstein

The trip to Beijing was a long one. For me it started around January 1994 when Pennsylvania Peace Links and the United Nations Association of Pittsburgh first got together to talk about Pittsburgh's part in the upcoming conference.

Then something very exciting happened in the spring of 1994. Barbara Lochbihler came to Pittsburgh from Geneva to tell us about plans for the Peace Train.

The idea was electrifying, and Pittsburgh's enthusiasm for the project helped make the dream a reality. Peace Links began raising funds to send a young woman on the Peace Train, because we strongly feel the need to support young women who plan to make peace work a significant part of their lives.

How can I convey the essence and spirit of those days on the train! First, its passengers. They ranged in age from eighteen to eighty-six, with the majority over fifty. There were about six married couples and several mother-daughter pairs. About 45 percent were from the United States. Other large groups were from Canada, Switzerland, Germany, and Australia. There was representation from every continent.

All religions were represented—there were a Methodist minister, an Anglican nun in habit, and a Catholic nun without. One woman was blind and at least three had severe difficulties in walking. Among the Americans, the largest group was from Minnesota and the second largest was from Pittsburgh. The official language was English. Almost all could understand it, and most could speak it relatively well. But the strain of having to think and express oneself in a different language was clear. By the end of each day many were exhausted.

Although most people on the train had a basic commitment to working for a more peaceful world, there was not unanimity on any particular issue, including the definition of peace itself. For some it meant inner peace, for others, survival. Some thought of it as an environment; for many it was a political concept. There was a wide range of attitudes expressed on an even wider range of subjects. These attitudes often related to one's age, national origin, race, sexual preference, or political orientation.

We boarded a relatively new Russian train for our exclusive use. It had sleeping cars at both ends and three restaurant cars and two meeting cars in the middle. One of the sleeping cars also housed a medical compartment, and there were two physicians on call.

We were relieved to find the two toilets per car were Western style and the train was air conditioned. There were nine compartments per car; some slept two in a compartment; others housed four. Each car had two female attendants who took good care of us and with whom we developed warm relationships. Each car also had a large hot water boiler and a refrigerated storage tank for the cold boiled water. There was adequate storage space; linen was changed every five days; and we were really very content in our small homes.

Organizationally, WILPF had a steering committee made up of its executive committee and travel agency staff. They met separately and then in a larger group with the spokesperson from each color-coded car to pass information and concerns back and forth. The passengers in each car, in such proximity, formed close relationships, and many are now involved in postconference correspondence.

Also on board were two video crews, one from the United States, which WILPF had contracted with to document the Peace Train, and one from Germany. There were photographers from several countries, and we found ourselves facing cameras and microphones on booms anywhere we might wander on the train.

Throughout the trip, WILPF generated press releases, which they attempted to fax at each of our stops. Communicating with the outside world was difficult and expensive, and in some cases it was impossible.

The cities were chosen as representative of societies in transition, and most of them are in either former Soviet or Soviet-bloc countries. We stayed in hotels in each city and met formally in a large group with our hosts. Usually we were also able to have smaller meetings in workshops dealing with the environment, violence toward women, health, education, and so on.

As we assessed our meetings in the seven cities, we realized we weren't always able to tell who our hosts were. True NGOs? Government-sponsored NGOs? Former party leaders who were trying to carve out new roles for themselves? What groups and leaders were included and who was left out? At best we had only partial answers.

I was very interested in the nature of leadership. Older women, in their fifties and sixties, who had been in leadership positions, with funding and resources provided by the state, seemed ill prepared to deal with the realities of grassroots organizing. They realize they'll have to develop new skills, but I have a sense they're floundering.

I wondered whether this was a generational phenomenon, since we had met with some very impressive young women, such as trade unionists in Romania and the Turkish women who had such noticeable organizational skills.

At the Chinese border we left the Russian train, went through Chinese security and customs procedures, and boarded our new, Chinese train. The atmosphere immediately changed. Traveling with us were so many additional security personnel, in uniform, with walkie-talkies, patrolling the cars and our brief stops to take on food and water that we doubled up in four-person compartments to make room for them.

During our stops over the next three days, all platforms were cleared of people, and attempts to talk to anyone on the other side of barriers were prevented. We were literally sealed off from contact with any Chinese not on the train. Although the foreign ministry had sanctioned the Peace Train, the Chinese still seemed suspicious about its purpose and what unexpected actions we might take.

An Example of Solidarity

Regina Birchem

Passengers on the WILPF Peace Train often said they "were changed forever" by the experience. Many women say that about the Beijing conference itself.

We learned from each other and from the women and men we met along the way. I offer one example of an experience that illustrates the long-term knowledge and solidarity that came from this historical train ride: meeting with the Mothers of the Russian Soldiers in St. Petersburg. Traditionally, the soldier-hero concept is used by the state as a tool to support military objectives. In Russia, soldiers' mothers are given medals, invited to special events, and receive the body of the dead soldier son. To try to protect one's son from the military service is seen as a challenge to national security. The Mothers of the Soldiers movement challenged the soldier-hero myth. The organization started before the Chechnya war as Mothers Rights Foundation, which assisted mothers who lost sons in the military.

In St. Petersburg, train participants had an opportunity to meet with members of the Association of Mothers of the Russian Soldiers. The organizers of the WILPF train had to insist that our Russian hostesses in St. Petersburg include the Mothers of the Soldiers in their program, because these brave women in the association are not accepted by all in their country.

Solange Fernex wrote in *Paix et Liberté*, the WILPF France newsletter, an editorial that encapsulates the impact of global solidarity and sisterhood. Fernex was not a passenger on the Peace Train, but she vividly tells the story of this group of women who, acting in solidarity, succeeded in accomplishing the seemingly impossible.

This group of brave women [Association of Mothers of the Russian Soldiers] who rebelled against war's madness was formed toward the end of the 1980s to fight against abuses in the Russian army as well as the neglect in awarding deferments to students. They succeeded in obtaining the return of the 170,000 conscripts who were enabled to complete their studies.

At the start of the Chechnyan war they denounced the war and became true pacifists, insisting on resolution of the conflict by political means. With the help of voluntary donations only, they organized convoys to Grozny to seek out their children, dead or alive, and take them away, ransacking hospitals and prisoner-of-war camps, harassing the army to locate the records of those who had been killed. In sisterhood with Chechnyan mothers, they demanded loudly and clearly that the killing must stop, confronting equally the Russian authorities and the Chechnyan leaders. As mothers they succeeded in keeping their sons alive, in seizing them from certain death, in persuading them to desert the army—even while the shells were exploding, even in the midst of battle in the besieged city.

Radicalized by this grievous war, they set up offices in over forty cities to counsel young men of military age and to help them avoid service.

They join with the Women in Black of Palestine, Israel, Bosnia, Croatia and of Serbia, the Meres de la Place de Mai, the Corsican women against the violence of war.

To demand equal representation in society need not signify for us, in France, and in the time of peace, that women imitate the murderous stupidity of men and serve equally in the army. We who have borne our infants for nine long months and who have guarded these fragile lives in order for them to grow as harmoniously as possible must work for the transformation of a society which pits its children one against the other, armed with deadly weapons which become more and more sophisticated. We who have daily experience of mediation, of nonviolent resolution involving family, school, place of work, must resist this violence, strive for conversion of armies, strive against war as citizens (women citizens) seeking a world which is viable and in solidarity.

At the risk of their lives, the Mothers of Russian Soldiers have set us an example. We thank them with all our hearts.

More than a year later, on October 3, 1996, the Alternative Nobel Prize (Right to Livelihood Award) was awarded to the Association of the Mothers of the Russian Soldiers.

Crossing Borders

Teresa Wilson

The first border we cross is from Finland to Russia. Though the train stops twenty minutes later because our passports have been left behind, it does not, as it would have a few years ago, produce a deadly fear of the armed guards of a police state: this is Russia 1995, and the mix-up only means an annoying delay.*

The Finnish and Russian sides of the border have only their birch forests in common. The homes, the gardens, the fences, the roads—all seem to deteriorate the farther we move into Russia. Dachas with rusted corrugated roofs replace well-built wooden cottages. Now we see dirt paths instead of paved walks. But the rough Russian tracks do become smoother as we approach the stations of suburban St. Petersburg.

At each stop we will be meeting with local women. In St. Petersburg we hear stories—they will be repeated at each stop ahead—about unemployment and women's loss of status as the society suffers in its shift from a socialist to a capitalist economy. "Women have no property, no money, no children, no social contacts," a professor of women's studies tells us. "Older women have now lost the state safety net of medical care, pensions, and guaranteed housing." Women veterans and the mothers of soldiers express nostalgia for a society that is gone. Their city now is corrupt, controlled by the Mafia. They have gained the freedom to discuss their fears and frustrations, but one of them asks, "What are we to choose, now that we are free to do so?"

New to my ears is the extent of public dissent and disagreement. I'm heartened to hear fierce denunciations of the war in Chechnya, though not all the Russian women join in. They are as one, however, in asserting that domestic violence is on the rise.

Except for the general decay of streets and buildings and the westernizing of some things fondly remembered from earlier visits, St. Petersburg seems little changed. But then, on an early morning walk, I observe an

*Excerpted from an article first published in *Cross Currents*, spring 1996.

old man sweeping the street, while nearby an old woman begs, and I am reminded that in earlier years there were always sweeping assignments for older women in exchange for a pension. Now they are considered useless. Women of all ages make up 70 percent of the unemployed. Last night, though, there was a floor show in our hotel dining room in which singers and dancers performed a Las Vegas–style adaptation of ancient folklore. The music was amplified, the emcee sounded like the barker for a circus sideshow, and the women's costumes were transparent.

Our tour guide is quite unlike those I listened to in previous years. There is no obligatory bragging. "Thanks to God," she says, "the churches have returned to being churches." The Nevsky Prospekt, where our hotel, the Moskva, is located, is "the street that Dostoyevsky walked on and Tchaikovsky composed in. And while we cannot boast about many things, some things make us smile . . . and even bring tears to our eyes."

We have a new linear home in which to leave St. Petersburg, a freshly decorated private train. Jack and I are assigned a two-bed compartment in car number 4, the Yellow Car, which also contains two other married couples making the trip. (The arrangement provides Jack with some accessible male companionship, which will turn out not to be a bad thing.)

Twenty-six hours after leaving St. Petersburg, we arrive in Kiev and are greeted by, of all things, a military band. There follows a traditional Ukrainian bread-and-salt ceremony presented by a chorus of beautifully costumed women. At the Hotel Bratislava, we learn we have been designated official guests of Parliament. Instead of using public transportation, we will be whisked about the city in private buses complete with police escort.

Chernobyl dominates our discussions. The hospitable Ukrainian women describe their country as a dumping ground for nuclear waste. Attempts to clean up after the Chernobyl disaster have failed. Two and a half million people live on land that remains contaminated; increases in thyroid and digestive disorders are astronomical; leukemia and kidney failure are rampant. The people live in a climate of fear that they have named "radiaphobia." There is increasing evidence of congenital defects and deformities and a high rate of infant mortality. The story is grim and relentless but difficult to document since, as in Hiroshima, little hard data are available to confirm what individuals are experiencing. One woman is blunt: "Chernobyl is World War III and you, the people of the Peace Train, should tell everyone about it. Life and health are synonymous."

(We will later learn that neighboring Belarus shares Ukraine's fate and fears: there has been a 50 percent reduction in the birth rate, and Chernobyl-related effects cost a fifth of the GNP.)

At several of our stops on the way to the Chinese border, we will add newcomers to our train. The first of these is a woman from Kiev, a cheerfully upbeat kindergarten teacher. She tells us that the primary necessity in her life is to stay hopeful and buoyant for the sake of the small children in her class. But then she asks, "Hopeful for what?"

From Kiev, we travel a whole day until we reach Bucharest. Along the way, fields of golden wheat make it easy to see that this is indeed the breadbasket of Europe. The farther south the train rolls, the more bucolic the countryside becomes—richer, greener, dotted with orchards laden with ripening apples. The families working in the fields wave to us—and to the peace signs we've added to the train's windows.

Reminders of Nicolae and Helena Ceauşescu, Romania's megalomaniac leaders from 1965 to 1989, abound in Bucharest. Their palace, a world-class architectural atrocity second in size only to the Pentagon, built by twenty thousand workers (sometimes fed on animal fodder, we are told) on sixteen-hour shifts at a cost of 80 percent of the GNP, has been converted into an international conference center. We are brought there for a banquet in the main hall. The table, laden with garnished and decorated choices of ethnic dishes, meats, cheeses, vegetables, and sweets, is the most elaborate I have seen since the 1987 Orthodox Church celebration of Christianity's first millennium in Russia.

This display of opulence sits queerly with the people of the Peace Train. We know that as a result of a horrific inflation rate Romanians are going hungry. The tuberculosis outbreak is the worst in Europe. Why, we ask an English-speaking hostess, are we being given a banquet so in keeping with the hated architecture? Because of the size of our group and our official status, she replies, nothing less will do. If we return in smaller numbers, the appropriate welcome would be potluck suppers.

At our workshops and meetings, Romanian women stress the effects of the war in Bosnia. "Due to the embargo, navigation on the Danube River, an important asset for Romania, was stopped," Stana Buzata tells us in her opening comments, "We enjoyed good economic and trade relations with the former Yugoslavia. There has been an extreme loss for Romania, which big powers never consider."

Domestic violence, Romanian women say, is a major problem. One woman adds that violence thrives on the job and in the square, as well as in the home. It is a question of instinct, she feels, and needs to be controlled by laws stating that no one should be subordinate to another. The punishment for rape and murder is not strong enough.

Having spent fifty years under another system, the women suggest that their only expertise is in following orders. They feel like kindergartners, unable to find the way to initiate change. Can we give them advice on creating women's shelters and providing counseling for abused women? They have no civic organizations that will help them develop appropriate responses to violence. Women in Eastern European countries, they tell us, have great capacities for providing hospitality, but none for organizing at a grassroots level.

A woman I meet on the palace steps seems atypical. Active in the Romanian Association of University Women, she has prepared an analysis of the Plan for Action for the UN conference. It shows a crisp awareness of how women must take hold of solutions. Here as elsewhere, women's lives move at different paces in response to extreme change.

The tempo of our trip is speeding up—six cities in seven days. Yesterday's fields of yellow wheat, cabbage, pumpkin, corn, and sunflowers have given way to darkly green mountains and remote valleys. Here in Bulgaria, during World War II, more than a few Jews found refuge from their oppressors.

Older women—so often victims in the transition from socialism to capitalism—host our meeting in Sofia. They speak of a complete collapse of morality. Sex shops and prostitution are everywhere; hotel rooms supply condoms along with soap and towels; Western pop music "makes people stop thinking"; and TV imported from the United States turns values upside down. The ability to speak out, one woman says, is a poor trade-off for the family-centered culture she valued and the security she had under socialism. The Bulgarian women, more than any others we have met, blame the United States for the changes they detest.

The tone changes totally when we meet with young Serbian members of Women in Black—a group organized to protect and work with war refugees on the Bosnian border. They say the images of suffering they have seen will never leave them—and are grateful for their freedom to help. If men took visible part in their work, they would immediately be called up for military service.

Since trade embargoes have brought the ship providers to the edge of bankruptcy, our plans to sail across the Black Sea into Turkey have been abandoned; we'll have to go by bus instead. As we approach Istanbul, what seems like endless miles of new apartments finally give way to flocks of sheep grazing near the old city wall. The new and the old, it develops, are even more strikingly juxtaposed in the lives of Turkish women, who are imbued with Arabic culture but are simultaneously absorbing Western practices and values.

Many with whom we meet, the first in their families to be educated, left the countryside to study alone in urban universities. Those beginning their own families are learning to develop more open relationships than those based on traditional respect, distance, and order. They accept the burden of maintaining tradition while transforming it. On commuter trains, we are told, you will often see women in conventional Arab dress open their briefcases and pull out one of the forty or so women's magazines that reflect feminist positions.

"Take your hands off our friends" was the slogan of a successful feminist effort to pass legislation mandating respect and protection for women. We used it in a message to the Turkish government advocating justice for the Kurdish minority, including Turkish sisters who are suffering discrimination, jailing, and torture.

Eight days after leaving Helsinki, we board the buses and retrace our route. At the Bulgarian border, there are moments of anxious hilarity when it seems that our train has disappeared. But it's found soon enough, and to most of us, it feels like home.

After twenty-one hours, we reach Odessa. The resort seems tired and dusty and our hotel dingy. Warnings of pollution arm us against the temptation to swim. We wonder what it was like under the Soviet system when whole factories closed down for the vacation time their workers spent there. Now, gambling and prostitution abound. And the Peace Train will be delayed here for two days, since the Chinese government has, for reasons best known to itself, decided to postpone our arrival in China until August 26.

At our meeting with local women, seventeen people share the podium, each of whom has to be introduced and all of whom—except for the representative of the Orthodox Church, who wears a tall black-veiled headpiece and a huge gold cross—seize the chance to speak. In a formal address, Rusian Bodelan, deputy of the Ukraine Parliament, assesses the value of nongovernmental organizations—to which so many on the Peace Train belong: They are too many and too noisy; they think in slogans and care only about single issues; so long as different points of view are already represented in the government, the NGOs add no balance to political decision making.

(The translation is excellent, which has not always been the case. In Bulgaria, for example, translators had often lost the thread of what impassioned women unused to public speaking were trying to say. And peace trainers didn't help when they persisted in asking questions with which the Bulgarian women were clearly uncomfortable.)

Having engaged us with his frankness, Bodelan, I'm sorry to say, didn't wait to hear WILPF's Regina Birchem challenge those in political power to develop a culture of peace: "If your son kills my son, and my son is obliged to kill your son, how can I raise him so he will not kill your son?" We need a peace culture that "recognizes that no borders can protect us from poisoned air and water and the effects of military testing." How many governments, I wonder, take those principles into account when they attempt to make balanced decisions? Does Bodelan's?

The Chinese government doesn't. Attempts to persuade them to respect our agreement and reinstate the original Peace Train crossing date bear no fruit. We now learn what may be a part of the reason why. China has just exploded a nuclear device at their Lop Nur testing site just south of the route we are to travel.

The train is speeding through Kazakhstan. Though the scrub lands and desert seem barely populated, thousands of burial mounds—stupas—attest to the presence of life and the death of worshiping Muslims. The burial mounds with heads hold the remains of men; those that do not, women.

Three days of uninterrupted train time bring us together, often in useful conflict. Young women express frustration that their opinions are not taken seriously; older women point out that the younger ones undervalue their life experience. Black women feel that the issue of racism, particularly in the United States, has been given too little attention by peace advocates in general and the 233 of us on the train in particular. Europeans wish the percentage of Americans on the Peace Train had not been so high. Some women dislike having men aboard. A nun points out that forty-two years as a sister have taught her that community is a goal, not a given. It's unclear whether many of us have the ears to hear.

We are finding the -isms of our personal borders—age, race, sex—are as hard to cross as those between nations. None of us any longer assumes that our shared peace activism can automatically make us into a community. Krishna asks Jack how it feels to be—at least for the length of the train ride—a member of the disempowered male minority. It's a great experience, Jack says, to encounter so many women with so little in common, including their ideas of feminism, who are nevertheless a potential force for changing things for the better. Many are aggressive and ungraceful, personally selfish and quick to anger; they are also kind, versed in the issues, adept at handling ideas—creative, enthusiastic, optimistic. "Their success is in their constant pursuit of peace." Jack wrote a Peace Train song. It ends with hope:

> Now everyone is happy, and it's issues through and through
> Around about and in and out—there'll never be a few
> So on we go to Beijing town with spirits high anew
> And God, *she's* in her heaven, but some *men* may be there too.

Detraining in Almaty, Kazakhstan's capital, provides welcome relief. A few of us meet with a parliamentary deputy who is also a three-star general. He announces with pride that Kazakhstan is a nuclear-free state.

With help from the United States and backed by a petition signed by 4 million of Kazakhstan's 17 million people, they have negotiated an agreement to return all warheads to Russia for dismantling.

The burden of cleaning up after the Soviet nuclear-testing program—it dates back to Stalin—is another matter. Grassroots organizers tell us this is a key women's issue: 40 percent of those who become pregnant have miscarriages and the death rate during the first year of life is almost as high. The people are now concerned that they will be victimized by the Chinese testing program in nearby Lop Nur.

As we near the Chinese border crossing at Alanshankou, we are asked to put our cameras away. No pictures are to be taken during our time at the border. Most of us are busy anyway, packing our bags and reflecting on the journey. I am glad to discover that Jack and I are not the only ones who over the last three weeks have become attached to our train and to the staff who have been unfailingly cheerful in meeting our needs.

On the narrow-gauge Chinese train that will take us to Beijing, the white-gloved and white-jacketed attendants smile less, perhaps because of the hundred or so security people who have been assigned to accompany us. One woman—an American who works in Taiwan and holds a visa from Hong Kong stamped with the wrong date of entry—is turned back and escorted under guard to our Russian train on which, we will later learn, she returned to Almaty and, after a few days, caught a flight to Beijing.

We are unable to stop and meet Chinese women on our journey through western China. At our occasional ten-minute pauses for exercise breaks, people lean out windows or gather behind barricades to watch us. But the stations are locked and our own security personnel form a cordon at six-foot intervals lest we make any untoward contacts.

The pull toward Beijing, the NGO forum, and the UN conference, grows stronger. At our meetings and seminars, we feel the need to arrive prepared. Yet we are also drawn to the incredible diversity visible from our windows—the huge and heavily polluted city of Urumqi, a remote village when Owen Lattimore journeyed there by camel and met his bride in 1929 . . . the newly planted poplar forests outside Lanzhou . . . harvested fields in which stand rice stalks bound in double and even triple layers of sheaves (to me, they look like an art form, but later, when I show pictures of them to a Chinese friend, she says that all she can see is work) . . . Xian, with air so polluted I have difficulty breathing, but the site of the recently discovered underground clay army . . . the nearby hills where many of the caves have brightly colored doors . . . the terraced farms that climb the hills along the Yellow River, whose broad valley yields crops more stereotypically European than Chinese. Above all, though, we are impressed by the fact that almost everything we see is the result of human toil. The power of the machine has not yet come to dominate the civilization of China.

At Beijing, four women from the All China Women's Federation, together with a translator and members of the official Chinese press, stand on the otherwise empty platform to greet us—briefly. As our buses depart, there are crowds of people with banners and signs in front of the station. Even WILPF president Edythe Ballantine has not been permitted to approach the platform.

But soon we will be listening to Gertrude Mongella: "A revolution has begun. There is no going back. There will be no unraveling of commitments. Neither today's nor last year's, and certainly not this decade's commitments. This revolution is too just, too important, and certainly too long overdue."

A Peace Train from Helsinki
A Train Song (sung to the tune of "Ghost Riders in the Sky")

John M. Wilson

Described by one friend as "a very brave individual," Jack was one of only nine men on the long and arduous Peace Train journey. A strong presence in any context, Jack very seriously went about the business of making people laugh. Those who traveled with him on the train said he may have been the only one of the 233 passengers who never lost his sense of humor and playfulness, and he captured the spirit of the journey in this song.

> A peace train from Helsinki went south one sunny day
> On board were lots of women and they found to their dismay
> And a bolt of fear ran through them when they found some *men* on
> board
> Who signed up for the journey to make *plowshares* out of swords.
>
> Chorus: (sing after each verse)
> Yi-pi-yi-ay, Yi-pi-yi-yo
> The Peace Train to Beijing
>
> But all was not so peaceful for just a day or two
> They called each other *Girls* and *Boys* and that was not quite true
> So they gave out gifts to everyone like pins and posters, too
> And even passed out condoms, I think we all got *two!*
>
> The women on this Peace Train are not at all the same
> You can tell them by their colors and by their different names
> They come from many countries, and it's peace they're here to seek
> But the thing they have in common is they're not afraid to *speak!*
>
> The men are quite a docile lot, at least it seems to me
> They talk among themselves so much on what they hear and see
> So when they got to Istanbul, some people thought them weird

Jack Wilson with a young man from Kiev. (Photo by Teresa Wilson)

But they laughed because they found that Goddess Sophia had a
  beard!

Then there was Moldavia, I thought it was quite nice
The border guards kept coming round, I know they did it thrice
They gathered in the railway car, and on our doors did pound
I know nothing of their country since we never touched the ground.

From Finland to St. Petersburg to Kiev and Bucharest
The issues were a flowing so that women could be best
But now and then within the car you heard the music play
The women they were "living high" before they "hit the hay."

So onward to Odessa just to be close by the sea
Our hotel was quite a dingy place, as rundown as could be

The Chinese, they played ping pong, I'm afraid we were the ball
Seems they want us two days later and it's us who have to stall.

The train rolls on across the steppe, I could not ask for more
The sky is vast, the land is FLAT, just east of Volga's shore
There's sheep and horses on the plain, a village here and there
And gardens by their little shacks, well tended with much care.

Our little cabin's crowded and my clothes are on a hook
My water bottle's ready, and I do not have to cook
The atmosphere is cozy and my back is not too sore
And I'm glad I'm in a cabin that sleeps two instead of *four!*

Now everyone is happy, and it's issues through and through
Around about and in and out, there'll never be a few
So on we go to Beijing town with spirits high anew
And God, *she's* in her heaven, but some *men* may be there too.

Zina

Lois Goldstein

I am still haunted by a story I heard on the Peace Train. I first heard Zina in Helsinki at the WILPF Congress. A teacher from Kiev, Ukraine, she was dynamic and emotional as she addressed her first gathering of women from all over the world, speaking of what this opportunity meant to her.

I had agreed to cover Kiev for our Peace Links newsletter and was pleased I would have an opportunity to interview someone so articulate. I knew I would be able to find sufficient quiet time on the twenty-three day train ride to get a meaningful story.

In the meantime, I observed her upbeat and take-charge manner, as she interacted with other passengers and officials and our hosts in Kiev and Odessa. I saw passengers rely on her for her knowledge of Russian behavior and language as we stopped in several Russian cities along the way.

In a small workshop on peace education I learned of Zina's work in an alternative school in Kiev, which emphasizes conflict resolution. I saw her laboriously copying sections of a teacher's manual she knew she would be unable to find in Kiev.

Finally, I sat down in her compartment to find out how people's lives had changed since Ukraine became independent and what the Chernobyl disaster had meant to ordinary people. I was unprepared for her response:

There have been no great changes. Proclamations and language have changed, but life is the same. . . . To destroy is much easier than to build. . . . People are in despair and have no hope or belief in the future. . . . The people in power are the same ones who ran things before, only now under new titles. . . . The privileged children are receiving the fancy foreign educations and are returning to key jobs. . . . It's a closed circle. We were the slaves, we are the slaves, and I'm not sure we won't be the slaves. . . . You need to change people's hearts, or maybe a civil war will be necessary to accomplish real change.

Regarding Chernobyl, she showed me a picture of a beautiful nine-year-old boy with stumps for hands and feet. His father left the family after seeing him at birth, and his eighteen-year-old mother, unable to cope, was admitted to a mental hospital. Zina's friends, the grandparents, are now caring for the child, living on a tiny pension and even smaller allowance from the state for the care of the boy.

When I asked how she reconciles her true feelings with her publicly optimistic and cheerful attitude, she said, "The children are waiting for miracles; you must give them what they need. . . . Adults need the same thing."

iv THE FORUM

Looking at the World
Through Women's Eyes,
August 30–September 8, 1995

These, then, are [the] common hopes that unite us—that as the shackles of prejudice and intolerance fall from our own limbs we can together strive to identify and remove the impediments to human development everywhere. The mechanisms by which this great task is to be achieved provide the proper focus of this great forum.

—Daw Aung San Suu Kyi, Nobel Peace Laureate
Keynote Speaker, Opening Plenary

Change happens. . . . It happens . . . village by village, woman by woman, conference by conference.

—Sally Field, Honorary Chair of Save the
Children Delegation to Beijing

Noonday Prayer for Beijing

Sponsored by the U.S. Ecumenical Women's Network: Beijing and Beyond

O God, Creator of the heavens and the earth, we pray for all who gather in Beijing. Bless them. Help them and us to see one another through eyes enlightened by understanding and compassion. Release us from prejudice so we can receive the stories of our sisters with respect and attention. Open our ears to the cries of a suffering world and the healing melodies of peace. Empower us to be instruments in bringing about Your justice and equality everywhere.

This prayer, printed in five languages—English, French, Chinese, Arabic, and Spanish—was recited every day at noon in the Peace Tent on the grounds of the NGO forum. It was also read by people of faith around the world from August 20 to September 15, 1995, to express spiritual unity and a shared commitment to "look at the world through women's eyes."

Sistuhs Coming Together

Valerie Lawrence

We come from a long line of great, gentle, glorious
women generals, women healers, women teachers
women thinkers, women peacemakers, women dreamers
women creators, women builders, women sorcerers
women lovers, women warriors.

We come from the womb of mother God's most precious creation.

We are full blossomed women setting traditions that will stay
long after our ashes have been reabsorbed into the ground,
traditions that will be another layer on which children will
erect a world.

We are the ones children look to, to show them the way.
We are two sides of the same coin smelted civilizations ago
in the cradle of humanity.

Sistuhs, it's time to come together for each other, and for
our children who have hurt too long and keep dying before their time.

Experiences in Beijing

JoAnne W. Boyle

"So are you sitting in a circle singing 'Kum-by-Yah'?" The voice was my daughter's. I was talking to her from Beijing on the first of September, my fifth day in China, and she was guessing, from television coverage back in Pittsburgh of the NGO forum, at how my day had gone in Huairou. I was still recovering from having just seen Jane Fonda, shaking an upswept hairdo, and saying she felt old and out of touch with the young people who were attending the forum, and I paused for a moment wondering if the right generation in my family had decided to go to China. I wondered too whether the lasting memories any of us would have of the World Conference on Women would be those we actually experienced or those gleaned from CNN and the newspapers. I had spent days prior to my trip clipping out-of-sorts coverage with headlines such as Controversy Looms in Beijing and What in the World Do Women Want? The daily live news coverage now seemed an effort by the media to make the advance stories come true. Determined to compile for my own memory at least some other kind of record of the forum, I kept a journal and I find it useful now to dip into the facts and fictions I find there.

I started my journal in Narita airport in Tokyo where the young Japanese woman checking me in proudly told me her mother too had left that morning for the forum. According to most accounts, the Japanese delegation of five thousand women was one of the largest going to China. I was to learn later they were a mixed group. I watched Japanese women wearing masks, marching and chanting in forbidden demonstrations against nuclear war, and then rode buses with members of a social club from Kyoto who were much more interested in making new friends. Of such variety were the other delegations. Always the encounter with the new came with recognition of our common experiences.

The women from Turkey were exotically dressed and members, from my perspective, of an equally exotic organization, the Universal Brotherhood and Wisdom Association. They rushed into a conference room, hung posters, and wrote on the blackboard these lines from Wordsworth, "God for his service needeth not proud work of human skill; they please him best who labour most in peace to do his will"; a veiled Muslim woman talked about her computers and worried about a husband left behind to cope with child care; a Chinese woman, cooking a meal for me in her apartment in suffocatingly hot Nanjing, fussed about serving her American guest a cold drink.

The young and the old, the women garbed in black and the women dressed in many colors, in turbans, veils, vests, saris, and business suits that I met and talked to were well educated, well-spoken, and had means enough to get themselves to Beijing. Many were representatives of churches, social clubs, women's organizations such as AAUW, and educational institutions. Even the women from the grassroots movements were at the forum because they had become leaders in their movements and were already, in a way, part of a power structure that they wanted to make more powerful.

Our causes were many: equal access to education, political equity, economic opportunity, the right to inheritance, to name a few. I, like most of the women I knew at the forum, was most moved by the stories of child prostitution and other indignities and human rights abuses endured by women and children. I left one session determined to keep the topics alive wherever I could, encouraged that over the centuries other "customs" once thought too sacred or ingrained in a culture to be challenged had disappeared. Why not these too?

There was much talk among the delegates to the forum in Huairou about the Chinese women who attended the sessions with us. How had they been selected? How freely could they speak? Did they represent mainstream Chinese women (whoever they might be)? The consensus was that we were pretty much hearing the party line when these women spoke up (always in excellent English), even if they were not part of the official delegation at the conference.

I had the opportunity to take another gauge of the views of Chinese women during a trip I took to Nanjing University immediately after the forum. I had been invited by the president of Nanjing University, which has been exchanging professors with Seton Hill College for more than ten years now, on an official visit. Told upon arrival I was expected the next morning to give a two-hour talk to several hundred faculty and students of the English department—"perhaps on literature, since that is your field"—I had another suggestion. "Perhaps," I said, "on the women's forum and conference in Beijing since that is fresh in my mind." "Wonderful," they agreed, "literature *and* the conference." Knowing there was limited access for my Chinese hosts to news about the conference, but unlimited interest, I had thought they might go for the change in topic. But I also wanted to honor their request for a lecture on literature, so I inquired as to the syllabus for the current year. The students I would meet were reading *Jane Eyre, MacBeth,* and *The Scarlet Letter.* I was determined to make a connection—as I would had I been teaching in the United States—and the next morning I found my opportunity.

The students, far more interested in current events than in the reading assignments, were full of questions that reflected the mix of information, fact, and myth that comes to be news in most countries: What did Mrs. Clinton say? What do you think of human rights in China? What did you think of the acrobats at the opening ceremony? Why were prostitutes allowed to attend the conference? Is it true there were nudists running in the streets of Beijing? I responded as frankly as I could and then turned for some of the answers to their questions to the women in their reading assignments: the insane wife hidden in the attic in *Jane Eyre,* the bloodthirsty and ambitious wife of *MacBeth,* the fallen Hester Prynne, forced to lead a life of shame because she refused to name her lover and father of her child in *The Scarlet Letter.* I tried to connect the stories of these women to the misconceptions of the Chinese students about the women attending the forum. No wonder it was easy for them to believe that power-hungry, crazy women of dubious virtue were running unchecked in the streets of Beijing. We talked about the need for people everywhere to listen to women and to hear their concerns, in the words of the forum's theme, "to see the world through women's eyes." Remembering a preconference headline and news story I asked the students, "In China, what do women want?" They were eager to tell me. First of all equality; second, a clean country; and third, peace.

Later, at dinner with the faculty, we returned to the subject of the conference. The world had been editorializing, including the Asian *Wall Street Journal,* on the wisdom of holding the conference in Beijing. What did they think of that decision, I asked. Everyone wanted to speak and most said that although they were saddened by the negative criticism of their country, they were glad the conference had been held in China. One woman, still angry over my report of Mrs. Clinton's speech, said, "Let her come and live among us before she criticizes us again." The dean of the faculty had been quiet, but he spoke now, obviously pleased that this question had been asked. "When I heard the conference was coming to China, I was happy. I have a wife and two daughters and I want their lives to improve. I want the best for them. I want their lives to be better than my mother's. I thought that having the conference in China would be the best way for that to happen. I think I speak for the husbands and the fathers that I know." I think he spoke for the mothers in China, too. The women in the group at the table were nodding in agreement.

A Kaleidoscope of China

Patricia D. Wilson

China! A kaleidoscope of scenes, people, places, and meetings—an ever-changing pattern of color and sound that constantly bursts forth into something different, something new; a challenge for the senses and the mind.

Nineteen of us boarded Air China at the San Francisco airport. We would meet our other companion, a woman from Aotearoa, New Zealand, in China. We were a part of the Greater Anglican Network.

We began a two-week journey through China, prior to the opening of the NGO forum. It was a well thought-out trip designed to bring us in contact with successful women of China: founders of schools, managers of hotels, workers in factories. A new spirit of equality, development, and peace are evident as Mao's slogan, Women hold up half the sky, takes on a new, updated meaning in a new China rushing toward democracy.

From Shanghai to Wuxi to Nanjing and Xian and finally to Beijing, the chance encounters that I had with people who momentarily shared experiences with me have become jewel-like moments that flash through my kaleidoscope of memory. In an art shop, where I purchased a painting, the manager pointed to my cross and then to himself to say that he too was a Christian. Then very softly he hummed "America" to convey his dream and the language barrier was breached.

In Wuxi we visited an Elders Home of Fortune and Longevity, modern China's answer to working couples' concern for their aging parents. Once again language was breached by happy faces welcoming us, bowing and clasping hands, looking deep into eyes that spoke so much. Afterward, on a boat ride on the lake that faced our hotel, a man standing next to me mentioned that he had worked for Westinghouse in Pennsylvania; I in turn told him I had gone to Pennsylvania when my husband went to work for Westinghouse. Another thread of commonality linking our worlds.

In Nanjing we visited a Christian theological seminary, the Amity

Headquarters of the All China Women's Federation, Beijing. (Photo by Teresa Wilson)

Foundation Editing Company, then toured a silk factory and spoke to the working women. They were proud of their jobs, difficult as they were by our standards. At breakfast one morning, we heard a Dr. Zu who spoke to us about Chinese medicine. He had worked at the Pittsburgh Presbyterian Hospital and he knew Dr. Thomas Starzl.

In Xian, we viewed the archaeological dig of the famous terra-cotta army. We also visited Mrs. Shen's Girls College. The whole village turned out to welcome us and the girls happily led us to their rooms, classrooms, and all around campus. That evening a group of students from the university came to interview us. We broke into small groups. There were three lovely, serious young women in my group. We have since exchanged letters. Lu Jun-feng writes:

> From the other side of the ocean I receive your letter. I hear your voice and see your smile. The world becomes smaller when we can say hello to each other in a letter in spite of the distance between us. The memory holds a never-to-be-stained picture for me. I am studying hard; there are too many books to read, too many questions to answer, too much

knowledge to grasp, to analyse and convey. I LOVE MY WORK. Yours sincerely, Lu Jun-feng

On a Sunday in Beijing we attended a Chinese church that overflowed with people, into the courtyard and beyond. The service was in Chinese but many of the hymns were tunes we knew, so we sang along in English and the two languages blended in praise. We felt privileged to be a part of that congregation that has as one of its ministers the Reverend Gao Ying. She says, "I am aware of the risk involved in publicly offering a western feminist theology. Such an attempt on my part may result in grave consequences, jeopardizing my future as a minister in the Chinese church." Women from all levels of society come to her for counseling. Despite a ban on publicity, the number of Christians in China has multiplied to an estimated 9 million.

China: ancient, civilized, owners of two of the Eight Wonders of the World. China, I look forward to your future. I have seen a glimpse of this future in your people. I have seen the hope of the future shine in the eyes of your young. I am connected by a silken thread of words that flow back and forth between me and three bright, serious young women who are halfway around the world and yet seem very close. I feel now that I too, in a small way, am a part of your kaleidoscope.

Recollections

Sande Hendricks

I attended the U.S.-China Joint Conference on Women's Issues in Beijing from August 25 to September 2, 1995, as a delegate from the American Association of University Women. The conference consisted of 550 professional American and Chinese women. I also attended the opening session of the NGO forum.

I first visited the Orient more than twenty-five years ago. Because of the Cultural Revolution taking place there at that time, the People's Republic of China, "mainland China," was closed to outsiders. Japan, Taiwan, and Hong Kong fascinated me with their culture, their religions, their history, and their political struggles. As one who grew up very much influenced by the Asian culture in Los Angeles, I was particularly interested in crossing the Pacific Ocean to see the origin of those local influences. And as much as I loved the colorful and picturesque life I found there, especially the art, I have wondered these many years since why I felt that something was missing. Traveling from San Francisco to Beijing, I found that it was the People's Republic of China that would move me and fill in that long-existent gap.

Our journey from San Francisco to Beijing was delayed for two and a half hours while we waited for Harry Wu to return to his adopted country, the United States, in an eleventh-hour arrangement between our government and China. During the Cultural Revolution, Harry Wu was placed in a forced labor camp, Laogai, and kept there for nineteen years. In 1995 he returned to China and was detained for sixty-six days, from June 19 until his return here on August 24, for having spoken out about conditions at Laogai. It was at the point of his return that my trip began and little did I comprehend then the impact of his continuous struggle to raise the world's attention to the plight of Chinese dissidents.

During my conference I heard the stories of three Chinese women who have overcome their years of exile to the fields, having lost everything they had during the Cultural Revolution. They were so humble and friendly and eager to share their histories with us. They have since over-come that ten-year tragedy and gone on to teach themselves the school they missed (all schools and universities were closed during that period), received their college degrees, and made great personal strides in ex-celling in their professions. But the imprint of their pain has been such that I found it very difficult to even look at Tiananmen Square as we drove by twice a day during the two weeks I was in Beijing. I asked my husband, who was there twice on business that year, if he had any feel-ings driving by the square, and he said he could not bring himself to look at it.

It was on the afternoon of the twelfth day that our bus took us to visit the Great Hall of the People and to see the square. It was raining steadi-ly, the first rain we had on our trip, and it seemed incredibly appropriate. As I walked the square alone, looking at the sculptures and thinking about the struggle for freedom that has gone on in that place for genera-tions, I was glad for the rain that was soaking my hair and clothes and hiding the tears I could no longer contain.

Women Weaving the World Together

Dorothy Hill

Quilts were everywhere—beautiful, colorful ones with flowers, houses, sunshine, and happy, carefree children; black, ugly ones with symbols of rape, wife burning, child brutalization, and deep anger. There were peace symbols on the one hand; bombs, tanks, fires, and destruction of war on the other. Women sewing together, to express some of the most profound emotions and concerns of their lives. Other women hearing what they were saying, even though there were no spoken words.

I did hear a young Irish mother talk of how moved she had been while creating, with women of all ages in Belfast, a quilt to bring from her war-torn country to Beijing, not because of the violence and futility of war or the hope for peace expressed in its squares but because she had gotten to know and appreciate her mother-in-law through the process of making that quilt. She said, "I never knew how to sew. In fact, I made silent fun of women who wasted their time in this way. As we sat and talked and stitched, I learned more than the skill of sewing. I learned to listen and to appreciate the experience of those who had gone before me."

Women from Africa wore fabrics they had made, handsome tie-dye and colorful batik, patterned with symbols of the conference and forum. The boldness of the patterns and colors seemed to be a reflection of the strong stands they took, the power they were beginning to feel. One of them wore a dress splashed with bright yellow at the Women in Black demonstration, a silent protest against all forms of violence. "I decided not to wear black because I am black and I wanted to wear a dress to show that the sun will rise. There is hope no matter how subjugated or hopeless we feel."

More than one thousand Chinese women from Shaanxi Province, an area well known in China for its long history of folk embroidery, created a huge canopy to welcome the women's conference to Beijing. Each of the 1,008 squares was different in design, harmonization of color, and techniques, but it all went beautifully together to portray a great red phoenix, ready to fly with its spread wings, the mythical bird that rises out of the ashes with hope for renewed or restored life. This seemed to me a powerful symbol for the conference, as well as for Chinese women, who, like women around the world, are just coming to appreciate some of their own value and worth. The quilt will be sold and the money used to set up women in development in the poorest areas of Shaanxi Province.

Women from central Pennsylvania sewed large rectangular quilt pieces that were tied together to form a ribbon of peace.* This was taken to the Great Wall in China and stretched out for miles. It was called "Women Weaving the World Together." That is the way I hope I will always remember the conference and my experience there.

*This weaving was connected to a project that began in Cambodia.

Falling Into a Sea of Women

Suzanne Polen

My experience at the NGO forum was perhaps best expressed by a woman from Africa who was speaking during a workshop on women's issues in the World Conference of Churches. She said, "Coming to Beijing [the forum] is like being a raindrop falling into a sea of women—but not losing your identity!" An apt metaphor for the rainy days we had.

I felt very much like that raindrop during the time I rode the bus back and forth between Beijing and Huairou, strolled down the avenue of posted leaflets from the main entrance to the tent areas, participated in a demonstration, tried hard to find out "who was in town today" and where the closing ceremony was to be held. My identity was clear: a white Euro-American with sharply limited language skills. Precisely because of my identity, I was able to converse with many others, as English dominated among the various languages used at the forum.

I was not a workshop leader and did not focus on a specific issue like peace even though it is an important issue for me. I went to listen and learn from other women, especially those from the Two-Thirds World (so often called the Third World by those who don't live there). I heard strong, vigorous speakers from the many countries struggling with colonialism, militarism, and other forms of foreign occupation, countries such as Tahiti, Cyprus, East Timor, and from countries with critical poverty problems, such as Peru and Jamaica. Any one of those women would be a leader if she came to the United States because of her clarity of thought and power of delivery. I heard a number of sharp comments about the dominance of English, the negative image of Muslims in the Western media, and the problems caused by the Structural Adjustment Policies of the International Monetary Fund, which is dominated by the northern First World countries. But I did not experience any direct hostility toward me as a woman from the north. I did not feel like an outsider when I joined a circle with black Caribbean women to sing "We Shall Overcome" in the grassroots tent, or when I joined in a demonstration against militarism with the Pacific Islands women.

I met a friend of a friend, originally from western Pennsylvania, who is now living in Chile and working with a South American ecofeminist spirituality collective. Part of our conversation was about some Nicaraguans we both know and the situation in that country. Like the woman from Ghana, I fell into a sea of women without losing my identity and experienced a new, much smaller world.

Letter from Beijing
Wednesday, September 5, 1995
Janice Auth

Every day seems like a week because of the wealth of information and activities that are swirling around the forum. We are busy walking, talking, thinking, singing, learning, and celebrating from early morning until the moment when our bodies simply cannot stay awake any longer. For those of us staying in Beijing, most days begin at dawn with breakfast and maybe some tai-chi. The ride to Huairou takes about an hour and a half by shuttle bus, a little less by taxi, so we leave the hotel at 7:00 or 7:30 and arrive by 9:00. This morning we left earlier because Hillary Clinton was due to address the forum at 10:00. Rain began to fall and was seriously coming down by the time we arrived. Originally scheduled to be held outdoors, the meeting was moved to the Huairou Theater, capacity fifteen hundred, where a substantial crowd had already gathered by 7:30. We moved in under the small awning and were almost immediately pressed up against the building by the growing crush of people seeking shelter from the rain. The doors were finally opened about 9:00 and we were swept inside. Shirley Mae Statten did a heroic job of keeping the volatile crowd under control by having us sing: "Gotta keep on movin' forward . . . never turning back, never turning back." Energy was high and soared higher as we sang and applauded our worthy Chinese host women while waiting for Mrs. Clinton to arrive. Banners were unfurled and signs shot up as she came onto the stage. Stop U.S. Imperialism at the World Bank; U.S. Support CEDAW; Free [Leonard] Peltier were a few of the more prominent ones. Hillary Clinton spoke forcefully, intelligently, and sensitively, being careful to stick to the issues but pulling no punches when it came to stating what those issues were: Women's rights are human rights and there are universally identified human rights that cannot and must not be violated anywhere on earth. Among these are women's right to health care, education, and education for their children. She praised the work of nongovernmental organizations, saying that the

Janice Auth and Sue Bayley exchanging literature with two Muslim women.
(Photo by Toni Conaway)

PBB participants with Japanese women in a demonstration at the NGO forum. (Photo by Toni Conaway)

real work of the conference and forum begins when we all get home. She urged the production of a document, perhaps just one page, that can be distributed, read, and understood by all the women of the world. She spoke of the need to break the silence around women's issues, and she closed with the universal prayer that has been read every day at noon. We came back to the hotel and watched it all on CNN. She is not the most powerful woman here but she is the most famous and she is using her fame to bring the issues of the conference to the attention of the world. And for that we thank her.

Finishing up this momentous day by sending a fax to the French Embassy here telling them what Peace Links members think of their nasty little exercise in the South Pacific this morning. Urging immediate boycott of all French goods and services. Pass the word!

Leone Paradise *(right)* and a new acquaintance from Russia. (Photo by Toni Conaway)

African woman wearing fabric specially designed for the conference. (Photo by Teresa Wilson)

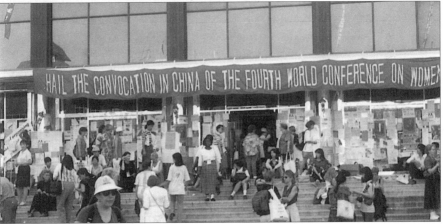

The front steps of the main meeting hall in Huairou, always humming with activity. (Photo by Toni Conaway)

An Open Letter to M. Jacques Chirac

Mon cher Jack:

Je suis a bit fromaged off avec votre decision to blow up La Pacifique avec le Frog bombes nuclears. Je reckon vous must have un spot in La Belle France itself pour les explosions. Le Massive Central? Le Quay d'Orsay? Le Champs Elysees? Votre own back yard, peut etre? Frappez les crows avec stones, Sport! La guerre cold est fini! Votres forces militaires need la bombe atomique about as beaucoup as poisson need les bicyclettes. Un autre point, cobber. Votre histoire militaire isn't tres flash, consisting, n'est-ce pas, of battailles the likes of Crecy, Agincourt, Poitiers, Trafalgar, Borodino, Waterloo, Sedan, et Dien Bien Phu. Un bombe won't change le tradition. Je/mon pere/mon grandpere/le cousin third avec ma grandmere/la plume de ma tante fought avec votre soldats against Le Boche in WWI (le Big One). Have vous forgotten? Reconsider, mon ami, otherwise in le hotels et estaminets de l'Australie le curse anciens d'Angleterre—"Damnation to the French"—will be heard un autre temps. Votre chums don't want that.*

On September 5, when the conference and forum were both in full swing, we learned that the French government had ordered another nuclear test in the South Pacific, in the vicinity of Tahiti. Pennsylvania Peace Links immediately sent a message of protest and outrage to the French Embassy in Beijing, calling for an immediate boycott of all French goods and services. Gertrude Mongella, secretary-general of the conference spoke out against the testing as did numerous other conference and forum participants, particularly the Tahitian and other South Pacific women and the Japanese women.

*First published in an Australian newspaper; found on the Internet and contributed by Sue Bayley.

The Beggar Woman of Bangladesh

Leone P. Paradise

The Grameen Bank was founded by Mohamed Yunis in 1976 to promote the economic independence of the poor by lending money to people who had no collateral. Initially, the bank loans were distributed to both men and women on an equal basis. But Yunis found that women were much more reliable about paying back the loans. Today, the bank loans 94 percent of its assets to women and they have a 98 percent payback rate. Yunis tells this story:

One day he approached a young beggar woman to offer her a loan of $2.50 to start a business. The woman refused the loan, because she felt that amount of money was way beyond her ability to repay. After weeks of discussion, he was finally able to persuade her to accept a loan of less than $1.00.

With the dollar, the woman purchased colored ribbons, which she decided to sell house-to-house. She knocked on the door of her first prospective customer. A woman answered, explained that she had no money to give and suggested she return on Friday, which was payday. The woman explained that she was not begging; she had ribbons to sell. The woman at the door then invited her to come in and sit down.

The beggar woman later told a Grameen Bank official that the invitation to come in and sit down was the first time in her whole life she had ever been treated with dignity and respect.

The $1.00 loan bought start-up inventory, but more important, it provided a way toward self-respect and self-confidence. This woman went on to become an entrepreneurial success. Her last loan was for $250.00.

Mother and Daughter

Lee Fogarty

Several months before the conference, I attended a board meeting of the Feminist Therapy Institute. We began to talk about our children and different ways we were attempting to bond with our daughters. One person was watching a television show every week with her daughter, while another rode bikes with hers. When my turn came, I said, "I'm taking my daughter to China for the women's conference." And I did.

The excitement began in the middle of the night, when we picked up our materials. Traciy and I began discussing which one of the hundreds of workshops we would attend the next day. Then, as we stepped off the bus in Huairou amid thousands of women from all over the world, it finally became real—we were here in China to participate in a historic event. We joined the kaleidoscope of colors—bright colors of clothing, of ponchos (it rained a lot), of languages, and of cultures.

Women's ways of working cooperatively have always impressed me, and I was pleased to see this evidenced in China where everyone was far from home and the familiar, yet reached out to help each other. Catholic nuns and Muslim women took part in the celebration of Mary's birthday. The Sabbath service at the end of the last day was attended by women of many faiths. People listened to each other. When one group ran into difficulty, another helped out. In the true spirit of cooperation, a group that had presented once, gave up its much-coveted spot on the program to a group who had been washed out of their space by the rains.

One particular program was memorable, as much due to the interactions as to the content. A group from Seattle presented a program on women's health issues. The content was rather delicate, focusing on women's health and knowing our bodies intimately. First, the presenters sent the ever-present Chinese man who was "helping" in our room to find some nonexistent projector. When he left, the doors were locked and the windows covered, so that the session was private. Following the presentation, Chinese women who were there spoke about how brave the presenters were to talk about the body, so openly and with examples, and to resist the establishment by eliminating a potentially dampening presence (the state-appointed watcher). "Brave" for performing in a way that most of us take for granted. A poignant reminder of how freedom of speech is not a universal concept.

Both Traciy and I were struck by the warmth of so many women and their willingness to listen. Though Traciy (at twenty-one) was one of the youngest in our traveling group, her opinion was elicited and respected. In listening to her interact, I was reminded once again of the way my daughter can listen, evaluate, and respond so thoughtfully to ideas. Even as a small child, Traciy was adept at analyzing information and thinking things out. She accompanied me to marches, demonstrations, and meetings about women's issues from the time she was able to walk. As she grew up, she continued to be interested in politics. While a student at Boston University, she helped to organize a pro-choice group and to produce a very well-attended rally for women's right to choose. At the end of our sojourn to China, she returned to Boston College to complete her master's in social work.

As a psychologist, as a feminist, and as an activist, I have worked for many years to help women become more self-actualizing and less encumbered by negative aspects of our society. I have felt that I knew and understood the issues women were facing. Through my trip to Beijing, my focus has been widened. I learned about the women in Bangladesh who have opened their own businesses; the women from Africa who are very strong and organized; the women of China, who are unable to express themselves freely without fear; the Tibetan women (in exile) who were so brave to even attend this conference, and then to confront the Chinese on their treatment of Tibet; and the playfulness of the Australian women. Issues such as domestic violence, poor education, and inadequate medical care are, unfortunately, evident in all countries and cultures. I had access to people I would never otherwise have met, to see different perspectives and embrace a new kind of accountability not only to American women but also to women and girls of the world. I brought home with me a need to understand and celebrate diversity, and a renewed commitment to speak out for those who cannot speak for themselves.

My favorite memory is of sharing the closing ceremonies with women from Canada and Japan and China and Sweden and Africa—all of us soaking wet and smiling. The most exquisite aspect of this trip was that I was able to experience this historical event in the company of my daughter, Traciy—to spend two weeks with her listening and learning and sharing in a way that I will cherish all my life.

Beijing '95
An Affirming Experience

Dorothy Jacko

Participation in the NGO Forum on Women was an overwhelmingly positive and affirming experience for me. One speaker at the forum called this historic assembly of women from around the globe "the largest gathering in the world of marginalized experts," and so it was. Listening to and sharing insights and experiences with so many competent and dedicated women made me more aware than ever of the tremendous potential women have for transforming the world. In this brief reflection on my experience of Beijing '95, I focus on three themes that particularly impressed me.

First, despite the varied and sometimes conflicting agendas of specific groups present at Beijing, one thing was very clear: Women from around the globe share a common experience of being women. That experience is one of women's exclusion and marginalization across cultures. This point was brought home to me in a session sponsored by the Episcopal Church Women of the United States, which presented a process for the empowerment of women that this group has developed. Participants in the session were asked to share negative messages they had received from their cultures and then to list positive contributions women made to society. Women from the United States, Mexico, India, the Philippines, China, and other countries had no difficulties whatsoever in identifying immediately with the negative cultural messages voiced by women from other cultures. Nor was there disagreement about the positive values and gifts women bring to society. Also clear in this session, as throughout the forum, was the fact that women are no longer willing to tolerate marginalization and exclusion as they have done in the past.

Second, Beijing '95 was a powerful testimony to the seriousness of the worldwide women's movement and of the issues it is confronting. This is an important point in view of the continuing trivialization of the women's movement by the political and the religious right. Because I am currently teaching a college course in Third World theologies, I decided to focus on sessions given by women from the Third World. Here the violence against women takes on a special poignancy because of its massiveness and "rawness." Women from various African countries, for example, spoke of the increased economic hardships suffered by women and their children because of structural adjustment policies imposed on their countries by the World Bank. Women who work in various Asian countries to combat the evils of trafficking in prostitution presented statistics and details about the sexual slavery into which young girls and women in Asia are sold. A video documented the sexual exploitation and violence against women in the current war between the Burmese army and various ethnic groups in Burma. These are but a few examples of the literally hundreds of NGO forum sessions that illustrated the worldwide violence against women and the courageous initiatives of women's organizations to expose and change these harsh realities. Clearly, the women's movement is not about anything trivial.

Third, the '95 NGO forum presented an opportunity to learn about the many invaluable contributions women are making to the building of a more just and peaceful world. There were many sessions on women's roles in peacemaking and nonviolent conflict resolution, including presentations by women from Northern Ireland, from the former Yugoslavia, and by Palestinian and Jewish women working together in Israel. There were also opportunities to hear courageous women whose work and example have become an inspiration to many others: women such as Wangare Maathai of Kenya, founder of the Green Belt Movement, an environmental group that has raised women's consciousness about the political, economic, and social power women possess when organized.

My experience at the NGO forum has left me with an even stronger conviction that, as an Australian poster I picked up there says, Liberation is in the hands of women.

Some Thoughts from My China Notebook

Edith Scheiner

I felt like the blind woman being shown an elephant. I knew it was an elephant, but when asked to describe it I can only describe that small portion I happened to touch. That is why I am so eager to share experiences with anyone who was there at the same time. Listen to all the stories, and eventually you too will be able to feel this giant colossus that was the 1995 NGO Women's Forum in Huairou, China.

It seemed as though a huge map of the world was put down at my feet, and with each small step I was privileged to enter another country, to dialogue with some of its women, to share some of its pain and its pride. I walked, in the sun and in the rain, from Kenya to Israel, from Pakistan to Japan, from Vietnam to Ireland, and back again to China.

I felt like I was again a thirteen-year-old groupie waiting to hear Frank Sinatra as I huddled with thousands of women in the pouring rain waiting for the auditorium doors to open to hear Hillary Clinton address the forum.

I knew such a surge of hope as I listened, in a small classroom, jammed with 150 women (including the Queen of Belgium), to Israeli and Palestinian women describe their arduous years of dialogue. What began in secret in 1986 through the efforts of a Belgian national has now become a working organization throughout Israel called the Jerusalem Link. "Peacemaking takes hard work. . . . Trust comes only *after* dialogue, not before. . . . We may sometimes disagree, but we now know we can work it out." These were the women's themes.

Women were networking in a more intense and direct way than most men. As I watched this sharing across borders, women showed a willingness to reveal their successes and failures so that others could stand on their shoulders to reach for the higher stars. For me, seeing the internationalization of the women's network was exhilarating, for this collection of strength will certainly empower women everywhere.

And now I ask myself: How can I be cynical about the present when I have seen such hope for the future?

Images of Beijing

Florence L. Johnson

Observing women from all over the world interact with one another and discuss issues and concerns that interest them all was overwhelming and very significant to me. To see women in plenaries, in small groups, in large tents, and in small circles in sunny spots discussing topics that impact their daily lives was invigorating. On this particular day, thousands of women are standing in the rain in front of the Huairou International Convention Center in Huairou, China, eagerly awaiting entrance to hear Hillary Clinton speak. They are hidden under umbrellas and shrouded in raincoats, ponchos, and head scarves.

In the chilly morning air, these women from all over the world huddle together. According to a Chinese saying, Women hold up half the sky. But on this day, the women at the forum are more interested in staying warm than in holding up the sky. Because of the closeness of the situation, a bond begins to form among the women, and the relaxed carefree conversation becomes serious as they begin to discuss many subjects such as violence against women, economic power, genital mutilation, dowries, families, and life in the United States.

I was moved by the sight of so many women—women from the largest cities of the world to the smallest rural villages; women who could easily afford the trip and others who had saved for years to come. An elementary school teacher from Kansas informed me she wanted to be at the forum so much that she had been saving her money for three years. Some of the women had received scholarships; others were representing their governments and thus had their way paid; while others were able to fund the trip themselves with no financial hardship.

Each woman at the NGO forum was conscious of the myriad of women who were not there and of the constraints that kept them away. The keynote address to the forum had to be delivered via video. Aung San Suu Kyi, 1991 Nobel Peace Prize winner just released from almost six years of house arrest in Burma for her advocacy of democracy, did not want to leave the women she had promised to serve. Women at this conference sent a message to the world that women are crucial to the development of any community. Women's development cannot be neglected and women's rights as human beings must be valued. Women want equality, peace, and development and they will continue their endeavor to realize their goals. The world has witnessed their dedication, determination, and enthusiasm for political participation and the goal of changing the world for the better.

A Night of China

Janice Auth

The sky begins to darken about 6:45 and the crowd gathers for a performance at the outdoor theater. A dirigible circles overhead trailing a banner that reads, Equality, Development, Peace, and Friendship. It is the close of another day in Huairou, China. Huairou is playing Worthy Host to the women from all over the world who have come here to hear and be heard. Part of being a host is to provide entertainment and that is what we are to have tonight. The printed program calls this evening "A Night of China." The young Chinese woman who introduces each act urges us to "please 'enjoin' it" and in predictable fashion, we are treated to a series of cultural showpieces including a Tibetan rural harvest dance, rubber-spined acrobats and gymnasts, and the requisite adorable children, in this case a gaggle of twirling five-year-olds dressed in white and billed as the "Snow White Flakes." Next a gorgeous woman in a slinky black gown takes the stage and begins to sing, in Chinese, a Western-sounding pop song. She sings high and nasal and with much gesturing and flirting with the audience. Many of the townspeople have come to watch this free performance, and this singer is obviously very popular here. The night is completely dark by now, a rice-bowl half moon shines, the blimp circles, and the three guys behind me are really "enjoining" this Chinese version of Mariah Carey.

My favorite part of the evening is a balancing act. A woman comes out with a candelabra on each outstretched palm. In each candelabra there are about ten or twelve lighted candles. She then lies down with her legs up in the air and two other candelabra are placed on the soles of her upturned feet. An assistant keeps adding candelabra until eight or nine are blazing and teetering all over her body. Clusters of light and heat emanate from her forehead, chest, shoulders. While the audience is cheering wildly for her acrobatic and balancing dexterity, I slowly realize that her act reminds me of my own life and the lives of so many women I know and have met here. The candles come to represent the myriad facets of female expectation and accomplishment. The candle acrobat becomes a metaphor for the quintessential woman who balances home, family, career, self; is volunteer, nurse, mother, daughter, counselor, manager, accountant, domestic, professional, writer, teacher, mentor, lover, arbitrator, artist, worker; using every part of herself to brighten the space around her.

English
The Universal Language
Susan C. Bayley

When a feminist lawyer and writer from Costa Rica began to speak about violence against women at a featured panel in Huairou, she spoke in English. However, Alda Facio soon threw down her microphone and exhorted her audience to listen to her in Spanish, her native language and her language of identity. As a native speaker of Spanish, she refused to accede to the imperial use of English. A dramatic moment, one that brought a few cheers and some applause from the worldwide audience.

I attended that panel on violence and women on my first day in Huairou. Right away, I realized the NGO Forum on Women was a powerful gathering of Third World women, not simply an international forum featuring academic sessions, erudite presentations, and "guests" from the Third World.

Women leaders from different regions of the world did not need their English-speaking sisters to address frontline issues of violence against women; the rise of conservatism in its various forms; obstacles to peace and human security; media, culture, and communication; institutional mechanisms and financial arrangements; and gender equity. They shaped and influenced panels on strategies and mechanisms used by women in the past decade to bring about change. They also dominated other formal and informal gatherings throughout the ten-day conference. But for the most part, these women did so, not in their different native languages but in English, their second, third, or possibly fourth language.

Although that feminist lawyer made a strong political statement by switching to the use of Spanish, women from around the world needed and used English to communicate their concerns and to address world-ranging issues. Conference literature, from the program book to the daily newspapers, was printed almost entirely in English. Placards at small and large demonstrations and fund-raising items such as T-shirts, hats, and pins may at times have been printed in two languages, but one of the languages was always English. And leaders, calling participants to their respective demonstrations throughout the week, used English. Probably the major criterion for selection as a conference or forum volunteer was a basic knowledge of English. It was fortunate, too, for the Pittsburgh contingent, that most services in Huairou and Beijing were in English.

While featured panels and speakers were provided with simultaneous translations, such a service was not feasible in smaller, less formal sessions. The real power of the forum in Huairou emanated from these sessions: scheduled workshops in small rooms, small group discussions in tents, informal gatherings throughout the forum grounds, and conversations on the buses that shuttled many of us back and forth from our hotels in Beijing.

Many of these smaller sessions were not in English as Leone Paradise and I learned when we attended a two-hour workshop on violence against women in Algeria. Only after the session had begun did we realize that it would be held in French. A lovely young woman, an Algerian American we later learned, extended a most-appreciated courtesy; she translated the session for us. Every few minutes she would turn to the two of us, the only ones in the workshop who did not know French, and tell us what had just been said, while the other participants had to wait patiently for her to complete her translation. At first, Leone and I were uncomfortable with this, not only because of our linguistic inadequacy but also because of the special attention directed only to us. After a few minutes, however, we realized this was another case of "women helping women," and English became the means by which we learned how traumatic being a woman in Algeria today can be.

Because of my career in the field of English as a foreign or second language, I believe that, as today's universal language of communication, English helps break down barriers between people. Neither I nor other native speakers from Canada, Australia, and the United Kingdom "own" the English language. It belongs to women from Costa Rica, China, and Algeria too. Women from all continents and regions of the world become connected and empowered by their knowledge and use of English.

The theme of the NGO Forum on Women was "look at the world through women's eyes," but only through communication could this theme be realized. The purpose of the forum was "to bring together women and men [yes, there were some in Huairou] to challenge, create, and transform global structures and processes at all levels through the empowerment and celebration of women." The success of the world's largest gathering of women ever was awesome, evidenced by the fact that so many people communicated through a universal language as powerful as English has become.

Dilemma of a Ghost

Linda Hunt

My hotel reservations somehow got changed and I had the good fortune to find a room at one of the many dormitories. For eight dollars a night you got a small room, double occupancy, clean, with a shared bath. There were six rooms to a floor and two women to a room. These were the economy accommodations so it wasn't surprising the complex was full of women of color, many of them from Africa. If you look at the economic status of white women versus nonwhite women around the world, you will understand why. That being said, I can only attempt to tell you what a wondrous and at the same time disconcerting experience it was. I was surrounded by women who looked much like me and yet were immersed in their cultures so different from mine. These women moved with an assurance about their ancestry, their culture, their traditions. This confidence was obvious in their garb (each pattern told what part of Africa they were from), in their language (tribal, French, or English). Daily I moved among them, not knowing my ancestry, my geographic patterns of dress, my language. There were times when I experienced the "dilemma of a ghost." I saw humans and remembered being human, but I was unable to cross over and reach out to humans or to become human again. Never had I felt so displaced; never had the term African American seemed so abstract to me. I wore my hair in a braided twist (African); I wore jeans (American); and I spoke English and Black English (African American).

The women would ask me where I was from and I would say, "I don't know. I was stolen away." They would nod their heads and smile, replying, "You are my sister, I know that. You didn't have to pay a fare to leave home, but you have to pay a fare to return."

Through a Woman's Eyes

Andrea Blinn

Thinking back over the last ten years of my life, it almost feels as if every decision I made was leading me to the 1995 NGO Forum on Women. In particular, to the incredible moment when I was told I had won a PBB scholarship to attend the forum. My interest in women's issues began on Koh Pangan, a small, beautiful island in southern Thailand. It was there, after watching a Thai woman be punched and kicked unconscious by her husband and four of his friends, that I truly began to fathom the problems women around the world shared. My Thai friend said to me, with tears in her eyes, "We are sisters. We must stop this."

Though I am a woman, I do not always live life as I see it, that is, through the eyes of my womanhood. Instead, my actions and way of life are influenced by dominant male perceptions that form accepted societal values. For me, I think my time at the forum was the first opportunity I had to truly look at the world through women's eyes.

A First Glance

It was time to dress for the plane ride to Beijing. I decided to wear my oversize black T-shirt with a huge white peace sign on the front of it. Though it was a peace sign, it was simultaneously a sign of my feminism. As I slipped it over my head and stared at myself in the mirror, I realized in sad wonder that this was the first time I'd felt safe wearing my feminism for the whole world to see.

Up until that moment, I had been ashamed to boldly admit, "I am a feminist." My feminism was something to hide, to admit only to other women who identified with the label, or to a few men, cautiously, and only after extreme deliberation. In graduate school, when I told male students my research focused on prostitution in Thailand, their attitudes toward me visibly changed. Their eyes instantly lowered—first to take in the size of my breasts, and then to slowly absorb the rest of my bodily curves. A moment later, eye contact resumed, but it was different, as if the study of prostitution had somehow made me a sexual figure in their eyes. (I often wondered if, in that brief moment, they'd imagined me naked, dancing wildly before them in some poorly lit, dingy club.) And if nothing else, I was no longer a smart woman capable of intelligent thought. No, I was a promiscuous feminist studying the intriguing sex acts of hot babes around the world.

On my way to the NGO forum, it was finally OK to be a feminist. On the plane, walking down the aisle to my seat, what did I see? WOMEN! An endless sea of beautiful women! Women in colorful saris, in faded Levis, in traditional African costume. After I put my rucksack in the luggage rack, I looked out at all of them. There was no need to ask. Their knowing, smiling eyes had already told me. Of course they were going to the forum.

Finally I could be proud that I had spent my graduate career studying how the impact of international development policies left 2 million women in Thailand with no viable economic alternative except to be prostitutes. And so I wore my shirt proudly for the whole world to see and to know: I am a feminist and I am going to the NGO forum. For now, I thought to myself, I am safe. I am protected by women from around the world, women who fought their way to get here, some who sacrificed greatly just to come together, and all who care deeply about the lives of other people.

What a relief that plane ride was for me. It was as if a sudden shift of power had occurred in the universe. And I felt so safe. To be seen, for the first time, only through the eyes of women.

The Sounds

Luckily, the Chinese made a big mistake with me. Instead of placing me in the U.S. dormitory in Huairou, they accidentally assigned me to the African bloc. When I stepped out at the Nanking Towers, I was greeted by hundreds of African women, dressed in the brilliant colors of traditional African costume, singing and dancing in the courtyard. I quickly learned they were celebrating the coming together of so many of their sisters from around the world, and almost nightly, they joyously celebrated.

One of my six suitemates was Veronica, an African woman from

Kenya. Veronica and I quickly became friends, and almost immediately she made a habit of bursting through my door at 6 A.M. Already showered and dressed for the day, she barged right into my room, completely ignored the fact that I was in a deep sleep, and announced in a loud, but very pleasant voice, "GOOD MORNING, ANDREA! WHAT ARE YOU GOING TO DO TODAY?" Then she would begin to sing. She sang out loud and clear, with no hesitation or embarrassment. To the sound of her strong voice, I dragged myself out of bed and into a freezing-cold shower.

Veronica sang the same song every morning and evening. Two days after living with her, I learned that she had written the song while still in Kenya, in honor of all women from around the world—those who were able as well as those who were not able to attend the conference. (I met an elderly woman who had sold homemade bread in Africa for three years to earn the money to get to China.) I still remember the song's chorus by heart. Veronica made me promise to teach it to my sisters in Pittsburgh.

I wish you could hear the tune. I wish you could hear Veronica sing it. You would love the way her voice carried, the way she moved her arms and hands to its soulful rhythm, and the way she danced to it, like it was the only song she'd ever known.

> So sing a song for women, everywhere
> Let it ring around the world, never ever cease
> Sing a song, for women, everywhere
> Equality, development, and peace.

At the forum, I listened to women share their anguish and their triumphs. I watched the peaceful demonstrations of women and men, dressed in black, mourning for the loss of their dead sisters. I applauded mothers and daughters who performed dances and songs together. I attended workshops from which I learned organizing strategies to bring home to my sisters in Pittsburgh. I fought my way (through the violent pushing and shoving of the Chinese police and reporters) to the auditorium where Hillary Clinton, the only First Lady I've ever respected, spoke out for the rights of women around the world. I cried, several times, at the sense of relief and joy I felt at being present for the coming together of thousands of people in the name of women around the world.

I learned that solidarity does not mean that women share exactly the same beliefs and ideas about life. Rather, solidarity describes what was achieved when women of different classes, colors, and cultures, with different individual needs in their everyday lives, bonded together at the NGO forum and united for a higher purpose, as sisters. We were all so different, and yet at the forum, if only through our sheer numbers and the passion with which we argued and debated issues, we shared one voice.

Now that I'm home, sometimes late at night I find myself quietly humming the tune of Veronica's song. I like to hear myself singing her song. I like to know that Veronica is still with me.

Eye to Eye

On my way home, I stopped for one night in Bangkok. I had conducted so much research about prostitution in Thailand, I was finally going to visit Patpong Road, Bangkok's red-light district. I rode a tuk-tuk there, alone.

The streets were lined with sex clubs. In an effort to attract customers, men stood outside each club holding signs about the kinds of sex shows women performed nightly. There were dart shows and balloon shows and cigarette shows and pencil shows and egg shows and fucking shows. When I peered in from the sidewalk, each club featured the same highlight: young Thai women wearing only bikinis, dancing on bars, for a mostly male audience.

I picked a small, approachable-looking club. Inside, six young women, who looked to be between sixteen and twenty-five, all dressed in green bikinis, danced on the bar. Each girl had a number pinned to her bikini so that a man could easily identify her should he choose to buy her for the night. The girls just kept moving, and smiling faintly, and dancing endlessly, and looking bored out of their minds, waiting for a rich farung (foreigner) to buy them.

The toilets were in the dancers' dressing room. While waiting in line, I watched as a Thai prostitute (I knew because she wore a half-zipped black leather jacket with a green bikini underneath) touched up her makeup in the mirror. Finally, I realized, one of the women whom I had spent two years of my life studying, was standing right before me.

I was keenly aware of three very huge differences between us: She is Thai and I am American. She speaks Thai and I speak English. She is a prostitute and I am not a prostitute.

And then suddenly—she must have felt me staring at her—she had just finished applying a thick coat of red lipstick—her eyes met mine in the mirror. She looked me right in the eyes for a long moment. I found that I wanted to talk to her and tell her about the forum and all the women who had gathered there. But I remained silent. And as I stared back at her (her eyes were such a deep brown), all our differences seemed to instantly dissolve. And she was just a woman. And I was just a woman. And we smiled knowingly, and nodded in recognition of one another.

And then the moment passed, and she went back out into the night, and I went home.

Fellow Citizens in the Household of God

Elizabeth Vann Hobbs

While attending a church service in Beijing, I was so moved by the beautiful singing of the choir, I felt called upon to give out copies of our ecumenical prayer. Quietly, as the last hymn was being sung, I walked over and gave the prayer to members of the choir.

Three days later, while waiting for Hillary Clinton to speak at the NGO forum, I noticed a group of Chinese women entering the auditorium while we were singing "Keep on moving forward, never turning back." As we continued singing, the whole auditorium of about eighteen hundred people from hundreds of different nations began joining hands and my hand was placed in the hand of Zhang Jian. She suddenly recognized me as the one who had given out the prayer cards in her church, and she told me this in excited, broken English—with gestures. I was so happy to see her again. I gave her a copy of my "One Over All" booklet, which I had brought with me to give out to new friends. In the booklet was my address and a special message about the importance of international friendship.

It was so crowded that I did not see her again, but much to my delight, I heard from her at Christmastime and discovered that she is a senior lecturer in a Chinese women's college in the department of social work. My profession is in the same field. In her letter she said, "I felt your hand was placed in mine and I was no longer alone when I read your booklet." I have written to her and hope to hear from her again soon. How wonderful to discover that we "are no longer strangers and sojourners, but fellow citizens with the saints and members of the Household of God" (Ephesians 2:19).

Glimpses of the Church in China

Bebb Wheeler Stone

Yes, I did get in to see and hear Hillary Clinton. The morning of September 5 was dreary with a steady downpour. Had it been sunny, everyone could have heard her because the venue would have been a large, outdoor stage before thousands of chairs. But drizzle forced the event into an auditorium designed for fifteen hundred. When we arrived by bus, hundreds of opened umbrellas colorfully greeted us. I approached the building on the left-hand side and was soon held captive by the crush of a crowd. When the crowd began to move, I was swept through the door, and I was one of the last to gain entry. About twenty of us stood in a back doorway. While the security issues were being resolved, we women were getting acquainted. Next to me was an attorney from Nigeria dressed in her African caftan and headdress; behind me a social worker from Jordan; in front of me a Presbyterian pastor from the Philippines. The Nigerian attorney finally inched her notebook out of her closely held bag, saw me observing her readiness to take notes, and offered, "I'm a Hillary follower."

Excerpt from a sermon at Third Presbyterian Church, Pittsburgh, Pennsylvania, September 24, 1995

God/Awful; God/Wonderful

Bebb Wheeler Stone

The Asian Women Human Rights Council held a tribunal. On one side of the stage was seated the court of wise women—seven international leaders in health and human rights issues. On the other side of the stage was a simple podium, to which woman after woman came to tell her story, to bring her case before the court.

This is but one of those stories: A Korean woman was kidnapped from her home when she was fourteen years old by Japanese soldiers during World War II. She was moved from place to place as the army moved, forced into—no euphemisms—sex slavery. There were many of these women; they are now aged, and they were and are called "comfort women." They have been in hiding since World War II out of their sense of shame at being—by their culture's standards—so unclean. Only now, decades after that war, are those so terribly abused women beginning to find each other, as one after another hears her own story being told publicly by a sister. The diminutive Korean woman I heard was dressed in her beautiful Korean gown. She spoke of her experiences in a direct and quiet voice, shielding us from nothing. What I will share with you is that at one point she was taking five shots of morphine a day to kill her pain. . . . The Korean woman told us that after the war was over, after she had been set free, she spent seven months alone in a cement-floor hut coming out of her morphine addiction. So strong was her pounding on that floor in her pain that when she got to the other side of it, she found holes in the cement.

Excerpt from a sermon, Third Presbyterian Church, Pittsburgh, Pennsylvania, October 8, 1995

We Are All Connected

Vail E. Weller

Originally, the forum was to be held in Beijing, but fortunately, for us, it was moved to Huairou. Beijing was teeming with life and historically significant but also extremely polluted and industrialized. Huairou was simply beautiful! It is a small city nestled in the mountains near the Great Wall. Many groups were stuck with a daily commute from Beijing, so we felt very lucky to be staying in Huairou.

Our delegation was made up of twenty-five women connected to the Center for Women and Religion of the Graduate Theological Union (students and graduates of the GTU, ministers, community activists, teachers, authors). We created and presented a workshop entitled "Celebrating Woman's Spirit: Sharing the Sacred," which facilitated personal storytelling focusing on spiritual inspiration and struggle. It incorporated music, meditation, art-making, and movement, and was well attended. I went to presentations that were very diverse in focus, ranging from "Architecture: The Spirit of Space" to "Farming and Genetics: Questions of Future Sustainability, Ethics, and Spirituality" to "Environmental Racism." The workshops, surprisingly, were not the highlight of the forum for me. Rather, it was the informal, unplanned events that were most important.

I would get on the shuttle bus (from the hotel to the forum grounds, about a fifteen-minute ride) and be seated next to a woman from India, or Africa, or Jordan. We would immediately begin talking about the workshops we had attended, or the facility, or our careers at home. In the process, I learned a great deal about what women around the world are accomplishing. A number of friendships developed out of these casual conversations.

Spontaneous demonstrations took place every day. These demonstrations ranged in focus dramatically. The element they all had in common, though, was the spirit in which they were undertaken. At these gatherings there was a feeling of vibrant energy unlike anything I have ever been in contact with. Additionally, these demonstrations felt strong and, at the same time, very peaceful. It was just amazing. One group I remember in particular was from Korea. They would alternate between chanting slogans and dancing. They were accompanied by a horn and a drum. The music and the resulting dance were haunting—simultaneously melancholy and joyous.

The forum was not without controversy. I attended a workshop on Tibetan women in exile, at which there was a dispute between the workshop facilitators and the Chinese authorities. This led the authorities to confiscate the video that had been shown, which was a breach of security and against the forum rules. This specific event was highly publicized, and I listened to the coverage when I got home. It felt strange to be involved personally in something that commanded so much international attention.

What have I brought home? A new appreciation for political situations worldwide. A deep love for the Chinese people I met. They were nothing but helpful, sincere, and generous. Mainly I came away with a painful awareness that our own consumption patterns and consumer policies intensely affect people—real people—living in other countries and here in our own as well. Their voices are not usually heard. I have now seen their faces. They have shared their stories with me and I have no choice but to remember them.

I have also returned with another gift from the amazing women at the forum. I am energized with a new strength, because they reminded me of the fact that we are all connected and our choices really do make a difference. This is a most radical notion (if acted upon!). It was the most important thing I learned.

The participants of the forum have also shown me the dire necessity for community involvement, vigilant political awareness, and above all, gratitude and joy for all that we already have. The things I learned there will continue to enrich me for the rest of my life.

Inspiring Young Women to Action and Advocacy

Susan Homer

When I was chosen as Chatham College's student representative to the 1995 World Conference on Women, I had no idea how this event would change my beliefs and motivations. I thought in the beginning I would learn about international policy and UN interactions. What I really learned in Beijing was what it means to care about women's issues. To care means to work to create change, to work to make a difference.

I was honored to receive a scholarship to travel to Beijing. Chatham president Esther Barazzone and I made plans to attend the NGO forum with several other students from American women's colleges. Like women all over the world, our group began to research this voyage on which we were embarking. Many of my fellow students and I were just babies during International Women's Year in 1975, and this history of the international women's movement was a new subject for us.

As I read about the evolution of this international women's community since the first women's conference in Mexico City, I realized this conference would be different from any before it. For the first time, the NGO forum was as important and as promoted as the actual conference itself. Grassroots organizers, NGOs, and ordinary women from all over the world would come together and make statements and create networks that had the potential to be more effective than the promises coming from governments. Even more of a change, however, was that young women would be a force on the international stage as they had never been before.

Young women were a prime audience for the messages of Beijing. After all, the discussion would be about the current status of women, but the Platform for Action would outline the goals that would define the future for young people. Each country made an attempt to include young women in its official delegation to the conference, and NGOs brought young members, daughters, and rising feminists to the forum. In addition, one of the twelve Platform for Action areas focused on the girl-child. Obviously, women of my generation were targeted as both subjects and participants in this event. It was this new recognition of our very real involvement and participation that inspired change in the lives of the young women who traveled to Beijing.

At the forum, one of the main organizing and meeting areas was the youth tent. Beginning early in the morning with a daily press conference and lasting well into the night, young women came together to share stories, talk, and laugh. I was awed by the excitement and enthusiasm of the other young women there and inspired by the commitment and passion of my peers. These women were amazing and had already worked on so many issues for women and their communities.

One of the highlights of my trip was meeting Marjorie Margolies-Mezvinsky, former U.S. Congresswoman and director of the official U.S. delegation. One afternoon in the youth tent, Marjorie had initiated a meeting with American youth to listen to our concerns and ideas. As we huddled under the tent, trying to protect ourselves from the wind and rain, other young women and I told Marjorie what we wanted to see done to help women our age in the United States. We told her our concerns about finding college financial aid, guaranteeing access to reproductive services, and the continual fear of violence against young women on campuses and in the cities. We told her what we were already doing to empower ourselves and our peers. Marjorie listened to our ideas with respect and interest, and I was impressed that our government delegation was taking time to consider the perspectives of young women.

That a member of the U.S. delegation would take time to just talk and listen demonstrated to me the weight that governments were placing on the youth perspective. What really impressed me with this conversation (as with all my interactions at the forum) was that these young women were talking about what they wanted to do in their communities to act on the lessons learned in Beijing. They didn't just talk about problems and the hardships of being a woman. They asked themselves and Marjorie, "What can we do about this and what will our government do about it?"

In the end, every discussion and workshop at the forum came down to *outcome*. Every day, my friends and I considered how what we had learned would make a difference or shape our actions when we returned home. While I was there, I was continually thinking about what would happen later. What would I do? What would our government do? And finally, what would young women as a whole do? I hoped we would be motivated and energized to act and make our government respond to the promises made in Beijing. I wanted to change—I wanted to become more involved in the process that will make women's lives better by giving them more choices and more access to precious resources like education, credit, and health care.

Although I spoke about my trip and the Platform for Action when I returned, I had a difficult time expressing what changed inside of me during those short weeks. I have always been interested in politics and issues. What is new is this desire to get out into my community and work with other women on these issues. I realize I have to start acting now—it is no longer enough to ride on the coattails of the earlier women's movement as my generation has done for so long. I need to put some personal effort into all these ideals in which I believe.

That's why it is so important that young women—girls and students and daughters—went to the conference and forum in Beijing. Young people are often overlooked when policy and activism are discussed. But we have the desire to be included, and we are acting and organizing and volunteering. Being in Beijing inspired me to act and made me realize that it is my generation that now has the responsibility to carry out the commitments made there. The torch has been passed on. I like to think that the older women at the forum heard our ideas and saw our enthusiasm and decided we were indeed worthy to carry on this movement they started long ago. We will honor this legacy and not forget that we must not just talk, but act, to make stronger women and stronger communities.

I haven't accomplished even half of what I wanted to do after Beijing. But the forum experience continues to be a daily inspiration for me to work toward my own personal commitments from that time. And, most important, it renews my desire to organize women my own age to act for ourselves and for the future.

Beijing
An Illuminating Experience
Adelle M. Williams

Never in my wildest dreams would I have imagined attending a major international conference and having the opportunity to provide an international presentation and network with women from all over the world. However, early in 1995, it became abundantly clear that a variety of different organizations within the Pittsburgh area and within the United States in general were actively involved in the planning and potential attendance at this phenomenal event.

When it was brought to my attention that all these activities were taking place, I became an active participant in the process. I began to attend local planning meetings and to make plans to attend the NGO forum. My participation in the health component in a series of local presentations set the agenda for the various discussions that would ensue in Beijing. My aspirations became reality through the generous support and assistance from Pittsburgh/Beijing '95 and Beyond, the Heinz Family Foundation, and Slippery Rock University. Obtaining the scholarship from PBB was an utter surprise because I had never imagined I would be selected. The scholarship was "icing on the cake."

There were times during the months preceding the conference and forum when I thought I'd never get there. A major problem was obtaining a visa. I have never been through such an exhausting experience in my life. In the end, I had to pay close to two hundred dollars to send, via Federal Express, for the application and additional documentation necessary to obtain the visa. I will never forget the experience and the relief I felt after I learned that a United Nations representative had obtained it.

Lower Socioeconomic Status Women: A Global Health Concern
Synopsis

The majority of individuals in a disadvantaged position in various societies around the world are women. Due to this position in their respective communities, their health status and that of their offspring are adversely affected. There is difficulty focusing on improvement of their health due to a basic need to survive. A high level of illiteracy plagues many women in developing countries, which interferes with their understanding and communication of healthy behaviors to family members. Violence, AIDS, infant mortality, and maternal mortality plague many women in these areas as well. My presentation addressed issues of poverty, illiteracy, and selected health concerns while offering recommendations to decrease or eliminate unhealthy practices and encourage participation and collaboration among various influential constituents within their societies. The strengths and weaknesses of the U.S. health care delivery system were highlighted as they were relevant to the topics. An attempt was made to display both an understanding of and an appreciation for the difficulties that developing countries are experiencing.

Impressions

The presentation was well received as evidenced by encouraging remarks, a standing ovation, and requests for photo sessions. Participants remained after the presentation to query me on government involvement in health services delivery, AIDS and its impact on youth, and issues related to advocacy for women and girls. This event was a rewarding experience, personally, culturally, and professionally.

In addition to presenting this workshop at the forum, I was fortunate to be able to attend the phenomenal opening ceremonies. I was one of approximately two thousand individuals who had the opportunity to listen to First Lady Hillary Clinton's speech, which emphasized the need to continue to focus on women's issues as part of basic human rights issues.

As a participant in the forum, I witnessed the intense commitment to improving the quality of life everywhere as evidenced by the attendance of women and men from all over the world.

Beyond Beijing

Upon arrival in Pittsburgh, I was mentally and physically exhausted. It took approximately ten days for my body to return to some degree of normalcy. I never anticipated such a long recovery because in other international traveling, I have been able to rebound in approximately two to five days.

I was invited to share my forum experiences within the Pittsburgh and surrounding areas. I have been interviewed by representatives from the *Pittsburgh Post Gazette,* the *Butler Eagle, Rocket,* the *Slippery Rock Eagle, Focus Newsletter,* and the *Rock.* In addition, articles have appeared in the *Allied News* and *Our World.* I was interviewed on the *Larry Berg Talk Show* and *Let's Talk,* hosted by Lorraine Williams. I have been a panel participant at Magee-Womens Hospital Celebration of Women and at Carlow College. I have also spoken to classes at Slippery Rock University, the University of Pittsburgh, and Westminster College.

I expect to continue to relate my experiences as my schedule permits. Thanks to the generous support of the Heinz Family Foundation, Pittsburgh/Beijing '95 and Beyond, Slippery Rock University, and my family, my dream became a reality.

The Anglican Women's Network

Elizabeth Vann Hobbs

More than five thousand Chinese greeted their foreign visitors at the Workers Stadium in Beijing on August 30 for the spectacular opening ceremony of the NGO forum. The twenty thousand doves that were released at the conclusion of the performance gave us the overwhelming feeling that equality, development, and peace would follow the conference as never before.

At Beijing, through the eyes of women, women testified to the fact that the world is a poor and violent place. They proclaimed that through the energy of women, a difference can be made.

The atmosphere of friendliness was apparent everywhere as people strove to overcome language barriers and extended handshakes and smiles. The Peace Tent, a lively place, was a gathering point for noonday prayers for the Anglican Women's Network and anyone who wished to participate. The workshops were enlightening and inspiring.

The Anglican Women's Network joined the worldwide gathering believing that through prayers, their power of presence, and advocacy, a change could be brought about regarding violence against women. We went to take our place beside our sisters—raising our hands in protest and praise—to listen, to learn, and to network.

A statement of commitment of the Anglican Women's Network concludes with this sentence: "God has blessed our network with vast potential, locally and globally. We commit ourselves through daily prayer, continuing dialogue, collaborative planning, and concrete action to work for equality, justice, and peace."

It becomes more and more apparent that challenges facing women everywhere are universal. To build a more peaceful, harmonious, and prosperous world for our families, we must all work together.

The following phrases, seen at the conference and forum, continue to remind us of our mission now that we've returned to our respective homelands:

Unity in diversity
The New Millennium is ours
Break the silence
Commonality discovered
Women hold up half the sky
Keep on moving forward—never turning back
Challenges to women are universal and global
Sisterhood   Solidarity
March for peace, vigil for hope

Don't Let Anyone Ever Tell You That You're Anything Less Than Beautiful

Toni Conaway

Since my return from China I have decided that at the core of all the issues—peace, development, equality—is the universal imperative to recognize all creatures on this earth as "beautiful." The litany of horror stories repeated by people from all over the globe—everything from domestic violence to serial murders to nuclear testing—is only possible because one group feels superior to another and has the power to dominate it. I believe it started with the patriarchal paradigm that has come

Toni Conaway and a new African friend inside the Peace Tent. (Photo by Janice Auth)

down through the centuries in virtually all cultures. It has been propped up by legal, medical, and religious arguments and rationalizations. It has survived because of the use of force, violence, conquest, and war. As a result, 70 percent of the poor in the world today are women. Violence is increasing—more than 80 percent of the women in Quito, Ecuador, say they have experienced physical abuse. In the United States, more than one-third of the police calls are a response to domestic violence. More than 80 to 90 percent of the deaths in wars raging today are civilian deaths. In World War I it was only 5 percent. Clearly, the patriarchal paradigm must be replaced by a new way of thinking and acting. The interactions in Beijing hinted at the answer. In the dialogues, where people were respected and listened to, a great deal of the talk was about partnership, cooperation, consensus, and conflict resolution. This means saying no to nuclear testing and nuclear dumping, especially on indigenous lands, and saying no to war as a solution to conflict. The twentieth century has been the most violent one in world history. The Just War theory has become just that—a theory. As we approach a new millennium we must find another way. The women in Beijing made a start.

Faces

Dorothy Hill

"The logo depicts eight women dancing. Each has her own energy and dynamism. Each one is tied to the other through a common center. Thus, they all together generate more energy and power than each of them could generate singly."

When I read what the logo of the nongovernmental forum signified, I found it compelling. At the forum itself, it took on deeper meaning, as I found myself caught up in the energy and power of those thousands of women gathered from the far corners of the earth. The eight dancing women had faces I would recognize—the beautiful young mother from Burkina Faso denouncing female circumcision; the Irish woman who questioned whether her political activism was depriving her daughter of any chance for a normal childhood; the passionate Muslim from Thailand, crying to other women of Islam, "Think of what we're doing! Bosnia can happen anywhere!"; the Japanese woman who demanded that her government apologize and grant compensation to the Korean comfort women; the Tahitian overwhelmed with anger at the French for using her precious small corner of the world for testing nuclear weapons; the white-haired great-grandmother sharing the wisdom of the Maori elders; the elementary school teacher from inner Mongolia who quietly pressed on us her gift, a Chinese fan with a tiny cross, the symbol of her Christian faith; Hillary Clinton, urging courage and commitment: "You are here. Your faces mirror the faces of millions of women who are not here and their voices will be heard through yours."

Eight, sixteen, countless other individual faces are there, representing most of the races, religions, cultures, traditions, and enormous shared concerns of the women of the world. The individual faces *are* there; yet the logo itself remains faceless, reminding us that while we are unique, we are equal and we are *one*. "Each one is tied to the other through a common center." Some of us were surprised at the degradation, pain, lack of opportunity, and injustice in the lives of our global sisters; some of

"Eight women dancing . . . each one . . . tied to the other through a common center." Banner at the NGO Forum opening ceremonies (Photo by Molly Rush)

us were surprised by how universal and common are the problems women from around the world face. All of us know that our "center" is the belief expressed in the African platform and echoed again and again in Beijing, "Women's rights are universal and indivisible from human rights."

Back in Pittsburgh, the logo is a constant reminder of the promise many of us made to ourselves and to each other in Beijing—somehow, we *will* make a difference. Our voices *will* be heard. Mary Leigh Touvell, who worked with the logo in making a banner for PBB to take to Beijing, said the circle of dancers sometimes made her think of a whirling dervish, with all that energy, teetering on the brink of going out of control. Part of the challenge is to make sure our energy is put to good use. Many people have questioned the conference and the Platform for Action as mere rhetoric—fairly elusive goals and not legally binding on governments.

Women gather in the rain at the Kuumba Stage area of the NGO forum site in Huairou. (Photo by Dorothy Hill)

Friends have challenged me: "What can you really hope to accomplish?" Chinese wisdom says, "A journey of a thousand miles begins with a single step" (Lao-tzu). I know I'm not alone in taking that first step.

Each one of us from this area who traveled on the Peace Train, attended the NGO forum or the UN conference, or did both is sharing her unique experience with many varied audiences and finding men and women eager to learn and respond. Each person we touch and influence with the messages of Beijing touches many others, and on it goes. This is happening all over the world. I believe in the Hundredth Monkey phenomenon that says that when a critical number of monkeys (or people) have learned a certain habit, it becomes accepted knowledge and practice. I also believe in the bumper sticker that says, "If the people lead, eventually the leaders will follow."

What are some of the other ways our energy and commitment will surface here in Pittsburgh? Each of the women who traveled to Beijing with Pittsburgh/Beijing '95 and Beyond will have different answers. Those of us who have been active with Peace Links will continue, with renewed energy, our work in nuclear nonproliferation and disarmament, in conflict resolution, in citizen diplomacy, in pressing for cleanup of nuclear sites, in demanding that resources are used for social needs instead of for weapons. We will uphold platform actions that outlaw land mines and make wartime rape a crime. We are excited by a new idea for creating national guardianships of nuclear waste repositories, establishing active monitoring of these time bombs that exist in our communal "backyards." Pittsburgh Presbytery will be distributing buttons from the Women in Black movement, urging western Pennsylvanians to join women around the world in wearing black every Thursday to protest violence against women in all its forms, local as well as global. I personally want to address the issue of domestic violence in a more direct way and will be more active in local gun control.

Kuumba Stage area on the final afternoon. Thousands of empty seats provide a stark setting for the forum logo. (Photo by Dorothy Hill)

Women came here with their own power and go back home with the power of women from all over the world.

This statement by Ugandan Kemenia Alinernay says the forum lived up to the symbolism of its logo. We all have that power. Let's use it well.

v THE CONFERENCE

Equality, Development, Peace

September 4–15, 1995

Because we are talking about issues that matter in the lives of women and girls, that does not mean we are ignoring issues of concern to men and boys. If as a nation and as a global family we truly care about strong families, strong communities, and strong societies, we have to recognize that economic, political, and social progress depends on women and girls having access to the opportunities they deserve. When women flourish, families, communities, and nations flourish. And every one of us, men and women, boys and girls, stands to gain. What we are striving for is the day when every person who graces this earth is able to pursue his or her dreams to the fullest because the opportunities and encouragement are there and the barriers have been torn down.

—*Hillary Rodham Clinton*

I am convinced that as we get farther and farther away from the conference, over the next couple of decades, people will be saying, "It started in Beijing."

—*Marjorie Margolies-Mezvinsky, Deputy Chair,*
U.S. Delegation to the UN 4th WCW, Former
Member of Congress from Pennsylvania

One of the official posters from the conference. (Photo by Janice Auth)

Observing the Governments of the World at Work

Roseann P. Rife

This was my first chance to attend a UN conference, and I was fortunate enough to attend as an observer for an accredited nongovernmental organization, the World Federalist Association (WFA), which meant not only could I participate with thousands of others at the forum but I could also attend the official government conference. I had many preconceived notions as I left for Beijing. Reality both surpassed and fell short of these expectations.

The official UN government conference was a serious affair. One half suits, one half every other type of garb imaginable. The first morning was pomp and ceremony. We were greeted by heads of state; UN representatives made speeches; the president of the conference, Chen Muhua of China was elected; and we were officially welcomed by Gertrude Mongella, the secretary-general of the Fourth World Conference on Women. When I say we, I mean the government delegates and many media representatives along with a handful of lucky NGO representatives who had waited in line for the few leftover seats inside the plenary hall. The rest of us, who couldn't get in, were watching on a large screen and several other monitors in the hallway. Each day there were plenary sessions, at least until every government had had a chance to make a statement. Eventually toward the end of the conference there was one plenary session where NGOs were allowed to make statements. But the plenary hall was not where the action was.

The final product of the conference was to be the Beijing Declaration and the Platform for Action (see appendix D). Many people all over the globe had been working on these two documents for more than two years. There were many preparatory meetings on all continents. Yet when the more than seventy-page Platform for Action reached Beijing, approximately 30 percent of the text was still undecided. These sections were in brackets. The negotiations began on the premise that only text in brackets was open for negotiation. There would be no further discussion on text that had already passed by consensus.

Two working groups were established to negotiate the remaining bracketed sections of the platform. These groups met from about nine in the morning until ten or eleven at night.

There were many different issues represented by the still-bracketed language. The qualifying term "universal" was bracketed before each mention of human rights. References to displaced women were preceded by the term "internally" in brackets. All proposals directed toward transnational corporations were in brackets. There was no agreement on the need for adequate, new, and additional resources for the implementation of the platform. The term sexual orientation was in brackets in all lists of discrimination criteria. And large sections of the health language were in brackets, including consensus language already decided upon in the declaration from the UN Cairo Conference on Population.

The trend over the years at UN conferences has been to allow ever-increasing participation by NGO observers, and at this conference we were permitted to sit in on the working group sessions. (Our only hurdle was getting into the room early enough to get a seat and one of the even fewer translation earpieces.) Discussion on one sentence could last for half an hour. Even then the chair often had to stop debate and assign the contrite sentence to an "informal group." Those observers like myself, sitting in the back, unable to speak yet hanging on every word, were always a bit disappointed when they created an informal group because we were not permitted to observe those discussions, which would meet in between and after the working groups, often arguing into the small hours of the morning.

When the official negotiations paused, however, we had our own meetings, one after another. We were constantly trying to get the most updated language, cheering or swearing depending on the outcome and one's point of view, writing and constantly rewriting. Can we get this issue into this sentence of that paragraph? Which country is sympathetic? Who do you know? Can you influence them? The pace was dizzying. All the observers had their own issues; each was passionate about his or her own cause. The energy level was exhilarating, the work exhausting. We began at 8 A.M.; we ended sometimes after 1 A.M.

As an observer, my day usually began with a briefing session given by NGOs for NGOs at 8 A.M. This session allowed us to find out what had happened during the previous day in informal groups and in working group sessions that we had perhaps missed while we were in other meetings. Then I went in search of the day's agenda printed daily by the UN Secretariat. I would choose which working sessions I wanted to attend and also check who was scheduled to speak at the plenary. Then I would search for the list of unofficial meetings scheduled for the day. For the most part this was a list of caucuses. Most of the NGOs had formed themselves into groups based on their organization's interest or an affinity group. There was for instance an Asian Caucus, a Refugee Caucus, a Disabled Persons Caucus, and a Human Rights Caucus.

The other WFA representatives and I had divided our duties so we could cover as much as possible. One of the focus issues of our organization currently is the establishment of an International Criminal Court (ICC). An ICC would be a permanent judicial tribunal with global jurisdiction to try individuals for gross breaches of international humanitarian law. Unlike the International Court of Justice, whose contentious jurisdiction is restricted to nation states, it will have the capacity to indict individuals. In order to follow this issue, I became part of the Human Rights Caucus.

The Human Rights Caucus was perhaps one of the largest at the conference. Human rights by definition being universal, inalienable, integral, and indivisible, the caucus dealt with almost every section of the platform. Within the Human Rights Caucus we were divided into groups on universality, equality, violence against women, economic structures, racism, and others. My task was daunting. To date there was no mention of an ICC in the platform. I found some allies and set about finding sections of the document where language about an ICC could be inserted.

Every day we would find out which sections were being negotiated, discuss these in the larger caucus meetings, and then get together in smaller groups to draft language and lobby government delegates. Frequently the Human Rights Caucus would meet again at 9 P.M. to discuss the day's happenings and plan strategies for the following day. Unfortunately these meetings took place in a hotel off-site and it required a fifty-minute taxi ride for me to reach this hotel from mine. I often returned to my hotel after midnight, long after the restaurant had closed for the day. Yet despite these inconveniences, everyone was giving their all; no one gave up. There was always tomorrow and yet another piece of the document to debate.

One interesting place was the NGO lounge, a room set aside for NGO use with several donated computers and one copying machine. It was always full of people trying to create a last-minute draft. Although many individuals had brought their laptop computers, there were not many printers to be found. We were often scrambling for someone who knew someone, in some office, somewhere, with a printer. Then in order to make copies you had to supply your own paper and wait in line with the other dozen or so individuals who were rushing to finish their jobs. There was a limit to the number of copies any one individual could make, but even so I spent a considerable amount of time in that line. It also provided me with one of my most interesting encounters.

One day while I was waiting in line, I saw a woman who looked very familiar to me. It took me quite awhile to remember where we had met. Suddenly I remembered that we had stood in another line together at the Chinese Embassy in Washington, D.C., waiting to get our visas. We had both left that line empty-handed and figured we would never get to Beijing, let alone see each other again. After we exchanged stories about how we had finally made it to Beijing, we began to talk about our work here at the conference. Originally from the Middle East, my friend worked with an organization that was very involved in the issues facing women within Islam. It was a chance for me to look outside my self-imposed narrow focus and hear an in-depth account about the work of another organization. Most startling to me were the stories she related about some of the women with whom she worked. Like her, many were refugees from their birth countries and were continuing to work on issues affecting individuals back home. Several of these women had been harassed and threatened by representatives of their home governments. When they themselves could not be threatened because they were already living in exile, these government representatives threatened their families still at home. It was a horrifying glimpse at the hardships women around the globe face as they work for peace, equality, and development.

As negotiations began on the "women in armed conflict" section of the document, those of us working on the ICC saw a chance. There had been much debate on a paragraph that reaffirmed that rape in the conduct of armed conflict constitutes a war crime and the next phrase in particular that, under certain circumstances, it constitutes a crime against humanity. What was key for us was the end of the paragraph that urged measures be taken to protect women and children in these circumstances and also to strengthen mechanisms to investigate and punish all those responsible. What better mechanism to accomplish this than an ICC? We carefully rewrote the paragraph and went out to see whom we could convince.

As a U.S. citizen, I took the opportunity to approach a member of the U.S. delegation, who was an employee of the State Department. It soon became apparent this was not considered a high priority by the U.S. delegation, but I gave it my best shot. I argued that several rather enigmatic comments made by the U.S. administration in the past several months "made it clear that the president supported an ICC." I got a skeptical look. I felt vindicated when on October 15, 1995, President Clinton, in a speech at the University of Connecticut, appealed for a permanent international tribunal. Unfortunately this was too late for the Beijing conference. Other allies had some success with a Scandinavian delegate, but in the end it wasn't a high enough priority on anyone's list to push for inclusion in the final document.

The Human Rights Caucus did however support our work, and when the caucus had a chance to speak, on September 13, those of us who had been working on the ICC were included. This was the chance for everyone who had lobbied hard for their issues but had been unsuccessful in getting language into the final draft. It might appear that certainly those of us within the Human Rights Caucus could easily agree among ourselves and quickly write a strong statement. Clearly that was not the case. It was naive to think that because we were all "working for human rights," we would all share the same opinions. After two days of debate, we did finally reach agreement and I was exhilarated to hear our statement read from the podium before the plenary.

It was much easier to get a seat that day. I didn't even need to wait in line for a ticket. There were no heads of state speaking. Even the media was scarce. But the audience was full of NGO representatives like me who had waited for this moment to hear their concerns expressed before the official UN plenary. It was a highlight of my two weeks of work to hear Hina Jilani, of the International Human Rights Law Group, and Alda Facio, Center for Women's Global Leadership, speaking on behalf of sixty-five organizations including the World Federalist Association. We called on the international community and the UN to, among other things, "cooperate fully with the ad hoc war crimes tribunals and quickly establish a permanent International Criminal Court which will fully integrate consideration of gender-based violations into its operations."

After two weeks, negotiations ended and a final Platform for Action emerged. No one was 100 percent happy with the final draft. That is the usual outcome of consensus compromise. The bracketed language contained some very controversial points and not all sides were pleased with the final version. The final Platform for Action stated clearly in its mission statement that "the human rights of women and of the girl child are an inalienable, integral, and indivisible part of universal human rights." Most other mentions of human rights within the document dropped the adjective "universal," with the argument that human rights are by definition universal and therefore overuse of that descriptor weakens the definition. The final draft urged governments, international and regional intergovernmental institutions, and NGOs to "provide protection, assistance, and training to refugee women, other displaced women in need of international protection, and internally displaced women." In the final document transnational corporations were urged to "recruit women for leadership, decision-making, and management, and provide training programs, all on an equal basis with men." The final financial arrangements of the platform state that "mobilization of additional resources, . . . may be necessary" but more emphasis is placed on "identifying and mobilizing funding sources" and the "reformulation of policies and reallocation of resources." There is no mention in the final platform of sexual orientation as a basis of discrimination.

The health section was a large area of heatedly debated and carefully drafted compromise language. One compromise in the health section, between the rights of young people wanting information and services, and the rights of parents wanting influence over their children, devised this final language: "Governments, in cooperation with NGOs . . . should disseminate accessible information to ensure that men and women can acquire knowledge about their health, especially information on sexuality and reproduction, taking into account the rights of the child to access to information, privacy, confidentiality, respect, and informed consent, as well as the responsibilities, rights, and duties of parents and legal guardians to provide appropriate direction and guidance."

The negotiations resulted in a final Platform for Action that addressed these twelve areas

women in poverty
education and training of women
women and health
violence against women
women and armed conflict
women and the economy
women in power and decision making
institutional mechanisms for the advancement of women
human rights and women
women and the media
women and the environment
the girl child

Advances were made and many battles were lost. It was the long-fought outcome of hours of negotiations by government delegates, with the heavy lobbying of NGOs and no small amount of compromise.

The nongovernmental forum was different. These people were not observers but passionate participants, also true to their issues but without the official status, therefore less constrained. The discussions were larger, more vivid, more emotional, more varied. By the time I went out to the site in the second week, the security posts were haphazardly manned. Protesters were everywhere and had free rein of the site, as long as they did not stray into the town. Women in mourning, women in anger, women in fear, all marching. Protesters not only had to contend with the local security but also with threats from their own governments back home and their government representatives in Beijing. But still no one stopped. Everyone, everywhere, was talking, sharing, compromising, cheering, laughing, singing, crying, writing, arguing, eating, painting, dancing, learning, and always doing.

I felt discomfort at the official conference because although progress was being made, it was never enough. I was pleased, yet frustrated. Here at the forum was the energy, the action, the future. These thousands of women and men who came to gather and share and teach and learn were the ones making the progress. They were the ones breaking new ground. It was not the diplomats making the news, but these individuals out here, forty-five miles from the conference site, who held the world's attention.

It is this energy, this sense of action and progress that we must hold on to. In the end the diplomats created a substantial document. But who will carry it out? It is the individuals who must make the document become reality. Whatever the issue, it is the action that is important. The future will not be created by the words of a document or even the reports of journalists who were there but missed it still. It will be created by those individuals and the people they reach at home and the government officials they influence and the children they teach. Theirs is the future.

Representing Hadassah

Judy Palkovitz

I had the extraordinary opportunity to attend the Beijing conference as the chair of Hadassah's six-member delegation. As the chair, I was an official observer to the conference and a participant at the forum in Huairou. Hadassah is the largest Jewish-Zionist organization in the United States and the largest membership organization for women regardless of religion. There are more than 385,000 U.S. members, 5,000 of whom live in western Pennsylvania.

Hadassah's interest in the Fourth World Conference on Women was twofold—Israel and women. Despite their intended purposes to promote the status of women, previous UN women's conferences often disintegrated into efforts to delegitimate the State of Israel. In fact, the infamous "Zionism is racism" phrase was first promulgated at the Mexico City conference in 1975.

Because of the history of anti-Zionism and anti-Semitism at previous conferences, my fellow Hadassah delegates and I spent the preceding year networking with other Jewish women's organizations who were sending representatives to Beijing. We met together on a regular basis to strategize ways to combat possible verbal and organizational attacks. We also met with the official Israeli delegation on several occasions to be updated on their activities, information, and plans. We formed a Jewish women's caucus, which was to meet in Beijing for mutual support. We intended to hold debriefing sessions in Beijing so we could share information about the conference sessions and the workshops in Huairou. We attempted to array ourselves in such a way that we would be present at any workshops that had to do with Israel, refugees, Muslims, Arabs, or the Middle East.

It was most pleasing to each of us (the approximately 250 identified Jewish women in Beijing) that the Beijing conference did not follow the pattern set by previous conferences. In Beijing, Israel was treated as a nation among nations, and the Israeli delegates were accorded the respect given to all others. I was personally overjoyed to be present at the official conference session when Ora Namir, the head of the Israeli delegation, took her turn at the podium to address the conference. She spoke well concerning the problems of women in Israel and throughout the world. She was well received and no one walked out.

In several forum workshops, Israeli, Arab, and other women were able to discuss topics of mutual concern to women without the intrusion of political concerns. The discussions were often heated, and very different perspectives were expressed, but this is the nature of these types of workshops. In general, the discussions transcended the political differences that historically have been divisive.

I think there are at least three reasons why this happened. First, the peace process has greatly improved the attitude toward Israel throughout the world, particularly the Arab world. Second, the demise of the former Soviet Union has left potential protagonists without a major backer. Third, and most important, Arab and Muslim women were determined not to let their agendas be hijacked. Very often, we heard that they were interested in the major themes of the conference—equality, development, and peace. They wanted to engage us in discussing the legal, social, economic, and cultural barriers to women's well-being and achievement.

Hadassah's second reason for attending the conference and the forum was of course to address the issues related to women. Our organization is devoted to the health and welfare of all women and their families. We went to become more familiar with the topics of greatest concern: the education of the girl child, rape as a war crime, the right of women to inherit property, women's economic equity, the right of women to say no to sexual relations, domestic violence, access to health care (including abortion), and the prevalence of HIV/AIDS in women.

I was particularly fascinated by the posters around the forum that illustrated the seemingly endless political and ethnic conflicts in the world and their impact on women. Although I consider myself to be rather politically astute, I became aware of the many situations of which I was ignorant.

I consider the time I spent in Beijing to have been mind-altering and very thought provoking. While walking through the official conference site, I was stopped by a television crew that was recording the reactions of random delegates. To my surprise, the crew was from Jordanian television. When the interview was concluded, I added the comment that I had been in Jordan within the month, had been to Petra, Amman, and Jerash and found my time there fascinating. The woman interviewer wished me a return visit and I assured her I hoped to do that. The encounter symbolized for me that many perspectives can be changed if we allow ourselves the opportunity to be open to new experiences.

As an American, a white woman, and a Jew, I was a member of several minorities among the participants. I am used to being a minority as a Jew but the other designated minority status was new to me. Combined with all the events of the forum and the conference, this experience certainly caused me to view the world through different eyes.

Women Defining the Future
A View from Beijing
Tanya Kotys Ozor

Although I have been working in international women's health and development for the past five years, the United Nations Fourth World Conference on Women and its attendant NGO forum, Look at the World
Through Women's Eyes, brought me closer to the essence of global sisterhood than ever before.

As a part of the Magee Womancare International delegation that included Irma Goertzen, president and CEO, Magee-Womens Hospital;
Rachel Mays, Russia field administrator; Melissa Zahniser, program coordinator; and Yelena Burtseva, director, Magee-Savior's Family Planning
Clinic in Moscow, I spent two weeks immersed in a whirlwind of energy,
strategic planning, political passion, and international diversity.

The goal of both the nongovernmental forum and the official UN conference was to create and adopt an international platform that will ensure
women's equality, health, development, and peace into the twenty-first
century. As part of our dedication to global women's health advocacy,
Magee presented two workshops: Womancare 2000 and Beyond:
Magee's Vision for Comprehensive Women's Health, and Magee Womancare Russia: An International Model in Women's Health Education
and Service. In addition, Yelena Burtseva was invited to copresent a
workshop with the Alan Guttmacher Institute of New York on reproductive health in the former Soviet Union.

I was deeply moved to meet with women of all nationalities and religions to find common ground, to learn to see beyond economic, racial,
and political difference in order to arrive at peace and progress. Serbian,
Croatian, and Bosnian women together held daily candlelight vigils for
peace; women of all religions and backgrounds found respectful and productive ways to discuss reproductive health; and everywhere groups of
women sprang up to celebrate diversity and to create models for successful conflict resolution.

I am not sure to what extent the UN Platform for Action itself will dramatically and permanently affect the lives of women around the world, but I am convinced that the three weeks spent by women united in Beijing touched us all individually, deeply, and irrevocably.

I will never forget the personal histories related to me by sisters from around the world who face the daily starvation of their children, the murder of their daughters, the mutilation of their genitals, domestic violence, and inhumane poverty. Their stories fed my conviction for change, for participation in politics, and for a continued career in women's development.

Recollections from Beijing

Carol Campbell

Because Pittsburgh/Beijing '95 and Beyond was accredited as an official nongovernmental organization, we were allowed to designate two "representatives with observer status" to the official government conference. Mary Rusinow and I had this designation.

As an observer at the conference, I checked in early each morning for updates of all the prior day's activities, attended plenary sessions and caucuses of interest, and checked with my press contacts for the latest information from a media perspective. In the plethora of activity surrounding the conference, contacts were everything, and I was fortunate to have a former classmate situated in China whose husband is deputy director, UN Development Program, Regional Bureau for Asia and the Pacific. They live in Beijing and offered insight and entrée. Other friends and acquaintances from my work in international and intercultural communications and with United Nations Association-U.S.A. facilitated information gathering.

Although the conference was a United Nations event and therefore on "neutral" territory, there were always reminders that we were physically in China. During my last day at the conference, curiosity got the better of me. Despite the inclement weather, I finally decided to take advantage of the daily free gift coupons that were a promotional part of the conference package. I trekked a circuitous route through the driving rain to arrive at display booth number 263, the Mongolian booth. I was presented with three gifts—a small flip-top can of Seaweed Drink; several small boxes of White Rabbit Candy, "the only candies recommended by the Fourth World Conference on Women," manufactured in Shanghai; and a box of one dozen vials with ministraws to ingest Ladies 888 Donkey-Hide Gelatin Super Oral Liquid. The ingredients of the potion included "dark cock, American ginseng, Chinese caterpillar fungus, human placenta, the root of membranous milk vetch, and tangerine peel." The function of the oral liquid is "to nourish the Qi and blood, thus, rejuvenating and blackening the hair and beautifying the skin." Donkey-Hide Gelatin also helps "to strengthen the immune system of the fragile person due to long illness and female syndromes due to deficiency. It also helps in treating bronchitis, coronary heart disease, frigidity and cancer." For the record, digesting three vials a day as recommended, did not darken my hair; however, it did seem to rejuvenate me for the long trip home.

I noticed a tremendous contrast between facilities at the conference and at the NGO forum where I was invited to make a presentation. Security at the conference consisted of UN personnel, while security at the forum was all Chinese. There was a more relaxed atmosphere at the conference than at the forum. Following the Tiananmen Square massacre in 1989, the Chinese government kept tight control over demonstrations at the forum.

Logistics at the forum, separated from the conference by being located at a makeshift site thirty miles outside Beijing, proved to be difficult. Inadequate bus transportation and almost daily unseasonable monsoon rains created time-consuming and exhausting hazards. However, the resplendence of the ambiance, created by women from all over the world, dressed in their native saris, chadors, silver head ornaments, and tribal robes, created an atmosphere that was compelling. And there was opportunity to meet women from almost everywhere.

I seized the moment to attend workshops conducted by women from war-torn countries such as the former Yugoslavia, Somalia, and Rwanda; acquired insights from women who represented the Islamic fundamentalists nations, women who came from countries whose cultural values still include female genital mutilation; and even attended a seminar on the first study being conducted, by a young Chinese woman now living in Canada, concerning the custom of crippling Chinese women by binding their feet.

My presentation at the forum was as part of a United Nations Association-U.S.A. national panel, American Women, International Concerns. My topic—Pittsburgh, Pennsylvania, U.S.A.: Implications of Economic Restructuring for the Status of Women—is pertinent because the Pittsburgh region provides an excellent context in which to study the impact of economic restructuring on the economy. As the *New York Times* has stated, Pittsburgh is America's most promising postindustrial experiment. The city has survived the collapse of its steel empire in the late 1970s and early 1980s with the disappearance of a hundred thousand jobs in ten years and a population base that shrank to half its former size.

At the time of the forum, it was not yet empirically known (although there were indicators) exactly what effect this restructuring has had on the status of area women. What we do know, however, is that the changing demographics of the "new" Pittsburgh indicate a shift from manufacturing to service industries. Because it was men who were displaced from the mines and the mills, this created the need for the dual-income family. Women went into low-paying service jobs out of necessity. According to a 1990 report, *Women in Management,* done by the Pennsylvania Economy League, Western Division, this change, coupled with a greater share of employment held by women in service industries, has increased the share of all employment held by women. However, increases of women in the labor market have not yet been distributed evenly through all occupations and industries. Women are still concentrated in lower-paid and less-influential positions. Women make up only 30 percent of the executive, administrative, and managerial work in Pittsburgh. Few women serve as CEOs and board members of Pittsburgh's major manufacturing, health care, financial, educational, business service, and government organizations. Women are well represented only in the nonprofits, service sector, and the arts.

In November 1995 Pittsburgh's Carlow College hosted an event called "Conversations Beyond Beijing." As co-convener of PBB, I presented an overview report entitled "The Status of Research on Women in Pittsburgh." In this report, I cited a number of local studies that have been done in recent years. The National Education Center for Women in Business (NECWB) at Seton Hill College in Greensburg, Pennsylvania, was founded in August 1992 with a $1.8 million grant from the Small Business Administration's (SBA) Office for Women Business Ownership. The SBA committed another $3.2 million for the center over a five-year period. Its purpose is to get more women interested in entrepreneurship at a younger age and to persuade women-owned businesses to expand, particularly into manufacturing. As the first program of its kind in the country, the center sponsors a variety of courses to help female entrepreneurs in cities across the nation. An NECWB study concluded that there is no evidence women are less skilled or less competent in carrying out tasks or managing in various functional areas; however, there are indications that such stereotypes still persist and that to be more successful in their careers or business, they must adopt male behaviors (NECWB *Source,* April 1994). The center is devoted to research, education, and information about entrepreneurs, a group often overlooked in academic and business circles. It is also involved in the curriculum at Seton Hill, a Roman Catholic women's college with an enrollment of about nine hundred. The center allocates about $250,000 each year for research on such topics as the difference between male and female management styles and the success and failure of widows who take over their husbands' businesses.

According to yet another study, *Taking Women into the Twenty-first Century: Issues Facing Pennsylvania Women,* published by the Pennsylvania State Data Center, Institute of State and Regional Affairs, in January 1994, women represented 46 percent of the total workforce in Pennsylvania, up from 42 percent in 1980. Between 1980 and 1987, the increase in women-owned businesses was three times greater than among men and continues to be the fastest growing segment of the economy. Pennsylvania ranks sixth in the nation among states with women-owned businesses, and Allegheny County (in which Pittsburgh is located) leads the state with the largest number (18,297) of women-owned businesses.

In spite of these encouraging statistics, women who sit on the boards of major corporations are rare. While there is at least some female representation in boardrooms, many women are concerned that the "token" woman is where the representation often ends. As Chatham College president Esther Barazzone says, "We'll know when we have really made progress when women are included on boards because their voice is valued, not because there is a gender issue" *(Pittsburgh,* August 1995).

An analysis done by the Women's Leadership Assembly in 1995 revealed that Pittsburgh has a better-than-average track record of putting women on boards—16.5 percent, as opposed to 10 percent nationwide. The study has been criticized as skewed because some of the board members are not based in Pittsburgh and because the not-for-profit sector is included in the total. However, task force chair Cindy Rothenberger, associate professor of business at Carlow College, defends the study's findings. "Everyone was surprised that the numbers came out as positively as they did. It shows that Pittsburgh isn't in the dark ages" *(Pittsburgh,* August 1995).

The Pittsburgh study followed a bipartisan federal commissions study on the issue (U.S. Department of Labor, Lynn Martin, 1992). The national study found that the glass ceiling still keeps women from top management ranks in the nation's corporate world. White males, for example, make up 43 percent of the U.S. workforce, but hold 95 out of every 100 senior management positions, defined as vice president and above *(Pittsburgh Business Times,* April 13, 1995).

A 1995 survey of Pittsburgh-area women-owned businesses conducted by Mary T. McKinney, director of the Duquesne University Small Business Development Center, identified five major themes concerning women-owned businesses in Allegheny and the surrounding counties. Women-owned businesses:

impact and contribute positively to the Pittsburgh regional economy
are growing and are poised for growth
are employers
are active participants in government and corporate contracting
are creative in financing their businesses

However, a lack of communication between banks and women business owners leads to underutilization of the banks. Although women business owners judge their banks positively, they typically have a limited relationship. In addition, the study found that Pittsburgh area women-owned businesses are not at national levels for sales or employees, and from a financing standpoint, Pittsburgh lingers behind the national average.

For a long time Pittsburgh has had an overabundance of organizations and government agencies devoted to attracting new or growing businesses. They overlapped in responsibility and duplicated efforts. It is significant that the Greater Pittsburgh Chamber of Commerce, Penn's Southwest Association, the World Trade Center Pittsburgh, Regional Industrial Development Corporation, and the Pittsburgh High Technology Council are forming a new umbrella organization to oversee their work. The recently formed Pittsburgh Regional Alliance will serve as a one-stop-shopping information clearinghouse for companies looking to relocate or expand here. It will also devise a uniform marketing plan for the region (*Pittsburgh Post-Gazette,* November 11, 1995; October 20, 1996).

The hope expressed by the Allegheny Conference on Community Development (ACCD) at their 1995 annual meeting, in a document entitled "Creating a Globally Competitive Region: Overcoming Barriers, Investing in Strengths," is that one hundred thousand new jobs will be generated by the year 2000 and that civic, corporate, and government leaders will now work together on the same team. The challenge will be raising the money. But there are no women on the ACCD executive committee, whose membership is composed of corporate presidents and CEOs.

In politics, Pennsylvania ranks forty-sixth in the nation for women elected officials; only Mississippi, Louisiana, and Alabama have fewer women in elected office. Few women have held office here, although some have achieved positions with significant power, including former mayor Sophie Masloff, State Auditor–General Barbara Hafer, who was the first female Allegheny county commissioner, and State Treasurer Katherine Baker Knoll. Carol Los Mansmann is a circuit judge, U.S. Court of Appeals, and Sandra Newman was elected to a federal judgeship in 1994.

Pittsburgh's conservative male culture was established during the days of heavy industry, creating a tradition that closed women out (*Pittsburgh,* August 1995). When heavy industry began to die out, the absence of women just moved from the mines and the mills to corporate headquarters.

It became apparent to me, while talking with and listening to other women at the forum, that women's projects, research, and activities are underfunded and understaffed on a global basis. Although each nation's workforce is shaped by its history and culture, the experience of Pittsburgh strikes a familiar chord with women everywhere. Whether a country is advanced or developing, nowhere in the world, not even in the United States, the most industrialized nation in the world, have women achieved equality with men.

Navigating the Conference

Mary Rusinow

United Nations conferences, unlike the parallel nongovernmental forums, are not easy to follow without experience, and it was for that reason I had been asked to be one of two representatives from Pittsburgh/Beijing '95 and Beyond to attend the conference itself, as an observer. In the 1980s I was working in Vienna at the United Nations Branch for the Advancement of Women, helping to produce the document for the UN Conference on Women to be held in Nairobi in 1985. I later joined the branch in a professional capacity, working for the chef de cabinet of the secretary-general of the conference, Letitia Shahani.* Together with NGOs, we disseminated information about the document *The Forward-Looking Strategies.* Even though I had not been able to attend the Nairobi conference, I had extensive experience at other UN conferences, and I was excited about participating in Beijing as an official representative rather than as a behind-the-scenes worker.

After the hassle of catching buses out to Huairou in the pouring rain, it was something of a relief to take a taxi to the conference center in Beijing and find my way to the registration tent in the tennis center.

The conference, of course, was a government conference, with members of nongovernmental organizations attending only as observers. Thus for the first two days security was so tight that it was impossible to approach the delegates at all on the second floor. It also meant a very undignified scramble for tickets to the opening ceremony—mine was snatched from my hand by someone even more eager than I to attend. I thus retired to the office of Virginia Sauerwein, an acquaintance from the days when I had worked in Vienna. She had been brought out of retirement to supervise the office that arranged the NGO speakers at the official plenary sessions. These speakers were very limited in number, with considerable pressure from above to ensure that all areas of the world, all religions, and all points of view were represented, not an easy task when

*Letitia Shahani, sister of President Ramos, is now a senator in the Philippines.

the numbers were limited to three or in some cases five speeches late in the evening. I was reminded of that when watching the video made by the Women's International League for Peace and Freedom, when their vice president, Manel Tiranagama, spoke on behalf of the Peace Caucus and the audience appeared to consist of some fifteen people.

It was a very different picture when First Lady Hillary Clinton spoke. Although she was not listed as an official speaker on the day's program, it was not difficult for those of us with experience to deduce at which session she would speak. It also involved a little blackmail on my part—either I stop helping Virginia (who at that time had no secretarial help) and go and stand in line or someone gets me a ticket for plenary. It worked, and my video camera and I were among the first into the room, thereby ensuring a place at the back where it was possible to stand up without incurring anyone's ire and film the proceedings, or at least part of them. I sat down next to a gentleman who was obviously of the press, only to discover that he was a member of the White House Press Corps and had an advance copy of the speech. A quick review made it possible to ascertain the key points, and I was able to stand up and film these very telling lines:

• It is a violation of human rights when babies are denied food, or drowned, or suffocated, or their spines broken, simply because they are born girls.

• It is a violation of human rights when women and girls are sold into the slavery of prostitution.

• It is a violation of human rights when women are doused with gasoline, set on fire, and burned to death because their marriage dowries are deemed too small.

• It is a violation of human rights when individual women are raped in their own communities and when thousands of women are subjected to rape as a tactic or prize of war.

• It is a violation of human rights when a leading cause of death worldwide among women ages fourteen to forty-four is the violence they are subjected to in their own homes.

• It is a violation of human rights when young girls are brutalized by the painful and degrading practice of genital mutilation.

• It is a violation of human rights when women are denied the right to plan their own families, and that includes being forced to have abortions or being sterilized against their will.

• If there is one message that echoes forth from this conference, it is that human rights are women's rights. . . . And women's rights are human rights. Let us not forget that among those rights [is] the right to speak freely. And the right to be heard.

That film sequence was to be used very frequently in the subsequent lectures that so many of us gave.

Chance played a part when most of the members of the U.S. delegation—there was only room for four people to sit in the designated chairs on the first floor—came up to our vantage point in the balcony and I was able to talk to Kathleen Hendrix of the State Department, who had come to Pittsburgh before the conference to brief us all on the issues. She had been part of the team that worked doggedly before Beijing with the thorny question of the word "gender," objected to by several countries. Even with so much work done beforehand, the draft document that became the Platform of Action came to Beijing with many words, phrases, and sentences in brackets, indicating that member states could not agree on the wording. Delegates and members of the staff worked tirelessly, largely in closed meetings, to eliminate the brackets, and it is a tribute to them that the document was finally agreed to, albeit with some reservations.

How agreement is reached is a mystery for those who have not observed the process. Government delegates have long experience in producing language that is acceptable to all of them. They are frequently approached by members of NGOs who informally lobby wherever and whenever they can for their individual issues. NGOs also meet in caucus on a daily basis so that, when only one speaker is permitted, that speaker presents the views of many. At the beginning of the conference so many people wanted to attend the caucuses that tickets had to be issued for those, too, but as the participants in the forum began to leave, it was easier to obtain access to the meetings.

In the end, in the small hours of the morning, consensus was reached on the final wording of the Platform for Action. It now remains for us to see that the provisions are carried out.

To quote from UN Secretary-General Boutros Boutros-Ghali's statement, read on the last day of the conference and reproduced in the Platform for Action:

> Despite the progress made, much, much more remains to be done. While women have made significant advances in many societies, women's concerns are still given second priority almost everywhere. Women face discrimination and marginalization in subtle as well as in flagrant ways. Women do not share equally in the fruits of production. Women constitute 70 percent of the world's poor.
>
> The message of this conference is that women's issues are global and universal. Deeply entrenched attitudes and practices perpetuate inequality and discrimination against women, in public and private life, on a daily basis, in all parts of the world. At the same time, there has emerged a consensus that equality of opportunity for all people is essential to the construction of just and democratic societies for the twenty-first century. The fundamental linkages between the three objectives of the conference—equality, development, and peace—are now recognized by all.

Because of the increased publicity given to women's issues, and the increased worldwide concern for human rights in general, governments are paying much more attention to this Platform for Action than they did to documents of previous conferences. Three hundred NGOs were represented at the Nairobi conference; three thousand were represented at Beijing. The tenfold increase, within the last ten years in the number of NGOs that will monitor the implementation of this platform will surely make a difference.

We've had lots of words on equality, now we want the music.
What is the music? The music is the action. This is the action
conference.

—*Bella Abzug*

My dear sisters and brothers, we have made it. We have managed to transcend historical and cultural complexities; we have
managed to transcend socioeconomic disparities and diversi-
ties; we have kept aflame our common vision and goals of
equality, development, and peace. A revolution has begun, and
there is no going back.

—*Gertrude Mongella of Tanzania,*
Secretary-General of the Conference

Where Do We Go from Here?

Janice Auth

Pittsburgh/Beijing '95 and Beyond served as a conduit for information from Beijing to Pittsburgh. The local people who went to Beijing helped acquire that information and to disseminate it once they got home. In the first six months following Beijing, more than three hundred presentations were made to church groups, schools, colleges, and universities, social and civic organizations, in libraries and in private homes. Reflecting the diversity of the conference itself were the groups that wanted to hear about it: the Asia Women's Institute, the Scottdale Reading Club, the Council of Jewish Women, Rotary, Boule, Friends of Tibet, the Twentieth Century Club, retirement homes and elementary schools, women's studies classes, communications classes, business and professional women's (and men's) organizations, women in prison, women in shelters, groups on the fifteenth floor of Gateway Center and in the basement of the Smithfield Street Presbyterian Church, the Pittsburgh Wellesley Club, the Community of Reconciliation, the Friends Peace and Justice Group. In addition there were interviews on radio, television, and in the local newspapers. Three Beijing attendees were on the University of Pittsburgh Semester at Sea program in the spring of 1996 and talked with the students and other passengers as they sailed. From Fox Chapel to Upper St. Clair, Homestead to Natrona Heights, Edinboro to Huntingdon, from Philadelphia to Albuquerque, and in fact around the world, Pittsburghers talked about the UN Fourth World Conference on Women.

The Beijing Platform for Action is aptly named. A platform is a clean surface, a little higher than the ground on which we stand, a solid foundation onto which we can climb. On a platform we can take action—we can proclaim; we can shout; we can dance.

"For the rising of the women brings the rising of us all." This line, from a song inspired by the 1912 walkout by women employees of a textile factory in Lawrence, Massachusetts, to protest intolerable conditions and unfair wages, comes to mind as we ponder the implications of the Platform for Action. As women climb onto the platform, we bring our children, our families, our communities, our nations, and our future with us as well. We can make the platform the place from which the bird with the two equally strong wings takes off.

This section outlines a few of the programs and initiatives that have come about as a result of the Beijing Platform for Action. With this platform as a base, these are examples of the things we can do to ensure that the recommendations made in Beijing come about.

> The woman's question has come of age. It is not a woman's question any longer. It is the survival question of the twenty-first century. (Joan Chittister, OSB, author; writer for the *National Catholic Reporter;* passenger on the Peace Train)

With Cup in Hand We Talk About Women Meeting in Beijing

Valerie Lawrence

Women develop ways and means to
save babies from diarrhea, measles
and no food.
Women grab on to each other and find
courage to raise our value.
Women commiserate to fertilize common
ground that nurtures revolution for schools, medicine,
clean water, sanitation, shelter, our right to dictate
language of our bodies.

**I wanna be Harriet Tubman
develop a way out of no way
freedom road for enslaved Africans.**

*Be like Mother Teresa like
Mary McCleod like Ma'at live
justice be righteous like
Ida Wells in rhythm with
Nature like harmony.*

MAKE ME YAA ASANTEWA,
QUEEN NZINGHA, HATSHEPSUT
RAISED WARRIORS, SCHOLARS TO
PRESERVE TRADITIONS, MAINTAIN
LAND, KEEP INTRUDERS OUT, SAVE
MY GIRL CHILD, RAISE UP MY BOY CHILD!

**Make me like women of kinship
aid societies to help my sisters**

**cause refugees don't always speak
foreign languages, but always flee
abuse, war, droughts, no work no
land no money no way out.**

Many women, girls, sisters can't
locate Beijing on a map didn't
know there was a meeting there didn't
know they were the subject didn't
know decisions were made about them didn't
know governments argued about them
being treated with respect, dignity, good
medicine; didn't
know women at the meeting looked like
them, cared about
them, hoped for
them, cried with
them, celebrated
them, and swore promises to return home to
them and make ways to talk, help, be with each
other, to work with each
other beyond a dot on a map too
many women girls sisters don't
know how to locate.

Women Without Borders

Regina Birchem

The Beijing conference was about women's empowerment. It was about equality, about development and social conditions for women, about peace and violence. It was not a conference *for* women—it was a conference *on* women for the world.*

Set in a series of global international conferences, the Beijing conference gives recognition to the importance of the role and status of women in addressing crucial global issues at the close of this century. Recent global summit conferences addressed environmental sustainability (Rio de Janeiro, 1992), the universality of human rights (Vienna, 1993), the growing human population and the ability of the earth's natural systems to support us (Cairo, 1994), excessive consumption by some and bitter poverty by many (Copenhagen, 1995), and human settlements—where it all comes together in our home communities (Istanbul, 1996).

The Beijing conference is a recognition that women must be equal players in decision making, in community and national development. They, as well as men, must be free from abuse and violence. Equal participation of women is essential in achieving a secure and sustainable society for all.

What is the situation of women around the world? What is the global context of the Fourth World Conference on Women?

There is no society where women have opportunities equal to men, according to the *Human Development Report* of 1995. Sweden, Finland, Norway, and Denmark come closest, with the United States fifth, having a ranking of 0.90 out of a possible 1.00.

Since the First World Conference on Women in Mexico in 1975 nearly every country has made some progress. For example, life expectancy

*First published in *Haversack: A Franciscan Journal,* winter 1995. All data and statistics are taken from UN Development Program, *Human Development Report* (New York: Oxford University Press, 1995).

has increased, high fertility rates have fallen, and literacy for women has improved from 54 percent of the male literacy rate in 1970 to 74 percent in 1990. Today, however, among the 900 million illiterate people, women still outnumber men two to one.

"Poverty has a woman's face—of 1.3 billion people in poverty, 70 percent are women" *(Human Development Report)*. The percentage of women in the labor force has only increased slightly. In many countries women have trouble getting credit and in all countries receive, on the average, a much lower wage than men. This severely diminishes their economic security, even more so in their later years. Women work longer hours than men and spend two-thirds of their time in unpaid activities.

Violence and discrimination accompany women all their lives, even before birth. In some countries the female fetus is selectively aborted and the girl child is abandoned.

During childhood and adolescence, sexual abuse is reported for one-third of the women in countries such as Barbados, Canada, and the United States. One hundred million girls suffer from the effects of genital mutilation.

In adulthood and married life, two-thirds of women in some countries report domestic violence. More than half the murders in Brazil are by present or former partners. In the United States, marital violence is the leading cause of female suicide.

The Fourth World Conference on Women addressed these issues. The resulting document, the Platform for Action, lists twelve areas of concern. It is not a perfect document, but it has plenty in it for us to work on worldwide. Some of the main issues are

violence against women as experienced all over the world
women's rights as human rights
structural adjustment policies for national debt problems
economic justice and strategies for getting out of poverty
a ban on landmines, nuclear testing, and nuclear weapons

The government of Australia issued a call that this conference be a "conference of commitments." This became a major objective. Throughout the meeting days, the speeches and statements of governments were tracked by NGOs to list the actual commitments, if any, each government was making to the Platform for Action.

The WILPF Peace Train was a special train journey originating in Helsinki, Finland, on August 7, 1995, and ending in Beijing, China, August 29, just before the opening of the NGO forum.

Why the peace train? Why would we plan such a journey? The idea came out of the goal to include more women and their concerns in the conference. Our intention was to cross borders through countries in economic and social transition and some countries afflicted by conflict and wars.

The WILPF Peace Train was an attempt to reach out in solidarity with our sisters in Eastern Europe and Central Asia and take their concerns to Beijing and home with us. Many regions are involved in ethnic and national conflicts. The voices of men and women for peace are not heard nor are the solutions they propose listened to.

What did we learn from this journey? We observed a definite overall economic deterioration for the life of the average person as we traveled through Eastern Europe. Only in Romania, one of the poorest countries of all, did people say that things were decidedly better these days after the removal of the dictator Ceauşescu. The environmental problems everywhere are serious. Water rationing is a frequently expected inconvenience.

The legacy and burden of heavy armament buildup during the Cold War years and continued militaristic policies, the development of nuclear weapons and their disposal have left a severe effect on the economies. During this journey the reality of the nuclear threat was brought to us again by the renewed testing by China and France.

Personally, each of us learned a great deal about herself and the societies from which we come. We take ourselves wherever we go. We tend to view the world from our own eyes, homeplace, history, and background. It takes a commitment to listen, to reflect, to experience in order to view the world through the eyes of the "other."

The "beyond" of Pittsburgh/Beijing '95 and Beyond is now with us. What are we going to do? The concerns of women, like environmental concerns, are without borders. By meeting together we found we have common concerns: we need clean water and fresh air; we need education; and we need peace. We found that the isolation, violence, and hopelessness so many experience need not be tolerated. The wars that are fought are not our wars. The weapons that are made are not made at our decision.

The very fact that so many women and men participated in this conference, or assisted others to do so, is in itself a means of changing the status quo. The work ahead involves implementation of the national commitments, the strengthening of weak commitments, and the design of new commitments locally and nationally.

The Platform for Action and the Beijing experience strengthen the work many are already doing. This is true of many who work for the relief of poverty and injustice. The global context of this conference strengthens and enhances their cause. It also gives new boldness in the awareness that the agenda for equality, justice, development, and peace is the agenda of millions around the world. It gives a new vision, a fresh boldness for new work beginning with the discovery of what the world looks like through the eyes of women, through the eyes of the other.

"Working Women Count" Honor Roll

One of the key commitments made by the U.S. government at the Beijing conference was under the area of economic structures. The commitment was announced by U.S. ambassador to the United Nations Madeleine Albright. The language of the commitment, now part of the permanent UN record, calls on the Women's Bureau of the United States Department of Labor to "solicit pledges from employers, organizations, and community groups to make systemic changes in policies and practices in the workplace." Women's Bureau director Karen Nussbaum was a member of the official U.S. delegation to the Beijing conference.*

The "Working Women Count" Honor Roll calls upon large and small businesses, state and local governments, and community groups across the nation to pledge to make real changes in the lives of working women and their families. All kinds of pledges can meet the honor roll's criteria, from large financial commitments, such as building a new child care center, to simple changes in office policy, like allowing newborns at work.

By the honor roll's official Labor Day 1995 launch, more than one hundred organizations had made pledges to provide new programs, new services, and new dollars in the areas working women care about most. At that time, the Women's Bureau set a goal of more than one thousand pledges in the ensuing year, which would ultimately affect more than 1 million people.

A sampling of pledges includes the following:

• The city of Kansas City, Missouri, granted city employees paid leave to participate in their children's school activities.

• A hotel and restaurant employees union in San Francisco established a child and elder care fund for employees.

• A construction company in Boise, Idaho, created new policies that allowed parents to work flexible hours and bring their children to work when child care is unavailable.

*From the *Honor Roll Update, October 1995,* a newsletter of the U.S. Department of Labor, Women's Bureau.

• A university in Tennessee reviewed gender equity in salaries and made salary adjustments based on the results.

• A job training center in Anchorage, Alaska, recruited, counseled, and referred women into nontraditional training and job sites across the state and established a support group for women working in the building and construction trades.

• The city of Hollywood, Florida, provided opportunities for management training, on-the-job training, after-school hours education, and apprenticeships to increase women employees' participation and marketability for other city jobs.

These are indicative of the kinds of pledges that came in from all parts of the country. Employers everywhere are realizing that by improving conditions for women employees everyone stands to benefit.

CEDAW
A Bill of Rights for Women
Roseann P. Rife

The United Nations Convention on the Elimination of All Forms of Discrimination Against Women (CEDAW), also known as the Women's Convention, has been likened to an international Bill of Rights for women. Human rights and the mechanisms created to actualize them are supposed to be equally available to men and women. There is, however, a sizable gap between the vision and the reality. For a number of years there has been increasing recognition that the international human rights movement has benefited men more than women. The mere fact that women are human beings too has not been enough to guarantee protection of their rights by the existing human rights standards and machinery. CEDAW brings together, in a single comprehensive international human rights treaty, the provisions of existing United Nations instruments concerning discrimination on the basis of sex and extends them further, creating a real tool for the elimination of discrimination against women.

Not only does CEDAW define discrimination against women for the first time but it also establishes rights for women in areas not previously subject to international standards. It calls for action in nearly every field of human endeavor: politics, law, employment, education, health care, commercial transactions, and domestic relations. Moreover, the Women's Convention establishes a committee on the elimination of discrimination against women to periodically review the progress being made by its adherents.

CEDAW was adopted by the United Nations in December 1979. For a treaty to enter into force it must be ratified by a certain number of members of the United Nations. Ratification of CEDAW was rapid, and it entered into force on September 3, 1981. To date more than two-thirds of UN member states have ratified CEDAW. Unfortunately the United States is not among this group. Despite the fact that the United States was heavily involved in the drafting of the Women's Convention, the

Senate Foreign Relations committee has yet to bring CEDAW to the Senate floor for a vote. Many of the U.S. citizens who attended the women's conference in Beijing have returned home with a renewed commitment to push for ratification.

Detractors of CEDAW frequently claim that the treaty lacks sufficient power to be a truly effective tool. Women around the world can attest to the fact that CEDAW has indeed made a difference in their everyday lives.

Ratification of CEDAW has affected different countries in different ways. Some, such as Brazil, have drafted new constitutions that reflect the goals of the Women's Convention. Others, such as Australia, have introduced legislation prohibiting sex discrimination or entrenching affirmative action policies. Still others have pursued the provisions of the Women's Convention through national plans and policy directives. Sweden has established an equal opportunity ombudsman.

In a number of countries, the convention has influenced legislation. In Tanzania, for example, CEDAW's provisions were used to reverse a discriminatory customary law relating to clan land. In Botswana and Zimbabwe, judges used CEDAW to prohibit discrimination against women in citizenship laws.

Furthermore, in some countries, the convention and its reporting and implementation process have been brought to life in domestic political activity and policy formation. For example, Sweden's third report was compiled by twenty-nine contributors representing nongovernmental organizations, political parties, and the government.

It is possible however that CEDAW has been most fully and powerfully brought to life by those nongovernmental organizations that have used it as the benchmark for women's equality and use it to campaign for women's rights at the national, regional, and local level. Those of us who went to Beijing certainly saw the Women's Convention brought to life. It was this living, breathing treaty that inspired so much of the work in Beijing and that continues to inspire our work now that we have returned home. By continuing this work, groups and individuals are truly proclaiming women's rights as human rights.

The campaign to urge U.S. ratification of CEDAW is one small but truly fundamental piece of the continuing work of Beijing. As a leading advocate for human rights, the United States has a compelling interest in improving conditions for women. Yet as one of the few nations that has failed to ratify the Women's Convention, the United States compromises its credibility as a leader for human rights. Moreover, if U.S. policy is to work toward the improvement of women's rights around the world, we would do so more effectively by joining CEDAW than by criticizing it from the sidelines. Indeed, President Bush took the position, when urging U.S. ratification of the Covenant on Civil and Political Rights, another important human rights treaty, that ratification strengthens the ability of the United States "to influence the development of appropriate human rights principles in the international community and provide[s] an additional and effective tool in efforts to improve respect for fundamental freedoms in many problem countries around the world."

The campaign for ratification needs your help. To effectively move the U.S. Senate toward ratification, each and every senator needs to hear from his or her constituents. Write to your senators and let them know how important it is for the United States to ratify the Women's Convention.

The international effort to improve the rights of women worldwide is making slow but significant progress. The experience of many countries teaches that the Women's Convention is an important component of that effort. It is time now for the United States to continue its international leadership and its advocacy in human rights by ratifying the Convention on the Elimination of All Forms of Discrimination Against Women.

Thursdays in Black

Toni Conaway

Most of the marches and demonstrations at the NGO forum were colorful and vibrant. Women talked. Women sang. Women chanted. And sometimes women kept the beat by tapping a drum. The most powerful demonstration for me, however, was the 5 P.M. *silent* gathering to protest violence against women. No one spoke, but the message was clear from the hundreds of black-and-white signs. Whatever the particular situation, the message was the same: stop violence against women. In addition to carrying the black signs, many women also wore black. This protest did not end at Beijing. It continues all over the world as women support Thursdays in Black. Pittsburgh women wear black on Thursdays in support of Australian women who wear black to protest treatment of Aborigine women; in support of Palestinian-Israeli women who wear black in support of the Middle East peace process; in support of Argentina's Mothers of the Plaza who wear black to protest their disappeared children. These protests received an international thrust when the World Council of Churches' investigative team of women returned from Yugoslavia. The personal stories they heard, from only a fraction of the fifty thousand to seventy thousand raped women, about public rape and forced pregnancies made them unable to sleep at night.

We came home from Beijing determined to connect these international atrocities to what women experience right here at home. Every nine seconds a woman, somewhere in the United States, is a victim of violence. We learned that every three days a woman or child dies in Pennsylvania due to domestic violence. Since 1990 there has been a 70 percent increase in the number of new victims. In 1995 more than eight thousand of the new victims were children. We have work to do—both locally and globally. And the work must start with education and consciousness-raising. We wear black on Thursdays. And we tell people why.

UNIFEM

Brenda J. Kagle

The United Nations Development Fund for Women (UNIFEM) was established following the First World Conference on Women. Since then it has been working in the developing countries to improve the quality of life for women. Its document *Women's Development Agenda for the Twenty-first Century* enumerated the challenges facing the world's women and some of the solutions that will bring equality and equity to them. This was the basis for their workshops and presentations at the Beijing conference. UNIFEM focuses on the economic and political empowerment of women.

Its political empowerment program aims at increasing women's control over their lives both within and outside the household and increasing the ability of women to influence the direction of society. Its economic empowerment program focuses on identifying, developing, and promoting alternative approaches to increase women's access to and control over the means of making a living on a sustainable long-term basis and to enable women to receive the material benefits of this access and control.

UNIFEM has achieved much during its twenty years because of its ability to work with other UN agencies, national and local governments, and grassroots organizations (especially existing women's organizations). Through this cooperative effort, UNIFEM has been able to bring the women's agenda into all issues facing our world—environment, human rights, peace, population, poverty, education, and employment.

Worldwide there are eighteen national committees that support the work of UNIFEM through education, advocacy, and fund-raising. The U.S. committee is headquartered in New York City and Washington, D.C. Although small by comparison to committees in other countries, it is growing in numbers and programs. The western Pennsylvania chapter of the U.S. committee was organized in October 1995 to support UNIFEM's work. There are now nine local chapters of the U.S. committee throughout the country. Through programs and newsletters, the western Pennsylvania chapter keeps the community informed on global women's issues as they relate to UNIFEM's programs.

An additional focus of the western Pennsylvania chapter is to bring together community leaders who are interested not only internationally but also locally in the need to increase the role that women play in our society. The chapter has been working closely with Pittsburgh/Beijing '95 and Beyond in this effort. The need for political and economic empowerment of women is the same worldwide. Many of the lessons learned by UNIFEM can be applied not only in western Pennsylvania but also throughout the United States—mainly the need to cooperate and work together to reach a common goal. In localities across the county there are many strong grassroots organizations, but others are not aware of their work. There is a great need to share ideas, accomplishments, and failures in an effort to address the ever-growing needs of our society—especially the needs of women.

Bringing Beijing Home

Louise Wilde

At Beijing, in September 1995, thousands of women from all over the world were energized by the experience of sharing their lives, their hopes, and their concerns with their sisters from nearly two hundred nations. Now, the crucial question is, *Where do we go from here?* How can we keep alive the enthusiasm, commitment, and momentum generated not only in Beijing but also by the entire twenty-year process of UN women's conferences?

The forum logo provides us with a ready answer to our question. It depicts a group of eight women dancing in a circle, with arms outstretched. Their energy radiates outward in all directions, widening the circle by reaching outward to the whole world. Those who "danced" in the circle at the Beijing forum and conference must now pass on its message: to the many millions who stayed at home, to grassroots organizations and networks in communities and workplaces, to our governments.

The Platform for Action approved at Beijing outlines twelve critical areas of concern. These are areas identified as main obstacles to the advancement of women. The platform offers objectives for and actions to be taken by governments, the international community, nongovernmental organizations, and individuals over the next five years to remove these obstacles, and it outlines specific goals to be achieved in each area. The twelve areas are

> poverty
> education and training
> health care
> violence against women
> the effects of armed conflict on women
> economic structures and policies
> power-sharing and decision making
> mechanisms to promote women's advancement
> human rights of women

the role of the media

the environment

the rights of the girl child

No single individual or organization can tackle all twelve areas. But we *can* set some realistic priorities. We can "bring Beijing home" by learning about the platform's goals and deciding which of these issues is most relevant in our own communities, what we can realistically achieve in terms of change, and how we can build networks with others who share our commitments.

Much of the action must be taken at the grassroots level. Here are some things you can do:

• Join the Women in Black campaign to protest against rape and violence against women everywhere (see "Thursdays in Black" above).

• Work with your local women's shelter to aid women who have been victims of violence.

• Work with an advocacy organization to advance women's equal access to economic opportunities.

• Cooperate with local schools to eliminate gender bias in education.

• Communicate with elected officials to pass laws and promote policies that will aid women and children (see "CEDAW: A Bill of Rights for Women" above).

It is better to light one candle than curse the darkness. (Motto of the Christopher Society)

The entire twenty-year history of UN women's conferences has taught us there is a lot of darkness in the world. But we have also seen what can be achieved when women work together, one small step at a time, to improve their lives and the lives of children. We can take heart from the energy and commitment radiating from the circle of dancing women. Each of us can add one candle to the light of millions of others. Through our individual commitments and actions, we can bring Beijing home.

Pittsburgh Success Stories

Janice Auth

> When you have more women in power, more money is spent
> on children, more money is spent on health care, more money
> is spent on education. . . . It has to do with the grounding in
> the family. Women politicians from all over the world got to-
> gether [in Beijing] and talked. What was perfectly clear was
> that we just handle . . . issues differently. . . . When we talk
> about making sure that there are more women [in politics], it
> has nothing to do with whether we are better or worse. It has
> everything to do with the fact that we are different.
>
> *—Marjorie Margolies-Mezvinsky, Deputy Chair, U.S.*
> *Delegation to the UN 4th WCW, Former Member of*
> *Congress from Pennsylvania*

The most encouraging discussions we have had (and continue to
have) in Pittsburgh involve identifying the many "success stories" that
are evidence of the creativity and commitment of women and men in
Pittsburgh to create a better world now and a better future for our children who at this time have no say in what is happening to the world they
will inherit. Following are descriptions of just a few of these successes.

• The Thursdays in Black violence awareness project, through the distribution of leaflets and buttons, invites women and men to wear black
on Thursdays to protest the intolerable violence in our communities and
around the world.

• The Check It Out—Breast Cancer Awareness project of Hadassah is
an education program for high school and college women to raise awareness about prevention of breast cancer.

• Pennsylvania Peace Links Puppet Show on Conflict Resolution is
based on the story "The Tree House" by Lois Lowry, which emphasizes
the value of solving conflicts peacefully.

• Just Harvest Women's Leadership Project identifies, trains, and mobilizes women living in public housing and other predominately low-income neighborhoods in Allegheny County as community leaders and advocates on public policy that affect their quality of life.

• City Theater of Pittsburgh operates a unique outreach program that sends artists out to schools or social service agencies to work with students and clients to write a play in their own words and perform it free on the City Theater main stage. Recent productions have included "Ashes," a moving performance piece with Holocaust survivors and liberators telling their stories alongside African American students, and "Through a Glass, Darkly," about the stigmas and issues facing welfare mothers.

• Pittsburgh Child Watch Program was initiated by women who went to the Beijing conference. In conjunction with the Children's Defense Fund, this program was organized to tell the story of the children in Allegheny County who are dependents of the juvenile court and Children and Youth Services and children who have been in foster care for an average of four and a half years.

• The YWCA Week Without Violence is a national effort that has received much more attention locally because of the women of Pittsburgh who went to Beijing and now participate in and support this effort more fully.

Although many of these initiatives were in place before the Pittsburgh participation in the UN Fourth World Conference on Women, it is safe to say that all of them received increased interest and energy because of that participation. Some, such as the Thursdays in Black campaign and the production of this book are a direct result of attending the Beijing conference.

Think Globally, Act Locally
Chatham College Initiatives

Esther L. Barazzone

A more compelling emotional or intellectual experience than the Beijing conference is hard to imagine. People from around the world, almost all women, were peacefully assembled to promote issues we cared about passionately. We were loosely, but effectively, organized to discuss and help adopt a platform of twelve issues that, if effectively addressed, would transform life on this planet.

That women's perspectives could make the world different was demonstrated time and again at the conference. The women's commitment to transformative values, and the significance of this commitment, were vividly expressed and vividly demonstrated. Certainly there were small nationalist and ethnic incidents at the conference, but more abundant and powerful were the instances given of overcoming these divisions when women's perspectives are involved. One such demonstration occurred in a session I chaired with participants from the STAR (Strategies, Training, and Advocacy for Reconciliation) project, the brainchild of Leall Stegall and funded by USAID to bring together women from Yugoslav successor states (Bosnia, Serbia, and Croatia) who are working on behalf of humanitarian projects throughout the region. A pediatrician, a teenager working on behalf of the displaced, the founder of a shelter for homeless girls, all from different ethnic groups, came together, literally embracing each other and the others' causes because of their shared concerns for women, youth, and families. Also on the same panel were women from tribes struggling with each other in the Horn of Africa, one with a babe in arms that was passed among the panelists and the audience for comfort while the women talked.

Our subject was, not surprisingly, peaceful conflict resolution. The session got off to an alarming start when one audience member insistently and stridently demanded a response to her shouted question, What about Macedonia? A young woman in the back of the room signaled to me her desire to respond. Movingly, she told a story that stood as a parable for the rest of us and reset the tone for the remainder of the session. She was an Israeli, and she told, calmly but with deep emotion, of interacting with Palestinian women and coming to realize that what joined them as people, as women, was more significant then what divided them and had led to her work in the region on behalf of a concept of justice based on sharing. Recalled to our goal and beliefs by the power of personal example, the session continued beyond its allotted time with thoughtful discussion of what has already worked and what could perhaps work in the future to resolve conflict without war.

The panel symbolized the whole conference for me. Both seemed to be a moment in time when new values were not only celebrated but also demonstrated. As a symbol, though I regret the comparison because of its detractors, the conference was much like Woodstock, which has assumed almost mythic status to commentators and historians as a moment epitomizing the emergence of a major shift in cultural and social values. Certainly it is only after the fact that one can tell if something has really been a symbol or not, as it took the sixties to demonstrate the suitability of Woodstock as the symbol it was thought to be, even at the time.

Beijing was also such a moment, full of promise and signs of change, and those who were there understood both the meaning of the moment and the hard work of implementation that must follow to fully realize the symbolic promise held out by the occasion. For me, the way of Beijing, the peaceful and collaborative assembly of so many diverse people with so many conflicting views, was the thirteenth platform point and the content of the symbol.

Because I am chair of the Executive Committee of the Public Leadership Education Network (PLEN), I went to Beijing as the titular head of a delegation mainly composed of students from around the country. PLEN is a consortium of nineteen women's colleges, under the excellent leadership of Executive Director Marianne Alexander. There were sixteen students from twelve women's colleges, two faculty, the executive director, and me in our group.

PLEN was founded in 1978 by Sissy Farenthold, then president of Wells College in Aurora, New York, because women's colleges have long excelled in the arena of preparing women for public leadership. For example, in 1992, 24 percent of the women in Congress were women's college graduates, despite the fact that fewer than 4 percent of U.S. college graduates attended women's colleges. PLEN's founding as a Washington-based consortium would permit each of us to give our students even more opportunities for leadership education than we already gave them on campus. Through providing seminars, internships, and opportunities to meet with women who are public leaders, such as members of Congress, Supreme Court justices, and executives, PLEN has served the women's colleges well since its founding.

By sponsoring students to go to Beijing, the organization made a new commitment to add a global focus for public leadership and fulfilled the commitment of the Nairobi conference to focus on youth at the next conference, to broaden the generational understanding of the issues, and to pass the torch.

Marianne Alexander set up an extraordinary program, coping with the tremendous logistical difficulties of attending the conference, managing not only to get visas and lodging but also to prearrange internships for our students in Beijing with NGOs that would be in attendance. The experience of the students was extraordinary (see, for example, Chatham student Susan Homer's essay "Inspiring Young Women to Action and Advocacy" in part IV). It was life transforming and not only raised consciousness, a familiar term to those of us from the 1960s, but created a sense of empowerment possible only in the 1990s.

For me, someone whose consciousness had already been elevated in an earlier generation, the major impact was on my thinking as an educator. I came away from Beijing with no new, but some strengthened and some slightly revised commitments. Two stand out. First, no study of women at our higher education institutions should ever again lack a global, multicultural perspective. Eight thousand women from the United States attended. But we were eight thousand out of more than thirty thousand participants. There is a global movement of women, and while there are many commonalities, there are many differences that must be recognized, both for true understanding and for effective cooperation. Women's studies, as Beverly Guy-Steftall pointed out in her 1995 report to the Ford Foundation, *Women's Studies: A Retrospective*, must in the future be firmly grounded in the perspectives of diversity and globalism. Chatham College had many follow-up activities to the conference, but perhaps the most important one was a new commitment to creating curricular and cocurricular linkages between our women's studies and African American and global programs. The first step that was taken was to expand the concept of our African–African American studies program to a Multicultural–African American studies program with joint directors, one especially immersed in women's studies.

Second, I came to believe that the best collegiate extra-classroom response to "bring Beijing home" would be a concerted effort to foster women's political empowerment in this country. The U.S. government, through USAID, proposed as one part of its follow-up activities to create an international initiative in women's political participation in traditional democracies around the world by offering assistance for women's political leadership training. I hoped higher education could be engaged in USAID's project, especially women's colleges, since we have such an outstanding track record of preparing women for public leadership. But I left Beijing particularly committed to work in my own backyard, especially with Chatham's students, and the Pittsburgh community as appropriate.

Several factors combine in my mind to make this seem to be a good case of its being best to think globally and act locally. The seventy-fifth anniversary of women's suffrage in this country was celebrated concurrently with the conference, an occasion I commemorated by having yellow roses delivered to our incoming students, whom I could not welcome because I was in China. The promise of women's suffrage can only be fulfilled by using it, and too few women are active in the political process, especially in Pennsylvania, which has the disgrace of ranking forty-sixth in the nation for the number of women in elective office.* Further, the diversity of women suggests that there can be no one definition of what the women's political agenda is, except that it is created through the full participation of women—all women—in the electoral process.

In the fall of 1996 Chatham College acted on these commitments.

* As of October 1997 according to data from the Center for the American Woman and Politics at Rutgers University.

Marjorie Margolies-Mezvinsky, head of the U.S. delegation to Beijing and former Democratic member of Congress from Pennsylvania, accepted our invitation to come to the college and team-teach a course entitled "Election '96" with Jacqueline Fish, an active Republican leader and experienced academic. The course covered the gamut of practical and theoretical political education and included not only our students but also alumnae and members of the community. Made possible by the sponsorship of the Elsie Hilliard Hillman Chair at Chatham, honoring the commitment to active political involvement of a distinguished Pittsburgher, and the Hollander Family Fund, the course gave participants the opportunity to have public officials, a pollster, candidates, a media consultant, campaign managers, fund-raisers, and others as faculty. The course had a "laboratory," which was participation in the process outside the classroom, and participants worked to register more than five hundred voters, created a Web page on gender politics in the election, took voters to the polls, attended fund-raisers, and had the opportunity to meet the presidential candidates. Their efforts were so imaginative and widespread that the *New York Times* reported on the activities of this small college in their special section on campus political participation.

Thus the Beijing conference, the conference that emphasized creating results through national commitments to follow-up, was continued at Chatham College, with outreach well beyond the campus and with effects beyond the focus on women through the emphasis on the political process. Like the conference itself, the follow-up activities demonstrated that women's rights and women's interests are indeed human rights and human interests and can have transformative results if we pursue them.

An Important Connection
Pennsylvania Peace Links
Ann M. Harty

On September 18, 1996, at the invitation of Pennsylvania Peace Links, a five-member delegation from the Chinese Peoples' Association for Peace and Disarmament (CPAPD) arrived in New York for a nine-day visit to the United States. Their meetings in Washington, D.C., Pittsburgh, and New York City put them in touch with organizations that are working to reduce armed conflicts throughout the world. Their visit culminated in a discussion at the United Nations with nongovernmental organization members addressing disarmament issues. In that forum Alice Slater of Global Resources Action Center for the Environment made a strong statement in which she congratulated Chen Jifeng, the Chinese delegation leader, on his government's leadership role in pushing for the UN's acceptance of the Comprehensive Test Ban. (We had just the day before celebrated the signing of the CTB at a rally in Pittsburgh's Market Square.) William Epstein, a forty-year dean of disarmament efforts at the UN, then challenged the delegation to request that their government offer the UN a "no first strike" resolution, which would include "no use against nonnuclear nations," a position China consistently promotes and one Epstein believes would find support at the UN now. Having just had a discussion about the ways in which NGOs can influence governments, the Chinese were being challenged to do just that.

How did it happen that Peace Links hosted this delegation from China? The initiative for formal exchange of delegations between Peace Links and the CPAPD was taken at the Peace Tent in Huairou during the UN Fourth World Conference on Women. It was the second contact that Peace Links had made with this group.

The first meeting occurred in the spring of 1991 when Teresa Wilson led a delegation of nine Peace Links women to China at the invitation of the All China Women's Federation. Seven came from the Pittsburgh area; Betty Bumpers and Sarah Murphy came from the national office in

Washington, D.C. Our group had requested meetings with Chinese organizations working on nuclear disarmament, so arrangements had been made to meet with the CPAPD. After one particularly animated and far-ranging discussion, as we assembled for a farewell photo, the CPAPD director exclaimed, "You ladies certainly do go straight ahead!"

After four years of little or no further contact, in the midst of a demonstration at the NGO forum in Huairou, Teresa Wilson found herself staring at a name tag bearing the letters CPAPD. Recognizing that this must be a representative from the Chinese Peoples' Association for Peace and Disarmament, she identified herself and suggested that the group meet with Peace Links at the Peace Tent.

On the appointed morning, Deputy Secretary-General Xie Zhiqiong brought Chen Jifeng, CPAPD secretary-general, and three women, to join five Peace Links and two members of the Women's International League for Peace and Freedom, one of whom was President Emeritus Edith Ballantyne, to discuss the challenges of worldwide nuclear disarmament. After outlining each country's role in the build-up of nuclear weapons, Edith Ballantyne proposed that China lead the world community on the path toward the abolition of nuclear arms. At the close of the meeting, Chen produced a magazine that contained the photograph taken back in 1991. Four of the Peace Links women at the meeting were also in that picture! Yes, we certainly do go straight ahead.

Following the meeting, Xie suggested to me that Peace Links and the CPAPD exchange delegations. I invited the CPAPD to send a delegation to the United States in 1996. In March 1996 Betty Bumpers visited the group's Beijing headquarters, where she discussed nuclear issues and the tentative itinerary for the upcoming trip. The plans were affirmed and began to move forward.

Upon their arrival in New York in September 1996, the Chinese visitors embarked on a nine-day adventure in citizen diplomacy. They experienced

four home stays with different families
a train ride between New York City and Washington, D.C.
meetings with representatives from the Center for Defense Information, the Peace Institute, and the Henry Stimson Center, with

whom ties had been broken in 1989 by the events at Tiananmen
Square

two day-long car trips filled with lively conversation covering a variety
of subjects—from serious to lighthearted

an overnight with dinner and breakfast planned as "downtime" when
personal stories were shared along with jokes both Chinese and
American; hilarity prevailed

two encounters with small Peace Links groups outside Pittsburgh, one
emphasizing acceptance of the Comprehensive Test Ban as a
prime example of how grassroots lobbying can be effective; the
other bringing attention to environmental issues, vocational–technical training, and a college classroom discussion with interested
students

a roundtable discussion at the University of Pittsburgh with Eastern
European and Asian studies students and professors

a UNIFEM meeting followed by a farewell party where a WILPF vice
president recognized Mr. Chen as a cohort at the UN Beijing conference where they had both been part of the round-the-clock sessions that finalized the Platform for Action

They also attended a WILPF meeting where Robin Lloyd's film about
the Peace Train was shown and discussed. Mr. Chen voiced strong disagreement with the segment of the film that dealt with Tibetan women in
exile and asked that it be edited out. It was also at this meeting that he
noted that hosting the UN Fourth World Conference on Women was of
great benefit to Chinese women in three ways: (1) it allowed them to
learn how to plan a major international meeting; (2) it allowed them
knowledge of women's lives and activities around the world; (3) it raised
consciousness in China about gender issues.

Hannah Wasserman, long-time peace activist and Peace Links representative to the UN, arranged a meeting at the UN with NGO professionals who are working for disarmament and are eager to share resources
and information. The Chinese had asked for help in contacting other
NGOs in New York and it was through Ms. Wasserman and the Peace
Links organization that this was made possible. The Chinese were fasci-

nated by the way in which an NGO, such as Peace Links, is able to facilitate such connections in our country.

There was palpable excitement among our guests as we left the UN building. Chen expressed keen disappointment that the visit was coming to an end. Many business cards were exchanged, information collected, and contacts made among people working toward common goals. A follow-up trip to China was offered to all present.

The potential for expanding this work for disarmament is clear. Through citizen exchanges such as this one, many doors have been opened, increasing the opportunities for promoting peace. Just as the UN Fourth World Conference on Women was about prodding the governments of the world toward more equitable treatment of women, so too, do all governments need prodding if peace is to become a reality. There are as many different approaches to prodding as there are countries in the world. Exchanges such as this one involve explanations of how each group works to prod its government. We learn from each other.

The members of the CPAPD were constantly remarking on the fine hospitality and extreme friendliness they experienced while they were our guests. In 1991 we had been given the red carpet treatment during our visit to China because, we were told, "You were the first group willing to talk to us after Tiananmen." I contrasted these sentiments with the frustration and anger we had felt at the way we were treated by the Chinese government on the Peace Train journey and I was reminded once again that this type of citizen-to-citizen diplomacy is important because it makes connections and builds trust where governments cannot.

In his thank-you note, Chen noted that this visit promoted understanding between our groups and gave the Chinese the opportunity to learn about the U.S. peace movement. But in a larger sense, the exchange "contribute[d] to the mutual understanding and friendship between the Chinese and American people." In a world increasingly cracking at the borders, a comment such as this carries much significance.

Pennsylvania Peace Links' Commitments to the Peace Agenda of the United Nations Fourth World Conference on Women, September 1995

Actions for Peace

1. Peace Links supports "Thursdays in Black," a protest movement demanding a world without rape and violence. This involves wearing black on Thursdays along with the "Thursdays in Black" button and disseminating the flyer that accompanies the button. Peace Links sells the buttons for $1.00 and distributes the flyer and buttons to appropriate groups in the city. The flyer and button are available at all appropriate Peace Links functions.

2. Peace Links continues its work in support of treaties to end the nuclear arms race, particularly a comprehensive test ban treaty (signed September 1996) and the Abolition 2000, a citizen-level effort toward the elimination of nuclear weapons by the year 2000. Peace Links cooperates with other local groups in this effort.

3. Peace Links continues to work on conflict resolution for children. This includes expanding the workshops for teachers to include a parenting component. It also includes continuing the productions of "The Tree House," a puppet show for young children, which is now also available on video. Peace Links also focused on conflict resolution at the 1996 annual dinner and was a sponsor of the National Conference on Peace and Conflict Resolution which was held in Pittsburgh in May 1997.

4. Peace Links has continued citizen diplomacy contacts, hosting representatives from the Chinese Peoples' Association for Peace and Disarmament in September 1996, and sending a delegation of five women to China in September 1997.

5. Peace Links continues to lobby to transfer funding from the military budget to the domestic budget.

6. Peace Links sent a representative to the United Nations Conference on Habitat in June 1996.

7. Peace Links continues to support a comprehensive ban on land mines and urges citizens to contact local government representatives to do the same.

Peace Links will continue to work in cooperation with groups in the city with similar goals, specifically the World Federalist Association, Physicians for Social Responsibility, the Thomas Merton Center, the United Nations Association, and women's shelters.

Peace Links, YWCA Building, 305 Wood Street, Pittsburgh, Pa. 15222; phone 412-471-0302; fax 412-471-4545; peacelinks@aol.com

A Woman's Questions

Linda Hunt

I've been asked many questions about how the Beijing experience has impacted me. The most interesting ones ask me how what I have learned or experienced from attending the forum is going to make a positive change in my community. People, many of them women, ask me these questions with wide-eyed anticipation of some deep revelation, some supreme insight or solution.

Many months after returning from the forum, I suffered from what I call sensory or cultural overload. Like a sponge, I had absorbed from those women with whom I lived, ate, debated, and networked. In that community, whose singular purpose was to improve the quality of life for women and girls worldwide, I was like a child locked up in a candy store, so in awe, so happy that it was impossible to decide what to eat. Like that child, I was so overwhelmed by the experience that the process of examining and categorizing it was difficult and slow. During this period my ability to articulate my experiences on anything but a superficial level was impossible. I would answer the many questions with answers like, "It was an experience of a lifetime." (And it was.) Or, "I couldn't believe I was really there." (And I couldn't.) For the most part, people were satisfied with that, especially if I told them about not being able to find a dog or cat in China. People wanted to hear stories about the Great Wall, the demonstrations, and of course, the shopping. And frankly, I loved to tell them about that. It was easy.

What wasn't easy was formulating answers for the questions that tug at my soul, like, "What is it about the socialization of blacks in America, from slavery until the present, that birthed the phenomenon of black on black violence?" And "What did I experience, learn, obtain, from attending the forum that will change things in my community?"

Fact: Allegheny County is ranked second in unemployment of black males in the nation. (I have three sons.) Fact: Seven black males in one community have been shot in as many weeks. Fact: Jonny Gammage was murdered by professionals sworn to uphold the law, and they may go free. Fact: In Pennsylvania, thousands of black women and children will be thrown off welfare without a net.

If we as feminists say we are going about the business of making the quality of life better for women and girls, then we must be inclusive of those women and girls who don't have a voice. If we are truly concerned about violence against women, we must understand that any violence perpetrated against my sons is violence perpetrated against me.

Many black women, as far back as Sojourner Truth and as recent as Angela Davis and Alice Walker, have voiced their concerns that the women's movement has disconnected itself from issues that affect black women in their communities. This was evident in the absence of these issues being addressed at the forum. Was the international conference not the appropriate format?

I returned from the forum rejuvenated but discontented, with more questions than answers. I am a creative writer so let me take license and put these questions to you.

- What did YOU learn, experience, or obtain from attending the forum that would have a positive impact on my community?
- What would happen if someone decided to sell their $30,000 car, buy a $16,000 car, and give the difference to help someone or some program in my community?
- What if someone decided not to leave everything to their children but set aside some of it and donated it to "Goods For Guns"?

Radical ideas? Take a minute. I bet you could come up with some what-ifs of your own.

Nicodemus was a godly, wealthy man who asked Jesus what he needed to do to get into Heaven. Jesus told him, "Sell all that you have and give it to the poor." The Bible says Nicodemus left, sad.

A Woman's Question

Linda Hunt

If we be sisters
let's tell of our union
of our dreams
of our nightmares
If we be sisters
let's embrace our differences
acknowledge our similarities
celebrate our rituals
If we be sisters
let's drink from the same cup
share of our bread
soothe one another's wounds
If we be sisters
If we be sisters
then let's sing with one voice
of our sisterhood

Or are we third cousins
twice removed?

Concerns

Louise Wilde

I have read the Platform for Action that was adopted at Beijing in 1995. I am familiar with the twelve areas of concern that it outlines. I have struggled in my own mind, and in discussions with others, with the question of how to "get a handle" on the recommendations—how to "bring Beijing home" here in our own community and in communities all over the United States.

I belong to a number of organizations and action networks related to the issues identified in the platform. I try to keep myself informed about public policy debates and actions, to write letters, to call my elected leaders, to work through several grassroots organizations to which I belong. I certainly understand the need to take stock of where we are.

Nevertheless, wherever I turn, as I look at the twelve areas of concern, I see us attempting to swim against an overwhelming current that is carrying us backward rather than forward; that is eroding our past gains rather than building upon them. The gap between rich and poor is widening, not narrowing, and the poorest of the poor are overwhelmingly women and children. Health care is increasingly being treated as an "economic good," a commodity to be bought only if one has the means, and not as a "social good," which should be provided on an equal basis to all. Our public officials argue that we lack the resources to provide even the most basic repairs to our decaying schools, yet they find the money to build more and more prisons and to increase the military budget by billions more than the Pentagon requests.

Public policy decisions are being made that starve us of even the modest resources that we need to work on solving problems at the grassroots level. The budget cuts of the eighties and nineties have created a situation in which those at the bottom are forced to fight against each other for ever-diminishing resources. The competition for scarce foundation and charitable dollars becomes ever more intense. Food banks, homeless shelters, women's shelters, and many other social service programs and agencies must focus their energies more and more on the battle for mere survival.

In a climate like this, I rebel at being told that the grassroots level is where my efforts should be concentrated. I resent being told that I should continue to hold my finger in the dike, when the entire seawall is crumbling around me. That seems to me to be simply a way to keep me from confronting the real problem. The seawall must be rebuilt. Public policy must change. That is where we must focus our efforts. Grassroots efforts alone are not going to be enough. We must pressure our governments to be accountable to the promises, the commitments that they made in Beijing.

UN Secretary-General Boutros Boutros-Ghali was criticized for spending money on international conferences. I think it is one of the best things he did because international conferences raise awareness of conditions around the world and they engage more people in the process of improving those conditions. We really need a unified mobilization effort and cooperation between nongovernmental and governmental organizations if we are going to establish some kind of balance in the world.

I think of the story of the Good Samaritan. We use that story as an example of how we should treat one another, as an example of compassion. The Good Samaritan was good because he stopped to help a fellow human being who was in need. However, if the Samaritan had passed on the same road day after day and had seen needy and suffering people day after day, at some point he would have had to ask himself, Why are there so many suffering on this road? What is wrong with this road? He would have had to seek help from those who were responsible for the road and others who were as concerned as he was.

To paraphrase a popular sentiment often seen on bumper stickers: Won't it be a wonderful day when we have all the resources we need for the twelve areas of concern—and the Pentagon has to hold a bake sale to buy a missile?

In the Image of God
Excerpts from a Sermon

Toni Conaway

The United Nations women's conference made clear to me that women from all over the globe, from all kinds of societies, from a variety of cultures, and from various religions have not been treated with dignity. They have not been treated as human beings created "in the image of God." As a result, they—and society—suffer.

But there is good news. And that is that there is another way. There is a Chinese proverb that says, "In hell, the chopsticks are one yard long and the people starve; in heaven, the chopsticks are one yard long, but the people feed each other." They found another way—a way of partnership, cooperation, and community. We, as Christians, have found this way, too. It is what the Gospels are all about. It is not an easy way. One has to say no to the old, in order to say yes to the new.

Of the thousands of women there, some . . . found their inspiration and comfort in Christ. But there were thousands of women there representing the world's other faiths as well. They, too, were trying to birth a new way of thinking. For the most part, the atmosphere was open and affirming and allowed for real dialogue. I think this was because women recognized that God has many faces and exists in all religions. Women were eager to share their life stories. In the words of a friend: "Women showed a willingness to reveal their successes and failures so that others could stand on their shoulders to reach for the higher stars."

A new millennium is approaching and it is obvious we need to find a better way of living. We can't have another century as violent as this one. Fortunately, for us as Christians, we have the inspiration of Christ, who, in his topsy turvy embrace of the weak, the despised, and the scorned—who were often women—came to Earth to serve life, all life. He did this,

Taken from a sermon which was delivered at the Westminster Presbyterian Church in Pittsburgh on Women's Sunday, November 19, 1995.

not through power, domination, or control over other people but through the awesome power of compassionate love. As a result, people were— and still are—able to transform and restore their lives. And when lives are truly changed, society is transformed as well. I can't imagine a better legacy to bequeath our children.

One Year Later

Louise Wilde and Janice Auth

On September 28, 1996, the White House Interagency for Women's Issues held a national teleconference to commemorate "America's Commitment: The UN Women's Conference One Year Later." In Pittsburgh, one of more than four hundred sites throughout the country linked by satellite to Washington, D.C., approximately 150 people participated in the day-long event.

The day began with a review of the conference, forum, and Peace Train, featuring three videos: *Cornerstone for the Future: Girls and Young Women* from the Center for Policy Alternatives; *Peace Train to Beijing* from the Women's International League for Peace and Freedom; and *Voices of Women* produced by Lee Heh Margolies and Martha Starr.

The second half of the morning was entitled "Bringing Beijing Home: Pittsburgh and the Platform for Action." Two important results of this connection between Pittsburgh and the international conference were identified: increased awareness of international issues on the part of the local community and increased communication among the various local nongovernmental organizations.

Panel presenters for the teleconference from Washington were Ida Castro, director of the Women's Bureau, Department of Labor; Donna Shalala, secretary of Health and Human Services; Thomas Kean, president of Drew University and former governor of New Jersey; Maureen Reagan, head of the U.S. delegation to the 1985 Nairobi conference; Connie Evans, president and CEO of the Women's Self-Employment Project in Chicago; Linda-Tarr Whelan, U.S. representative to the UN Commission on the Status of Women and director of the Center for Policy Alternatives; Geraldine Ferraro, U.S. ambassador to the UN Commission on Human Rights; Judy Heumann, assistant secretary of education for Special Education and Rehabilitation Services. The moderator was Judy Woodruff of CNN. First Lady Hillary Rodham Clinton, in her introductory speech, made the point that there is a tendency to assume that an international conference such as the one that took place in Beijing has little relevance to U.S. women. Yet she reminded us, we share the same aspirations and concerns with women from around the world. There is always more we can do in the United States to protect women from violence, to ensure equal pay for equal work, to guarantee retirement security, to help with family and work, health, credit, and economic opportunities. We are doing more, thanks to the Beijing Platform for Action, which is our blueprint.

A variety of programs from around the country, which have been initiated as a direct result of the Beijing conference, were described and discussed. The importance of education and mentoring were stressed again and again.

If there is one lasting message from the teleconference itself, it is that the effects of Beijing are still being felt and will continue to be felt in both grand and quiet ways. One example of this is the Heifer Project. Village women in developing countries are given an animal to care for, which in turn provides milk for their children and self-reliance for the family. When the animal gives birth, the new animal is given to another woman to help her and her family become more self-sufficient. The project is helping break the cycle of poverty.

Pittsburgh/Beijing '95 and Beyond was formed in an attempt to carry on the work of the previous women's conference in Nairobi. There was little interest or will to carry on after Nairobi, but ten years later PBB sent women to Beijing and in 1996 to the Habitat Conference in Istanbul. Although Pittsburgh/Beijing '95 and Beyond closed its doors at the end of October 1996, its task is not finished. Pennsylvania Peace Links, World Federalist Association of Pittsburgh, and UNIFEM are among the organizations dedicated to helping move the Beijing Platform for Action forward in the Pittsburgh area. And local organizations worldwide are keeping alive the commitment, the dedication, the energy, and the hope that was born in Beijing. Now the task belongs to everyone—including you.

Stand Up, Speak Out
Ten Things You Can Do to Improve the Lives of Women

This list is adapted from a similar list produced by the Center for Policy Alternatives, Washington, D.C.

1. Educate yourself on the United Nations conference in Beijing. Invite a participant of the NGO forum or the conference to give a presentation to a group of friends or an organization.

2. Don't underestimate the power of a letter. Contact your elected representatives and the media. Engage them in meeting the U.S. commitments to the Beijing Platform for Action. Urge them to support ratification of the Convention on the Elimination of All Forms of Discrimination Against Women.

3. Get involved. Call any of the organizations mentioned in this book or call the White House for an update on the now-evolving work of the Interagency Council on Women.

4. Stop the violence and negative images of women. Support the Women in Black by wearing black on Thursdays to protest violence. Monitor the media.

5. Organize a group that meets regularly to educate members on the status of women around the world and to take action at a local, national, or international level.

6. Participate in Take Your Daughters to Work Day. Encourage girls to take math and science; look at the curriculum and sports programs.

7. Share your time and expertise. Volunteer to be a mentor or coach. Open the door for other women.

8. Use your consumer power. Support companies that advance women and have family-friendly policies. Support companies and businesses that are owned by women.

9. Invest in women. Start or contribute to a women's campaign, organization, or scholarship fund.

10. Register and VOTE in every election.

vii TWO YEARS LATER

The Work Continues

Beijing was the tsunami of an earthquake. It is still making
waves.

—*Leone Paradise*

IN THESE TWO years following the Beijing conference, I have found my professional world in international women's health care peppered by references to the UN World Conference on Women. It has provided a background chorus to the ongoing lyric of making the world a healthier and safer place for women and their families. Although UN governments' follow-through on women's agendas has been slow, the momentum of the nongovernmental organizations and individuals who participated in the conference is continuing to build. The affirmation of community felt at the Beijing forum will energize our efforts well into the coming century.

—*Tanya Kotys Ozor*

THE GENERAL ASSEMBLY COUNCIL of the Presbyterian Church, at the request of its National Ministries Division Committee, agreed to request docket time at the 1998 General Assembly in Charlotte, North Carolina, for the final report of the Presbyterian Committee on the "Ecumenical Decade: Churches in Solidarity with Women," a comprehensive program sponsored by the World Council of Churches to call attention to the plight of women around the world.

I attended the Women's Pre-Conference to the Twenty-third Council of the World Alliance of Reformed Churches in Debrecen, Hungary, in August 1997. The theme of the conference, taken from a verse in the book of Isaiah (xii:6) was "Break the Chains of Injustice." Women at this gathering wanted to be heard. As they spoke about their experiences, I realized that the injustices that women in the Church face are the same as those that women all over the world face in all aspects of life. The ideas generated in Beijing are being taken up all around the world in many different contexts.

The World Alliance of Reformed Churches, founded in 1875, links seventy million Christians and 208 congregational Presbyterian reformed and united churches in 102 countries around the world. The alliance promotes unity, theological reflection, and ecumenical fellowship among its member churches. These goals are pursued at regional and international levels to assist churches in their mission and ministry in today's world. In 1990, Jane Dempsey Douglass, professor of historical theology at Princeton Theological Seminary, became the first woman to be elected WARC president. Her election underlined the commitment of the Twenty-second General Council held in Seoul, Korea, in 1989 to the partnership of women and men in church and society.

The theme of the council, "Break the Chains of Injustice," addressed the deep concerns of churches about the ongoing problem of human rights; unjust relations among people of different ethnic, racial, and gender groups; global economic injustice; and dangerous exploitation of the created order.

—*Florence Johnson*

CHILDREN AT RISK has been the emphasis of Episcopal Church Women of the Diocese of Pittsburgh (ECW) since Beijing, 1995. "United by Christ to Reach the Children and save the Families" is our theme and the heart of our mission. We have published a resource book, *United by Christ*, as an outreach tool to provide meaningful information to persons in our diocese, and across the country, who are seeking help for children and families at risk. Now we are getting copies of the book to people and organizations to help bring alive that message, that there is always a safe place to turn for help.

One example of national involvement reaching into the community and diocesan level is the Children's Defense Fund founded by Marian Wright Edelman. This organization lobbies for children nationally. On the local level, support is sought for people to march for children through Stand for Children, as witnessed in the recent Children's Sabbath Celebration. And Child Watch seeks organizations to band together as advocates for children. The Episcopal Diocese of Pittsburgh is a member of the Child Watch Coalition, and Child Watch was organized locally by the Children's Home of Pittsburgh.

The connection between ECW and Child Watch is evident in many parishes. ECW members serve as volunteers for the Kids Club at Church of the Savior in Ambridge. This group met initially to provide a family experience at least one day a week. Eighty percent of the children did not have a father at home. Many of their families had been devastated by substance or physical abuse, little supervision, or mental illness. Today, Kids Club is proud of their voluntary, racially integrated gathering of children and adults which provides a safe place for children when no one else will or can.

St. Stephen's Church, Wilkinsburg, has a Kids Club that has attracted ECW volunteers from several other parishes, including Fox Chapel and St. Andrews, Highland Park. The volunteers minister to the children while their parents are attending Narcotics Anonymous and Nar-Anon meetings. The parents can go about their recovery process knowing their children are in caring and loving hands.

The after-school program at St. Grace Church is Mt. Washington's response for at-risk middle-schoolers. A United Thank Offering grant, gifted teachers, and volunteers are making a difference in young people's lives from October through May. A well-structured program of homework, tutoring, games, crafts, drama, and a sit-down dinner (complete with manners and etiquette) make up their afternoons.

Statistics for children at risk are staggering. For children to even be able to think about taking advantage of some of the programs discussed here, they must be well enough and motivated enough to reach out. The Early Childhood Initiative, supported by the United Way of Allegheny County and the Allegheny Conference, and enthusiastically endorsed by the Pittsburgh ECW, expects to raise the quality of all infant, toddler, and preschool services in the county and to increase the number participating in those programs.

The ECW has made a pledge that as one person, and as part of a group in their local parish and in the diocese, they will:

See, hear, and communicate positively with children
Be a good role model for children
Support stable family life for children
Help build caring communities for all children
Speak out for children and support effective groups that help them
Vote to ensure all children fair opportunity
Make at least one child's life better by something they do
Pray for and see God in all children and youth

The ECW and the *United by Christ* resource book are small building blocks toward understanding the opportunities that are available for our children and families. The ECW members are volunteering to help make those opportunities a reality.

—*Elizabeth Hobbs*

WHAT DID WE HEAR? We heard about women and credit, about the problems connected with economic restructuring, about the efforts to keep girls in school, about learning to negotiate to help solve conflicts that might lead to war, about ways to empower women in many different countries, about how important NGOs are in developing leadership skills among women, and what specific groups of women, all over the world, actually are doing to make their lives better and to give the future to their children.

But the theme that emerged most forcefully for me throughout the forum, that cut across all national borders, all cultures, continents, classes, colors, religions, was violence against women, and particularly domestic violence. This was hardly discussed ten years before in Nairobi, and now it was addressed through countless workshops, posters, displays, banners, videos. I believe it was *the* definitive unifying issue of the forum.

A second major theme was economic and dealt with the need for greater resources for the environment, for education, for housing, for shelters, for clean water, and so on. And yet only some made the connection between cold war–mentality military spending and the lack of funding for social needs.

For me, there is a simple message from the NGO forum and the UN conference. I hope it will be carried around the globe and be understood and believed in and acted upon. The message? Because women's rights are human rights, the struggle must be engaged in by all of humankind—women and men working together to build a future.

My personal dream is to attend a *fifth* UN conference on women in 2005 with Jessa, my granddaughter, who will then be twenty-one years old, to see and hear how many of the hopes and visions expressed in Beijing will have become reality.

—*Lois Goldstein*

FOR MORE THAN HALF A CENTURY, I have been strongly aware of women's unique role in family and community and learned through my mother's example that we must become our own person. Therefore, for me, the Beijing Women's Conference was not an epiphany.

But I have found, in the past two years, that my presence at that conference has given me a new legitimacy to place women's issues on the agenda. I am constantly surprised at the envy and curiosity of most women when I mention this two-year-old event, and their eagerness to learn more about women beyond our borders.

For me specifically, the conference was an affirmation of the worth of my voice. For the first time I see myself as a real link in the strong chain of women of all races and cultures spanning our globe, speaking in the universal language of common joys, pains, and ideals.

Side by side with this identity I have developed a new openness, inquisitiveness, and sympathy as I look beyond my American/Jewish frame of reference. I remember vividly the women of the Asian-African panel who affirmed: "We are seeking to build *regional* models. We need to develop methods using our own roots and values, not necessarily western inspired."

I joined UNIFEM and read with special interest the many news stories of women's large and small victories (and defeats) around the world; I contribute to the New Israel Fund, which helps Arab and Israeli women forge links for peace; and China and her people have become real for me.

But deep inside me, when I rethink the stages of the struggle, I whisper this question to myself: *Did our powerlessness help develop the humanity of our sisterhood, the eager sharing of our ideas, the priority we give to peace and equality?*

Will power corrupt us too?

—Edith Scheiner

LET ME tell you about a few Chinese women I met who make me think that China may never be the same again, after having been through the UN Fourth World Conference on Women. I truly believe Pandora came out of the box. Five thousand Chinese women from all over the country, including all the semiautonomous areas, were introduced to the concept of nongovernmental organizations in a country where the centralized government is supposed to be everything. They were told that women's rights are human rights in a country where, to this day, a peasant woman will probably answer the door saying, "No one is home," and less than seventy-five years ago a wealthy woman could not even answer the door because her feet were bound. She was unable to do anything. And though women have supposedly held up half the sky since the communist revolution, yin and yang indicate that the female half is the dark, depressed side of life, whereas the male half is the good, light side.

We met two young policewomen-in-training at the peace tent who folded paper cranes with us, laughed and talked with us about a lot of things. They were wearing Aung San Suu Kyi buttons and they wanted to know all about this powerful, dissident leader of Burma, Nobel Peace Prize winner, who, though unable to come to Beijing, had sent a strong message of freedom to the conference.

Another woman we met, a Mongolian teacher, quietly handed us a fan with a cross on it, and told us she belongs to the newly redeveloping Christian church in China. She urged us to visit her the next time we're in Inner Mongolia, and we said we would. And at the time, we really meant it. Hundreds of women from Shaanxi province made a huge banner of a red phoenix rising out of the ashes, symbolizing hope for change, symbolizing power.

Power is what it's all about. There was a real sense of power that rose out of this women's conference. Not power for China or the United States or any other nation to dominate. Not power for women to dominate men—that would not be any better than men dominating women. No, it's the power to change things, the power to be born, to have enough to eat, clean water to drink, a home, however simple, to sleep in, a land free of fighting so that farming and normal living can be pursued, education for everyone, the right not to be poor.

—*Dorothy Hill*

"POST-BEIJING." That is the word that catches my attention on the news broadcasts and in the printed press. I am kept alert to the importance of the work still to be done on the issues raised in the Fourth World Conference on Women in 1995. With the privilege of participating in that historical event comes a heightened awareness of the milestone reached. Work at the UN is constantly referenced in relation to the Platform for Action and I find my Grail colleagues all over the world placing their development work in solidarity with Beijing objectives.

Joan Chittister was touring Australia with the Beijing message when I was there recently; and Mary Oto, Grail speaker from Nigeria here in Pittsburgh, focused her talk on the Beijing effort for the girl-child initiative. This was also the thrust of the League of Women Voters' questionnaire at the UN for the most significant work to be done on the Beijing Platform for Action. Post-Beijing efforts are on the agenda of major national meetings of women.

In our Peace Links work with the Chinese Peoples' Association for Peace and Disarmament, the question of the degree to which Chinese women shared in the results of the Beijing meeting met with a resounding response. Chen Jifeng said that Chinese women "found that they are not isolated but took their place with the women of the world in common concerns."

—*Teresa Wilson*

BEIJING has influenced the way we all live—from the international scene to our own personal and individual lives. The impact of Beijing was enormous—all those women, from practically every country in the world, sharing their concerns and hopes for the future. It was the first and only time I have felt that I was part of a historic event—it was like shipping out with Columbus. In fact, the new world analogy may not be all that far-fetched. The Beijing conference has had and continues to have the possibility of helping to build a more peaceful and equitable world.

On October 31, 1997, for example, about two years after Beijing, the *Pittsburgh Post-Gazette* carried three stories, which, while I don't suggest are the direct result of the conference, may well have more than a tangential relation to what the forty thousand women who gathered together in Beijing accomplished. The first article was about an international conference to abolish child labor held in Oslo, Norway; the second article was about an abused Kenyan Maasai woman, Agnes Siyiankoi, who defied her tribal and national mores by taking her husband, who beat her, to court; the third story concerned a Belfast woman, Mary McAleese, who was the front-runner in the race for Ireland's president. Last night I heard interviews with the two women who were running for the mayor of Minneapolis, Sharon Sayles Belton and Barbara Carlson. Locally, here in Pittsburgh, women are involved in citizen diplomacy, women in philanthropy seminars, and many organizations protecting the health and welfare of women and children. And, personally, I detect Beijing resonating in my own life. Although I was a serious feminist before Beijing, I notice I am more forthright than I used to be. For example, when I am with people with whom I am not well acquainted and who are discussing their work and, somehow or other (is it gender? is it age?), no one has inquired what I do, I now volunteer that I am a lawyer. The most fun is saying I'm a trial attorney in response to their question, what kind? Life's small pleasures.

It is no surprise then that it was my conversation with Janice Auth that initiated this writing. It was the conversation among forty thousand women that initiated some of the changes we observe in our world and in which we have the privilege of participating.

Beijing was the tsunami of an earthquake. It is still making waves.

—*Leone Paradise*

THE FOURTH UN Conference on Women held in Beijing, China, from September 4–15, 1995 is over. But it wasn't easy. Three-hundred and sixty-one paragraphs identifying twelve areas of critical concern to the role and status of women—poverty, education, health, violence, armed conflict, decision making and public participation, structural mechanisms, gender equality, media images, universal rights, ecology, and the rights of the girl-child—were finally negotiated at 5 A.M. on September 15, the very day of its ratification. The universal question, sometimes unspoken but always present at the edges of every conference conversation, however, remains: "So what?" "Who cares?" "With what effect?" The questions are well taken: What really happened in Beijing and was it worth it?

For one thing, men can breathe a little easier now: the world has not ended. Women have not left their husbands and children. Womanhood has not been impugned. Marriage has not been rejected. Everybody leaving Beijing looks exactly the way they looked when they walked in, a little more frazzled maybe, somewhat more tired, of course, but civilized, satisfied, and well-adjusted people. Whoever the crazies are supposed to be in the women's movement, detractors may be disappointed to hear, they didn't come to Beijing. Housewives came, nuns came, professionals came, politicians came, social workers came. In short, the women who came to Beijing were smart, experienced, and stable. This was not a fringe group of anything. At the same time, thanks to these types, there is now something very different in the air.

Twenty years after the first UN Conference on Women, which convened in Mexico City in 1975, Beijing has repeatedly been called "historic." For the first time in history, according to Gertrude Mongella, secretary general of the UN Fourth Conference on Women, women's issues have been recognized as societal issues, girl-children have been singled out for particular protection from sexual exploitation, and recommendations to make violence against women a criminal offense in all its forms have been accepted as necessary and just. Reality recognizes, however, that the UN can't mandate anything for anybody. So, after the dust settles and the participants go back to being teachers and mothers and delegates to nothing, will it have been worth the money, will it be seen to have merited the time, will all the paper generated by platform drafts and rewrites be justified?

There are many ways to measure those questions surely—in wages earned and public positions filled, in laws passed and quotas achieved, in terms of personal safety and human dignity and felt respect, in nutrition and education and self-determination. All those measures are sure and all of them are necessary. But all of them will take years to assess.

In the meantime, I draw my own answers to those questions from three simple indicators: a Chinese proverb, an ominous head count, and a challenge.

In a country where the Taoist symbol for the female is water, a Chinese proverb teaches: "Water wears away the rock." For twenty years women have persistently always, even perversely at times, insisted on their rights, raised their questions and complaints, demanded to be heard over the din of male militarism and religious machoism, not simply for themselves but for the sake of women everywhere. In a world where, twenty years ago, most of the countries of the world had no idea how women spent their time, how they sustained themselves, whether or not they could read, or even how many of them there were on earth, this conference drowned in information about refugee women and old women and little girls. The invisible woman is coming into focus. The picture may not be a pretty one, by and large, but for the first time in history it is a real one nevertheless. For the first time in history, the human race can ask questions about women and expect to get answers.

Now, thanks to the programs designed in Beijing, women are holding the world accountable on behalf of their daughters. The Beijing Document on Women calls governments to review and modify, with the full and equal participation of women, the macroeconomic and social policies that determine the world's distribution of resources.

The Platform for Action sets the year 2000 as the target date for the reduction of female illiteracy by half its 1990 level, and 2015 as the point at which the gender gap in primary and secondary school education ought to be closed.

The document leads governments to institute gender-sensitive health care, which gives priority to health programs in rural and poor urban areas.

To eliminate violence against women, the platform urges governments to condemn violence against women and to provide women with access to the mechanisms of justice that enact and enforce legislation against its perpetrators, as well as to provide shelters and support for the girls and women who are its victims.

Since women and children constitute 80 percent of the twenty-three million refugees and the twenty-six million displaced persons in the world, the platform calls for the inclusion of women in national reconciliation processes and reconstruction programs and for special steps to ensure refugee and displaced women safety, civil rights, and safe passage.

In most parts of the world, women are virtually absent from economic decision making. The platform calls for the end of economic discrimination, the valuation of women's unremunerated work, and equal pay for equal work.

Mechanisms for the advancement of women are called for at every level: local, regional and national.

Gender perspective is mandated in every arena.

The continued projection of negative, degrading and pornographic images of women requires balanced presentation and the access of women to the media.

The recognition that women's rights are human rights and not to be dismissed as a separate situation or a social gift of men to women requires the complete overhaul of systems and the total elimination of discrimination in all areas of human activity.

The involvement of women in environmental decision making, the platform insists, is necessary to the preservation of the globe.

The protection of girl-children from trafficking, sexual exploitation, domestic servitude, forced labor and the abolition of all forms of discrimination and cultural oppression, the platform states, requires national legislation and implementation.

Point: Accountability is coming to the whole human race, this time with a platform of specific priorities and clearly defined programs in hand. What Beijing began is a revolution that is more erosion than explosion. One small drop at a time, Beijing is a glimpse of the water wearing away the rock.

The second measure of the Beijing conference lies in its sheer size. According to UN sources, attendance in Beijing doubled the attendance record of the Third UN Conference on Women in Nairobi in 1990. Over forty thousand people—delegates, representatives of nongovernmental organizations, and observers—came to Beijing. The Fourth UN Conference on Women was the largest international conference in the history of the world. As you read this, one thing is sure: Beijing is everywhere now. In every country of the world, in every woman's organization anywhere. In the consciousness of every government, Beijing is a Greek chorus of warnings. If the men of the world do not heed the women of the world, women will suffer, yes, but more than that, that part of the human race that is killing itself, poisoning the globe, and wasting the planet will perish with them and at their own hands. The woman's question has come of age. It is not a woman's question any longer. It is the survival question of the 21st century. As a result of Beijing, feminism does not need to be apologized for any longer; it must simply be answered to. Everywhere.

Finally, the Beijing conference on women can be measured by the norms laid out by Gertrude Mongella, the Tanzanian secretary-general of the Fourth UN Conference on Women. "Women," Mongella pointed out, "joined men in their struggle against slavery; women participated with men in resisting colonialism; women fought alongside men to dismantle apartheid. "Now," Mongella pointed out, "men must join women in their struggle for equality."

It is time for men to stop being supportive to women in private but silent in public. It's time to see men walking alongside women for women's rights, as women walked with men in Selma and Belfast and Pietersburg and Shanghai.

We have signs of that, too. In Beijing, the Vatican emerged as a strong supporter of resource allocation for women's programs, a total life-span approach to women's health issues, supporters of family values and needs, and adherents of the Cairo Document on Population Control, with its awareness of the need to promote birth control. Gone was the acrimony of the Cairo conference and overt collusion between Vatican spokespeople and Muslim fundamentalists. In this conference, for instance, though the Vatican had reservations about the final document, rather than articulate them aloud in the plenary and be seen in cahoots with Muslim resistance, all reservations were submitted in writing to become a clear but very quiet addenda in the final publication.

At the same time, Joaquin Navarro-Valls, press secretary for the Holy See, when asked what steps the Vatican itself would take to assure women positions in decision-making roles in a church that limits authority to the clerical state, responded that the delegation "did not speak for the 400 citizens of the Vatican but only for the 90,000,000 Catholics around the world." The Vatican, it seems, will call others to honor the needs of women, but is hard put to say what it will itself do within its own confines to promote the full and equal participation of women, despite the fact that women are, in most part, missing from the decision-making processes of the church as well.

Forty Muslim countries, too, endorsed the Beijing Platform for Action but then, in the plenary, submitted public reservations against specific items in the document—the enlarged definition of family to include more than homes with both parents present, children's rights as opposed to parental control over sexual matters, inheritance rights of female children and reproductive self-determination for women—on the grounds that these elements "violate the Shariy'eh, Islamic religious law." What governments are asked to renounce, in other words, theocratic states claim the right to maintain on theological grounds defined by men.

At the same time, 180 governments of the world have signed a document calling for programs designed to increase participation for women in decision-making bodies; give reproductive self-determination to women who are being either forcibly sterilized or impregnated against their wills; provide for the punishment of rape as war crime; give public recognition and valuation of women's unremunerated domestic work; endorse gender sensitivity in all areas of decision making; promise the protection of the girl-child from trafficking, early marriage, and forced prostitution; enlarge economic and social roles; recognize that human rights are women's rights; and provide new access to economic resources.

What's more, Beijing describes the specific programs it will take to achieve equality in all these areas.

The women along the Peace Train route who wanted economic security, personal protective legislation, health care, and political power may at least take comfort in the legitimation of their needs, whatever the remaining obstacles to their progress. After all, the Berlin Wall finally fell when least expected, ultimately the Soviet Union disintegrated, even the Great Wall of China was eventually breached. And, in case you're still inclined to doubt the persistence of change in a reactionary climate, it is important to realize that it is impossible to buy a Mao jacket and black Chinese sandals in the newly Westernized stores of China.

If Beijing proves nothing else, it may prove that change is coming for women, too, however slow the process.

Was the Fourth UN Conference on Women a success? It is a strange and decisive moment. In many instances, the statistics describing the role and status of women are getting worse every day. On the other hand, the notion that discrimination against women is moral is also getting thinner every day as well. Maybe the Chinese are right: Maybe water really does wear away the rock.

—*Joan Chittister, OSB*

APPENDIXES

NOTES ON
CONTRIBUTORS

INDEX

Appendix A
Sources for Further Information

Documents and Online Sites

A copy of the complete Beijing document can be obtained from the conference secretariat at DC2-1234, United Nations, New York, N.Y. 10017 (fax: 212-963-3463)

The document is also available on the following email conferences:

un.wcw.doc.eng (English)
un.wcw.doc.fre (French)
un.wcw.doc.spa (Spanish)

A complete listing of the commitments can be found on the WomensNet World Wide Web site: http://www.womensnet.apc.org/beijing/scoreboard.html

Additional information about the conference is also available from the following electronic sites:

* Global Net/Global FaxNet: Offers a one-page bulletin carrying follow-up information on Beijing as well as news related to UN meetings and special topics produced by the International Women's Tribune Center (iwtc@igc.apc.org).

* Division for the Advancement of Women: Provides news on the work of the division and the Commission on the Status of Women, updates on CEDAW, follow-up to the Fourth World Conference on Women, and a calendar of events (daw@undp.org).

* Commission for the Advancement of Women, Interaction: This site features "Mobilizing Beyond Beijing" information and activities, including government commitments and NGOs' actions at and after Beijing. Interaction is an association of nongovernmental organizations working in development (interaction@interaction.org).

* UNIFEM: The United Nations Development Fund for Women (UNIFEM) provides direct support for women's projects and promotes the inclusion of women in the decision-making process of mainstream development programs. This site describes UNIFEM's mandate (melanie.roth@undp.org).

* President's Interagency Council on Women: Official site of the U.S. delegation to the Fourth World Conference on Women. Includes documents (U.S. and global), press releases, and reports (rubinson@usia.gov).

* United Nations Development Program: Find documents relating to the work of the Commission on the Status of Women, including background documents for the priority themes of the CSW and Beijing follow-up (gopher:// gopher.undp.org).

To obtain a copy of the Women's Bureau report on the "Working Women Count" Honor Roll, call 1-800-827-5335 or send an email to wb-wwc@dol.gov. The Women's Bureau home page is www.dol.gov/dol/wb/welcome.html. See part VI for a discussion of the honor roll.

For information about the Contract with Women of the U.S.A. contact Women's Environment and Development Organization (WEDO), 845 3d Avenue, 15th Floor, New York, N.Y. 10022 (fax: 212-759-8647; telephone: 212-759-7982; email: wedo@igc.apc.org). See appendix D for a discussion of this contract.

For information about UNIFEM, please call the U.S. Committee for UNIFEM, 800-55UNIFEM; 1619 Massachusetts Avenue N.W., 6th Floor, Washington, D.C. 20036. See part VI for a discussion of UNIFEM.

Additional Related Websites

The following website is a project of the Stanley Foundation, which is very involved in the follow-up activities: http://globetrotter.berkeley.edu:8080/CFR/ NAGD/StanleyFR.html.

The Platform for Action can be found at: http://www.un.org/dpcsd/daw/csw or http://www.un.org/womenwatch.

The President's Interagency Council on Women site is: http://whitehouse. gov/WH/EOP/Women/IACW/html/IACWhome.html.

Womansword: A Newsletter for Activists: http://www.feminist.com/wword. html.

Appendix B
Participants and Presentations

Organizations Represented in Pittsburgh/Beijing '95 and Beyond

Alliance for Progressive Action
American Association of University Women
Amnesty International
Baha'i Community of Greater Pittsburgh
Bethlehem Haven
Black Women's Leadership Conference
Business and Professional Women's Organization
California University of Pennsylvania
Carlow College
Carnegie Mellon University
Center for Victims of Violent Crimes
Chatham College
Church Women United
City Theater
Clothesline Project
Coalition to Counter Hate Groups
Community of Reconciliation
Duquesne University
East Liberty Presbyterian Church
Ellis School
Episcopal Church Women
Episcopal Diocese of Pittsburgh
Executive Women's Council
Fair Housing Partnership of Pittsburgh
Female Adolescent Drug Abuse Study
Girl Scouts of Southwestern Pennsylvania
Greater Pittsburgh Commission on Women
Hadassah
Hope Center
Islamic Center of Pittsburgh
Just Harvest

LaRoche College
League of Women Voters
Life-Work International
Magee Womancare International
Magee-Womens Hospital
National Council of Jewish Women
North Hills National Organization for Women
Pennsylvania Peace Links
Pittsburgh Peace Institute
Pittsburgh World Affairs Council
Planned Parenthood
Presbyterian Women's Association
Seton Hill College
Sexual Assault and Family Crisis Unit, City of Pittsburgh Police
Sister's Place Inc.
Slippery Rock University
Sojourner House
Successful Women
Thomas Merton Center
Three Rivers Community Fund
UNICEF
United Nations Association of Pittsburgh
United States Committee for UNIFEM/Western Pennsylvania Chapter
University of Pittsburgh
Westminster Presbyterian Church
Wheeler's Paints
WomansPlace
Women in Development Conference
Women's International League for Peace and Freedom
Women's International Network of Pittsburgh
World Federalist Association of Pittsburgh
YWCA
Zonta International

PLEN Beijing Conference Participants

Marianne Alexander, executive director of PLEN, Washington, D.C.
Heidi Arola, student, Newcomb College (Tulane), New Orleans, La.
Esther Barazzone, president, Chatham College, Pittsburgh, Pa.
Jennifer Chase, student, Wells College, Aurora, N.Y.

Justine Craig, student, Stephens College, Columbia, Mo.

Nancy Eng, student, Douglass College (Rutgers), New Brunswick, N.J.

Andrea Graybehl, student, Mount St. Mary's College, Los Angeles, Calif.

Susan Homer, student, Chatham College, Pittsburgh, Pa.

Nicole Junas, student, Trinity College of Vermont, Burlington, Vt.

Debra Leibowitz, political science doctoral student, Rutgers University, and faculty member for the program

Beth McMullin, student, College of Notre Dame of Maryland, Baltimore, Md.

Heather Montgomery, student, William Woods University, Fulton, Mo.

Kathy Phillips, student, Mount St. Mary's College, Los Angeles, Calif.

Wendy Reilly, student, Douglass College (Rutgers), New Brunswick, N.J.

Don Scruggs, political science professor and faculty member for the program, Stephens College, Columbia, Mo.

Manomi Tennakoon, student, College of St. Elizabeth, Morristown, N.J.

Pam Tevebaugh, student, Douglass College (Rutgers), New Brunswick, N.J.

Christine Turner, student, Newcomb College (Tulane), New Orleans, La.

Dawn Walker, student, Douglass College (Rutgers), New Brunswick, N.J.

Conversations After Beijing

The following is a partial list of programs presented in and around the Pittsburgh area by Beijing conference and forum attendees from September 1995 through April 1996.

9/18/95 Hebron Presbyterian Church

9/19/95 Interview with Anderson Little for WDUQ radio

9/22/95 Magee-Womens Hospital—"A Celebration of Women"

9/23/95 Interview with the *Pittsburgh Post-Gazette*

9/26/95 Ellis Middle School

9/27/95 Westminster Presbyterian Church

9/29/95 Pittsburgh Council for International Visitors

9/30/95 American Association of University Women

10/1/95 Trinity United Methodist Church

10/2/95 Wilkinsburg Women's Club

10/3/95 Clean Water Action

10/3/95 Diocesan Council Meeting, Episcopal Church

10/3/95 St. Thomas More Church

10/5/95 Baha'is of Pittsburgh

10/5/95 Mt. Lebanon Episcopal Church

10/5/95 Pittsburgh Church Women United

10/5/95 Seton Hill College

10/5/95 United Jewish Fund
10/5/95 Upper St. Clair Rotary Club
10/9/95 Friends of Tibet
10/10/95 Carnegie Library of Homestead, Pa.
10/10/95 Twentieth Century Club
10/11/95 North Hills NOW meeting
10/12/95 Friends Meeting House
10/12/95 Task Force on Women and Addiction
10/15/95 Boule (a men's social group), with spouses
10/15/95 Community of Reconciliation
10/16/95 Greensburg Book Club
10/16/95 Women's Professional Networking Group
10/18/95 Baldwin High School
10/18/95 Derry Area High School
10/18/95 Indiana University of Pennsylvania
10/21/95 Carnegie Mellon University student center
10/22/95 Friends Peace and Justice Group
10/23/95 Mount de Chantal Academy, Wheeling, W.Va.
10/23/95 University of Pittsburgh, Graduate School of Public/International
    Affairs
10/24/95 Equitable Life Association
10/25/95 Kirkpatrick and Lockhart law firm
10/25/95 Northeasterners (social group)
10/25/95 Zonta
10/27/95 Grail (international women's organization), Cincinnati, Ohio
10/28/95 World Federalist Association National Assembly, Philadelphia
10/29/95 St. John's Lutheran Church
10/30/95 King's College, Edinboro, Pa.
11/1/95 Westminster College
11/3/95 Unitarian Universalist Church
11/4/95 Asia Women's Institute
11/7/95 Scottdale Reading Club
11/8/95 California University of Pennsylvania
11/8/95 Moon High School
11/9/95 Council of Jewish Women
11/9/95 University of Pittsburgh, Asian studies
11/20/95 Carlow College
11/28/95 Pittsburgh YWCA
11/29/95 Sisters of Divine Providence, mother house
12/5/95 LaRoche College

12/5/95 Upper St. Clair League of Women Voters
12/11/95 Friendship Village
1/10/96 Temple Rodef Shalom, men's committee
1/17/96 Forbes Hospice Jack and Jill Group
1/30/96 National Association for Female Executives dinner
2/14/96 Duquesne University
2/25/96 Peace Links Reports on Beijing and Looks Beyond
2/29/96 Business and Professional Women's Club, North Hills
2/29/96 International Women's Association
3/6/96 Community College of Allegheny County
3/21/96 Federal Women's Program
3/21/96 Juniata College
4/3/96 Aurora Reading Club (African American social club)

This is by no means a complete list of all the times and places in the western Pennsylvania area where the women's conference was being discussed. In addition to these, hundreds of other presentations were made in schools, homes, meetings, and workplaces; at breakfasts, lunches, dinners; by individuals and panels; to large groups and small, young and old. This list is meant only to reflect the diversity and wide-ranging interest of the people who wanted to hear more about what happened in Beijing. It is meant to illustrate that those individuals who attended the conference, the forum, or both truly acted as conduits for the "water" and the "electricity" of Beijing. They brought Beijing home to Pittsburgh and in so doing, fulfilled one of the goals of this conference:

Let us tell the world—and let us tell it with pride: the empowerment of women is the empowerment of all humanity! (Boutros Boutros-Ghali, UN Secretary-General, Introduction to the Platform for Action)

Appendix C
The Peace Train Itinerary

City Meetings and Workshops

St. Petersburg

Central Meeting: Russia, Fifty Years After the Second World War
Parallel Workshops: Transition and Its Impact on the Lives of Women
Disarmament and Conversion Projects in Russia
Women and Entrepreneurship

Kiev

Central Meeting: Nuclear Disarmament
Parallel Workshops: Protecting the Environment
Visit to Chernobyl Victims in Hospital

Bucharest

Central Meeting: The Economic and Social Situation of Women in Romania
Parallel Workshops: Women and Health—with a special focus on HIV patients
Visit to a Training School for Nurses
Poverty and Prostitution

Sofia

Central Meeting: The War in Former Yugoslavia
Parallel Workshops: The Fight Against Organized Crime
Minority Rights in Bulgaria
Violence Against Women

Istanbul

Central Meeting: History of the Turkish Women's Movement
Parallel Workshops: Women's Human Rights
Fundamentalism and the Status of Women
Peace in a Multi-ethnic Society
Visit to a Women's Library

Odessa

Central Meeting: Peace Around the Black Sea

Almaty

Central Meeting: Women and Society in Kazakhstan
Parallel Workshops: Peace in Central Asia Nuclear Testing and Its Effects in
  Semipalatinsk

Urumqi—canceled by Chinese government
Central Meeting: Women in China
Parallel Workshop: History of the Silk Route

Appendix D
The Platform for Action

The objective of the Platform for Action, which is in full conformity with the purposes and principles of the Charter of the United Nations and international law, is the empowerment of all women. The full realization of all human rights and fundamental freedoms of all women is essential for the empowerment of women. While the significance of national and regional particularities and various historical, cultural and religious backgrounds must be borne in mind, it is the duty of States, regardless of their political, economic, and cultural systems, to promote and protect all human rights and fundamental freedoms. The implementation of this platform, including through national laws and the formulation of strategies, policies, programs and development priorities, is the sovereign responsibility of each State, in conformity with all human rights and fundamental freedoms. The significance of and full respect for various religious and ethical values, cultural backgrounds and philosophical convictions of individuals and their communities should contribute to the full enjoyment by women of their human rights in order to achieve equality, development and peace.

—*The Platform for Action, Paragraph 9*

A Summary of the Platform for Action

The Platform for Action has important implications for community action. The following is a summary of the most pertinent parts of the platform—the critical areas of concern, objectives, and strategic actions, as well as the commitments made by the U.S. delegation in its statement.*

* Compiled from a summary prepared by the Executive Committee of PBB, information received from the UN Department of Public Information, and "UNIFEM in Beijing and Beyond."

In May 1997, the President's Interagency Council on Women published a report, *America's Commitment: Federal Programs Benefitting Women and New Initiatives as Follow-up to the UN Fourth World Conference on Women.* This report is available, at no charge, from the interagency: U.S. Department of State, 2201 C St., N.W., Room 2906, Washington, D.C. 20520. Phone: (202) 647-6227; fax: (202) 647-5337; http://secretary.state.gov/www/iacw/index.html. The report will be updated periodically on the website.

The United States made specific commitments in seven of the twelve critical areas of concern identified in the Platform for Action.

1. Poverty

Findings

The number of women living in poverty has increased disproportionately to the number of men, especially in the developing countries. This feminization of poverty has resulted from rigidly ascribed gender roles and from women's limited access to power, education, training and productive resources, and economic opportunities.

Objectives

Governments, with the full and equal participation of women, are to review and modify macroeconomic and social policies to ensure women's advancement. Multilateral financial institutions such as the World Bank, the Asian Bank, and the Grameen Bank, which deal with development, need to help countries reduce their external debts without having a negative impact on the lives of women and children.

Strategic Actions

Review, adopt, and maintain economic policies and development strategies that address the needs and efforts of women in poverty.

Revise laws and administrative procedures to ensure women's equal rights and access to economic resources.

Provide women with access to savings and credit mechanisms and institutions.

Conduct research to address the feminization of poverty.

2. Education and Training

Findings

The right to education is a human right for girls and boys, men and women. Approximately 100 million children, including at least 60 million girls, are without access to primary schooling. More than two-thirds of the world's 960 million illiterate adults are women. Discrimination in girls' access to education persists in many areas due to customary attitudes, early marriage and pregnancy, inadequate and gender-biased teaching, sex harassment, and lack of school facilities. Women should have access to continuing education.

Objectives

Governments are to commit themselves, by the year 2000, to universal access to basic education and completion of primary education by at least 80 percent of primary school-age children, to closing the gender gap in primary and secondary school education by the year 2005, and to universal primary education in all countries before the year 2015.

Strategic Actions

Ensure equal access to education.

Reduce illiteracy among women.

Improve women's access to vocational training, science and technology, and continuing education.

Develop nondiscriminatory education and training.

Allocate sufficient resources for and monitor the implementation of educational reforms.

Promote lifelong education and training for girls and women.

U.S. Commitment

The administration is committed to ratification of the Convention on the Elimination of All Forms of Discrimination Against Women (CEDAW), article 10 of which addresses women's education (see "CEDAW: A Bill of Rights for Women" in part VI).

3. Health

Findings

Women have the right to enjoy the highest attainable standard of physical and mental health and the right to control and decide freely and responsibly on measures regarding sexual and reproductive health, free of coercion, discrimination, and violence. Women have different and unequal access to and use of basic health resources and different and unequal opportunities for protection, promotion, and maintenance of their health. Health policies and programs often perpetuate gender stereotypes and fail to take account of women's lack of autonomy regarding their health. Public health systems have deteriorated in many countries, especially developing countries. Sex and gender-based violence, including physical and psychological abuse, traffic in women and girls, and other forms of abuse and sex exploitation, place girls and women at high risk of physical and mental trauma, disease, and unwanted pregnancy; the increasing longevity of men and women also makes health issues of both a concern.

Objectives

Governments agree to provide women with more accessible and affordable health care services, including sexual and reproductive health care, which includes family planning information and services. They agree to reduce maternal mortality by at least 50 percent of the 1990 levels by the year 2000.

Strategic Actions

Increase women's access throughout the life cycle to appropriate, affordable, and quality health care, information, and related services.

Strengthen prevention programs that promote women's health.

Undertake gender-sensitive initiatives that address HIV/AIDS, other sexually transmitted diseases, and sexual and reproductive health issues.

Promote research and disseminate information on women's health.

Increase resources and monitor follow-up for women's health.

U.S. Commitment

The Department of Health and Human Services plans action on a range of problems of concern to women. Special attention is to be given to women of low income and from ethnic and racial minorities.

Plan to reduce smoking among children and adolescents by 50 percent.

Prevent teen pregnancy by improving access to health and family planning services and health education in schools.

Establish a Council on Children and Youth to develop a Children's Budget.

Support partnerships with governments and communities and coordinate research and evaluation.

Address health needs of older women through new Women's Health Initiative.

Establish a National Women's Health Clearinghouse and a toll-free health information line.

Conduct contraceptive research and development.

Develop public policy agenda on HIV/AIDS specific to women, adolescents, and children.

4. Violence

Findings

Violence against women nullifies the enjoyment by women of their human rights and fundamental freedoms. The term "violence against women" means any act of gender-based violence that results in or is likely to result in physical, sexual, or psychological harm or suffering to women, including threats of such acts, coercion, or arbitrary deprivation of liberty, whether occurring in public or private life, including the family. Knowledge has greatly expanded since the 1985 Nairobi conference about the causes and consequences of as well as incidence and measures to combat such violence. In all societies, women and girls are subject, to a greater or lesser degree, to physical, sexual, and psychological abuse whatever their income, class, or culture.

Objectives

Governments agree to adopt and implement legislation to end violence against women and work actively to ratify and implement all international agreements that relate to violence against women. They also agree there should be shelter, legal aid, and other services for girls and women at risk, and counseling and rehabilitation for the perpetrators.

Strategic Actions

Take integrated measures to prevent and eliminate violence against women. In particular, organize, support, and fund community-based education and training campaigns to raise awareness about violence; mobilize local communities to teach and use appropriate gender-sensitive methods of conflict resolution.

Study the causes and consequences of violence against women and the effectiveness of preventive measures.

Eliminate trafficking in women and assist victims of violence due to prostitution and such trafficking.

U.S. Commitment

The Violence Against Women Office at the Justice Department has been established with a $1.6 billion budget for the next six years to lead a comprehensive national effort to fight domestic violence and other crimes against women.

The director of the office is authorized to bring broader public attention to the problem of violence against women through meetings with law enforcement and advocacy groups across the country and through public appearances and media interviews.

5. Armed Conflict

Findings

Peace is inextricably linked with equality between men and women and development. Armed and other types of conflicts and terrorism and hostage-taking still persist in many parts of the world. Gross violations of human rights such as genocide, ethnic cleansing, and rape, now identified as a war crime, are strongly condemned and must be stopped. Equal access and full participation of women in decision-structures and their involvement in all efforts to prevent and resolve conflict are essential to maintain and promote peace and security.

Objectives

Governments are to convert military resources to peaceful purposes and to work toward ratification of international instruments that prohibit or restrict the use of landmines.

Strategic Actions

Increase the participation of women in conflict resolution at decision-making levels and protect women living in situations of armed and other conflicts.

Reduce excessive military expenditures and control the availability of armaments.

Promote nonviolent forms of conflict resolution and reduce the incidence of human rights abuse in conflict situations.

Promote women's contribution to fostering a culture of peace.

Provide protection, assistance, and training to refugee women, other displaced women in need of international protection, and internally displaced women.

6. Economic Structures

Findings

In most parts of the world, women are virtually absent from or are poorly represented in economic decision making, including formulating financial, monetary, commercial, and other economic policies as well as tax systems and rules governing pay. In the last decade, women's participation in remunerated work in the formal and informal labor market has increased significantly. Women still work in agriculture but increasingly have been involved in micro-, small-, and medium-size enterprises, and have become more dominant in the informal sector.

Objectives

Governments are asked to guarantee the right of women to equal pay for equal work and to integrate a gender perspective into all economic restructuring and structural adjustment practices. Sexual harassment, lack of affordable child care, and inflexible working hours need to be rectified.

Strategic Actions

Promote women's economic rights and independence, including access to employment and appropriate working conditions and control over economic resources.

Facilitate women's equal access to resources, including credit, as well as to employment, markets, and trade.

Strengthen women's economic capacity and commercial networks.

Eliminate occupational segregation and all forms of employment discrimination.

Promote harmonization of work and family responsibilities for women and men.

U.S. Commitment

The Women's Bureau of the Department of Labor will launch a campaign to solicit pledges from employers, organizations, and community groups to make thousands of changes in policies and programs affecting improved pay and benefits, work and family, and increased value for women's work (see "'Working Women Count' Honor Role" in part VI).

The Department of the Treasury has established the Community Development Financial Institutions to support community development through financial support, technical assistance, and training to microlenders. This fund will coordinate a new Federal Microenterprise Initiative to ensure coherence among the microenterprise programs in a number of federal agencies.

The Interagency Committee on Women's Business Enterprise in cooperation with the National Women's Business Council, a private sector group of successful women entrepreneurs and nongovernmental women's business advocates, has submitted its first annual report to the president and Congress emphasizing four areas:

(1) opening the public marketplace for free and open competition for procurement of goods and services by the government to meet 5 percent of women's business contracts in each participating agency,

(2) collecting data and conducting research on women-owned businesses and organizing a national conference in November 1995 at Northwestern University's School of Business to assess the situation,

(3) expanding the support of entrepreneurship through technical assistance, training, and information for women business owners, and

(4) opening capital assets for start-up and expansion of women-owned business.

USAID will continue to support microenterprise programming for women.

7. Power-Sharing

Findings

The Universal Declaration of Human Rights states that all people have the right to take part in the government of their country. Empowerment and autonomy of women and the improvement of women's social, economic, and political status is essential for the achievement of accountable government and administration and sustainable development in all areas of life. Despite the widespread movement toward democratization in most countries, women are largely underrepresented at most levels of government, especially in executive and legislative bodies and in international institutions.

Objectives

Governments are to commit to the goal of gender balance in governmental bodies and political parties and are to ensure gender balance in delegations to the UN and other international organizations.

Strategic Actions

Take measures to ensure women's equal access to and full participation in power structures and decision making.

Increase women's capacity to participate in decision making and leadership.

U.S. Commitment

The administration is committed to Senate ratification of CEDAW, several articles of which refer to political empowerment of women.

8. Institutional Mechanisms

Findings

National machineries (committees, councils, departments, or offices) have been established in almost every UN member state to design, implement, monitor, evaluate, advocate, and mobilize support for policies that lead to women's advancement. But these are often marginalized in national government structures and are hampered by unclear mandates and by inadequate staff, training, data, resources, and political leadership.

Objectives

Governments are to promote the advancement of women through such mechanisms as gender-oriented policy analyses and statistical compilations.

Strategic Actions

Create or strengthen national machineries and other governmental bodies.

Integrate gender perspectives in legislation, public policies, programs, and projects.

Generate and disseminate data and information for planning and evaluation that reflect a more accurate picture of the situation of women.

U.S. Commitment

An interagency council of ten federal departments and agencies is studying ways to implement the Platform for Action in the United States. The U.S. delegation to the conference will serve in an advisory capacity to the council.

USAID is supporting two programs, one on women's political participation and another on women's legal literacy.

9. Human Rights

Findings

A major goal expressed in the UN charter is the promotion and protection of human rights and fundamental freedoms without regard to race, sex, nationality, or religion. The protection and promotion of human rights is the first responsibility of governments. The gap between the existence of rights and their effective enjoyment derives from a lack of commitment by governments to protecting those rights and failure by governments to inform women and men alike about them.

Objectives

Governments should advocate equality and nondiscrimination under the law and promote women's legal literacy. They are asked to limit reservations to CEDAW and to withdraw reservations contrary to its purpose.

Strategic Actions

Promote and protect the human rights of women through the ratification and full implementation of all human rights instruments, especially CEDAW.

Ensure equality and nondiscrimination under the law and in practice.

Achieve legal literacy.

U.S. Commitment

The administration is committed to Senate ratification of CEDAW. The Justice Department is enforcing the 1994 Freedom of Access to Clinic Entrances Act. USAID is implementing the Women's Legal Rights Initiative.

10. The Media

Findings

In the last decade, advances in information technology have facilitated a global communications network that transcends national boundaries and affects public policy, private attitudes, and behavior. But gender-stereotyping in the media continues to project negative and degrading images of women and does not provide a balanced picture of women's diverse lives or contributions to society.

Objectives

The media are encouraged to create nonstereotyped, balanced, and diverse images of women. They will develop self regulatory guidelines to address violent, degrading, and pornographic materials.

Strategic Actions

Increase women's participation in and access to expression and decision making in and through the media and new technologies of communications.

Present a balanced and nonstereotyped portrayal of women in the media.

11. The Environment

Findings

Through their management and use of natural resources, women provide sustenance to their families and communities. As consumers and producers, caretakers of their families, and educators, women play an important role in promoting sustainable development. Women remain largely absent at nearly all levels of policy formulation and decision making in natural resource and environmental management, conservation, protection, and rehabilitation. Their experience and skills in advocacy and monitoring of proper resource management are too often marginalized.

Objectives

Rural women's traditional knowledge and practices are to be integrated into the development of environmental management programs. Women are to be given full and equal participation in control over resources.

Strategic Actions

Involve women actively in environmental decision making at all levels.

Integrate gender concerns and perspectives in policies and programs for sustainable development.

Strengthen or establish mechanisms at the national, regional, and international levels to assess the impact of development and environmental policies on women.

12. The Girl Child

Findings

In many countries, available indicators show that the girl child is discriminated against from the earliest stages of life, through childhood, and into adulthood. Harmful attitudes and practices persist, such as female genital mutilation, son preference, violence against women, sex exploitation, sex abuse, discrimination against girls in food allocation, and other practices related to health and well-being.

Objectives

Governments are to enact laws to ensure that marriage is entered into only with free and full consent. Steps will be taken to abolish traditional practices harmful to girls, including female genital mutilation, female infanticide, prenatal sex selection, early marriage, sexual exploitation, sexual abuse, and discrimination against girls in food allocation.

Strategic Actions

Eliminate all forms of discrimination against the girl child including discrimination in education, skills development, training, and health and nutrition.

Eliminate negative cultural attitudes and practices against girls.

Promote and protect the rights of the girl child and increase awareness of her needs and potential.

Eliminate the economic exploitation of child labor and protect young girls at work.

Eradicate violence against the girl child.

Promote the girl child's awareness of and participation in social, economic, and political life.

Strengthen the role of the family in improving the status of the girl child.

A Brief Analysis of the Beijing Declaration and the Platform for Action

The Platform for Action together with the Beijing Declaration was approved by 189 member states on September 15, 1995. These documents were significantly influenced by the global women's movement, women's networks, and nongovernmental organizations. They are the product of the most highly participatory and inclusive process ever organized under the auspices of the United Nations and may be the most widely read UN documents in history. While they are imperfect documents representing compromises on language, glossing over of conflicting views, and weakened or diluted action verbs, they are the strongest documents on gender equality, empowerment, and justice ever produced and agreed to by the world's governments.*

The Beijing Declaration and the Platform for Action represent a powerful consolidation of the most significant gains made by women in previous UN conference agreements in the unique context of seeing the world through women's eyes. The 135-page Platform for Action is 361 paragraphs of carefully negotiated text packed with action statements and ideas. It is a unique road map for action on equality, development, and peace, which can be used at all levels of decision making. It is a tool for accountability with governments and international institutions and a comprehensive agenda for progress toward a better future for all. It names the multiple problems facing women and girls of all ages including all kinds of violence and exploitation (child abuse, rape, genital mutilation, trafficking, etc.) and is filled with admissions of complicity and responsibility such as governments admitting that "the major cause of the continued deterioration of the global environment is the unsustainable pattern of consumption and production, particularly in industrialized countries, which is a matter of grave concern, aggravating poverty and imbalances." It pledges all governments to mobilize the political will and resources to implement the platform so as to be accountable to the world's women.

A preliminary list of commitments from fifty-six governments showed that the majority of actions are in the health and education sectors. Very few resource commitments were made although many commitments imply substantial new monies or resource reallocations. Only Cambodia made a commitment in the area of armed conflict. The United States made seven detailed commitments and has established the President's Interagency Council on Women as a mechanism for coordinating the implementation of the Platform for Action including the seven commitments. The UN conference Secretariat reported that most of the commitments fell into three broad categories: reform of national policies, numerical targets for the year 2000, and frameworks for international development cooperation.

The document leaves many issues unaddressed or inadequately covered. NGOs were extremely creative in formulating ideas for inclusion in the platform. There were far-sighted proposals put forth by NGOs that never made it into the

*This analysis includes excerpts from a paper prepared by the Women's Environment and Development Organization.

document, such as a ban on the patenting of life forms and imposing an immediate moratorium on such patents. Other excellent proposals introduced into the draft platform, such as a 1 percent cap on military expenditures were deleted in earlier stages of negotiation. However, a substantial part of what women demanded was included in some fashion in the Beijing documents.

All governments, the United Nations system including the International Monetary Fund and the World Bank, nongovernmental organizations, the media, and the private sector are urged to "take immediate action" and be "accountable" in their efforts to fully implement the relevant recommendations and targets in the platform by the year 2000.

The prime minister of Norway, Gro Harlem Brundtland, one of the last speakers to address the conference's plenary session, said:

> The views expressed here—and the news which escaped from here—will irrevocably shape world opinion. The story of Beijing cannot be untold. The measure of our success cannot be fully assessed today. It will depend on the will of us all to fulfill what we have promised.

The views were echoed in the concluding statement of Gertrude Mongella, secretary-general of the conference:

> The Fourth World Conference on Women is concluded, but the real work of transforming words into action is only now beginning.

> Disseminate the platform on your return home to your countries and let the message be loud and clear: Action now!

The United Nations Fourth World Conference on Women: The Twelve Critical Areas of Concern*

The Beijing Platform for Action lists 12 "Critical Areas of Concern" that are identified as the main obstacles to the advancement of women around the world. Governments, the international community, and civil society including nongovernmental organizations and the private sector are called upon to take strategic action in the following critical areas:

1. The persistent and increasing burden of *poverty* on women;

2. Inequalities and inadequacies in and unequal access to *education* and training;

3. Inequalities and inadequacies in and unequal access to *health* care and related services;

*From the *Platform for Action and the Beijing Declaration,* United Nations Department of Public Information, United Nations, New York, 1996.

4. *Violence* against women;

5. The effects of *armed* or other kinds of *conflict* on women, including those living under foreign occupation;

6. Inequality in *economic structures* and policies, in all forms of productive activities and in access to resources;

7. Inequality between men and women in *power-sharing* and decision-making at all levels;

8. Insufficient *institutional mechanisms* at all levels to promote the advancement of women;

9. Lack of respect for and inadequate promotion and protection of the *human rights* of women;

10. Stereotyping of women and inequality in women's access to and participation in all communication systems, especially in the *media;*

11. Gender inequalities in the management of natural resources and in the safeguarding of the *environment;*

12. Persistent discrimination against and violation of the rights of *the girl-child.*

Women's Environment and Development Organization

> The Platform [of Action], while not legally binding, represents a politically binding contract with the world's women.
>
> —Bella Abzug

In 1996 Bella Abzug came to Chatham College to talk about WEDO (Women's Environment and Development Organization), an organization devoted to monitoring the commitments made by the U.S. government to the platform for action. WEDO has created a Contract with Women of the U.S.A., which summarizes and adapts key elements of the Platform for Action that are relevant to U.S. women. The purpose of the contract is to ensure that the promises made in Beijing, as well as the funding, support, and structures outlined in the platform, are turned into reality for all women. The objectives of the contract campaign include the following:

* Promote women's political participation in cooperation with voter education and registration projects.

* Develop state and local contracts with women (in cooperation with the Center for Women Policy Studies and progressive legislators).

* Monitor local, state, and national legislation using contract scorecards and public hearings.

* Organize community strategies to implement the goals of the Contract with

Women of the U.S.A. in cooperation with women's organizations, advocates, and allies.

* Publicize the Contract with Women of the U.S.A. and United States–wide implementation efforts.

* Network with women's groups worldwide to share ideas, report, and build coalitions for action.

Contract with Women of the U.S.A.

As public officials, advocates for women's rights, policy makers, organizations, and individuals, we sign this Contract with Women of the U.S.A. to implement the Platform for Action adopted September 1995 at the United Nations Fourth World Conference on Women by consensus of 189 governments, including the United States of America.

We pledge our mutual commitment to the goal of equality and empowerment for [U.S.] women, who are the continuing majority population of our nation and states.

We pledge to work together to overcome discrimination based on sex, race, class, age, immigration status, sexual orientation, religion, or disability. We seek to end social, economic, and political inequities, violence, and the human rights abuses that still confront millions of women and girls in our country.

Looking to the twenty-first century, we enter into this Contract with Women of the U.S.A. for ourselves and for future generations to achieve our vision of a healthy planet and healthy nations, states, and communities, with peace, equality, and justice for all.

1. Empowerment of Women

We pledge to work for empowerment of women in all their diversity through their equal participation in decision making and equal access to shared power in government, in all spheres and at every level of society.

2. Sharing Family Responsibilities

We pledge to work for equal sharing of family responsibilities, recognition and respect for the diversity of families, and for practices and policies that enhance the multiple roles, security, and well-being of women and girls, men and boys.

3. Ending the Burden of Poverty

We pledge to work for economic justice and to end the increasing burden of poverty on women and their children, who are a majority of the poor. Recognizing the value of women's unpaid and underpaid labor to our families, communities, and economy, we support a living wage for all workers and adequate funding for welfare and other social safety nets, child care, education, and job training, and access to collateral-free credit for women-owned small businesses.

4. High Quality, Affordable Health Care

We pledge to work to reaffirm the rights of women and girls, regardless of income or where they live, to high quality, accessible, affordable, and respectful physical and mental health care, based on sound women-focused research.

5. Sexual and Reproductive Rights

We pledge to work to reaffirm and uphold the sexual and reproductive rights of all women, including their right to control their own reproductive lives free of coercion, violence, and harassment.

6. Workplace Rights

We pledge to work for guarantees of equal pay for work of comparable value and an end to discriminatory hiring and sexual harassment. We support family-friendly workplace practices, job training and opportunities programs, strengthening of affirmative action, employees' rights to organize unions, and to work in safe and healthy working environments.

7. Educational Equity

We pledge to work for educational equity for women and girls, including creation and strengthening of gender-fair multicultural curricula and teaching techniques, equal opportunities and access for girls and women throughout their lives to education, career development, training and scholarships, educational administration, and policy making.

8. Ending Violence

We pledge to work for policies and programs to end violence against women and children in every form and to ensure that violence against women and children is understood as a violation of their human and civil rights.

9. Protecting a Healthy Environment

We pledge to work to end environmental degradation and eliminate toxic chemicals, nuclear wastes, and other pollutants that threaten our health, our communities, countries, and planet. We uphold active roles by government at all levels and public and private sectors to continue and expand environmental protection programs.

10. Women as Peace Makers

We salute women's leading roles in peace movements and conflict resolution and pledge to work for their inclusion in policy making at all levels aimed at preventing war, halting the international arms trade, and eliminating all nuclear testing. We seek reductions in military spending and conversion of military facilities to socially productive purposes.

11. Honor Commitments and Ratify CEDAW

We pledge to support the commitments made by the United States government to implement the UN Platform for Action, which constitutes a contract with the world's women. We call on the U.S. Senate to ratify the Convention to Eliminate Discrimination Against Women (CEDAW), which the United States has signed.

12. A Long-Term Plan to Achieve Equality

We who are state and federal policy makers pledge to work in partnership with women's organizations to develop and enforce a long-term plan to achieve our goals of equality and empowerment for women. We support the reestablishment of a national advisory panel on women and the creation or strengthening of similar panels or commissions in each state, to ensure that governments at every level take the necessary steps to implement this contract.

Notes on Contributors

Janice Auth has had a variety of life and work experiences including teaching elementary and junior high school, raising her two daughters, writing, traveling, singing, and bringing people together. She is active in Pennsylvania Peace Links, both as a volunteer and as office administrator. She is a volunteer host for the Pittsburgh Council for International Visitors, and is on the advisory board of the International Poetry Forum. She traveled to Beijing to attend the NGO forum as a member of Pennsylvania Peace Links and as a representative from the Baha'i community of Pittsburgh and returned to China in 1997 as a member of the Peace Links delegation.

President of Chatham College since 1992, Esther L. Barazzone holds a Ph.D. and a master's in European intellectual history from Columbia University, where she was a Fellow of the Faculty. She serves on the boards of such national and state committees as Pennsylvania's Commission for Independent Colleges and Universities, the Women's College Coalition, the Commonwealth Partnership, and as national chair of PLEN (Public Leadership Educational Network, a consortium of women's colleges that sponsors leadership seminars, internships, and other learning experiences focusing on women and public policy. Locally, she serves on the boards of The Carnegie, Shadyside Hospital, the Historical Society of Western Pennsylvania, and other civic organizations.

Susan C. Bayley is originally from Pittsburgh. She became interested in the teaching of English as a foreign language while serving as a Peace Corps volunteer in Turkey. A graduate of Penn State, with master's degrees in linguistics from the University of Pittsburgh and in human resource development from George Washington University, she has lived and worked in Hawaii, England, and Beijing. She was the executive director of a TESOL (Teaching English to Speakers of Other Languages)

center in Alexandria, Virginia. She went to the NGO forum with Pennsylvania Peace Links and to travel with her sister, Toni Conaway.

Regina Birchem received her Ph.D. in cell biology from the University
of Georgia and is a professional biologist with special expertise in the
area of micropropagation of plants. She is the international vice president
of the Women's International League for Peace and Freedom (WILPF)
with the Geneva office and was one of the organizers of and passengers
on the WILPF Peace Train. Her diverse interests include writing and lec-
turing about international peace issues. She served as coordinator of
Pittsburgh/Beijing '95 and Beyond.

Andrea Blinn is executive director of the Fair Housing Partnership, an
organization dedicated to eliminating housing discrimination in the
greater Pittsburgh area. When she was twenty-two she spent a year
teaching literature at Zhengzhou University in the People's Republic of
China. In 1991 she spent a year studying Chinese in Taiwan. She has a
master's degree from the Graduate School of Public and International Affairs at the University of Pittsburgh. Her research there examined the impact of international development policies upon the lives of women, with
a particular focus on the prostitution industry in Thailand.

JoAnne W. Boyle is the president of Seton Hill College, a Roman
Catholic liberal arts college for women in Greensburg, Pennsylvania. She
is also the vice president of the Women's College Coalition and vice
chairman of the World Affairs Council of Pittsburgh. She received a B.A.
in history and English from Seton Hill, a master's in the teaching of English from Harvard University, and a Ph.D. in English from the University
of Pittsburgh. She has been awarded the Medallion of Distinction by the
University of Pittsburgh and the Golden Cauldron Award by Nanjing
University, China. In 1995 the governor of Pennsylvania named her a
Distinguished Daughter of Pennsylvania.

Carol Campbell, who has a background in foreign languages, special-
izes in international and intercultural communications, specifically inter-

national business etiquette and protocol, women in international business, and international business development. She earned her M.Ed. in international education, M.P.I.A. in public and international affairs, and a post-master's certificate in international-multicultural studies from the University of Pittsburgh. She also attended the University of Florence, Italy. In 1984 she initiated the Beyond Nairobi Conference for Women in Southwestern Pennsylvania, a forward-looking strategy session at the close of the UN Decade for Women. In 1995, she co-convened Pittsburgh/Beijing '95 and Beyond.

Joan Chittister, OSB, is executive director of Benetvision: A Resource and Research Center for Contemporary Spirituality. A member of the Benedictine Sisters of Erie, Pennsylvania, she is a widely published author and noted national and international lecturer on women in church and society, human rights, peace and justice, contemporary religious life and ecumenism. She holds a doctorate in speech communication theory from Penn State University, an M.A. in communication arts from the University of Notre Dame, and a B.A. from Mercyhurst College. She is a social psychologist, communications theorist, consultant to religious communities, and has taught at all levels of education. An elected fellow of St. Edmund's College, Cambridge University, she was a passenger on the Peace Train and attended the UN Fourth World Conference on Women as a delegate of Pax Christi and as a correspondent for the *National Catholic Reporter.*

Toni Conaway has a B.A. in history from the College of Wooster and a master's degree in history from the University of Pittsburgh. She is a founding member and past president of Pennsylvania Peace Links and has traveled to Germany, Russia, and China doing citizen diplomacy work. She has been active in the Presbyterian Church's peace work for many years. She has also served as a member of the Colloquium on Security Issues at the University of Pittsburgh in the 1980s, as chair of the League of Women Voters study on common security, and as a board member of the World Federalist Association of Pittsburgh.

Lee Fogarty received her Ph.D. from the University of Pittsburgh and is a psychologist in private practice in Pittsburgh. She has worked extensively with women and men in psychotherapy and with women's issues in the workplace and in medicine. Her professional activities include holding offices in the local Regional Task Force on Women and Addiction and the International Feminist Therapy Institute, as well as membership in the Association of Women in Psychology. Locally, she does volunteer work at the women's center and shelter and with the Three Rivers Community Fund. Her daughter, Traciy, who accompanied her to China, recently completed a master's degree in social work and is working with adolescent girls in a rehabilitation center.

Margaret E. Galey is a policy analyst and consultant, lecturer, and author. She was a staff member, Committee on Foreign Affairs, U.S. House of Representatives, from 1977 to 1989, where she conducted research, synthesized information, and reported to the chief of staff and committee members on the range of U.S. government relations with the UN system. She was a member of the political science faculty at the University of Pennsylvania from 1965 to 1977. She has a B.A. in political science and history from Vassar College, and an M.A. and Ph.D. in international relations from the University of Pennsylvania; she has numerous publications to her credit including journal articles, book chapters, speeches, and congressional committee reports.

Lois Goldstein, a former elementary school teacher, worked as administrative consultant for Pennsylvania Peace Links from 1984 to 1997. She has traveled extensively in China and was part of the Pennsylvania Peace Links delegations to China as guests of the All China Women's Federation in 1991 and as guests of CPAPD in 1997. She has served on the boards of the Thomas Merton Center and Educators for Social Responsibility. She was a passenger on the WILPF Peace Train.

Ann M. Harty is past president and a thirteen-year board member of Pennsylvania Peace Links. She has participated in a number of Peace Links cultural exchanges, including those with the Chinese People's Association for Peace and Disarmament. Founding president and board member of the Job Advisory Service and first director of continuing education at Carlow College, she has also served on the board of the Three Rivers Shakespeare Festival. She was a passenger on the WILPF Peace Train and attended the NGO forum in Beijing.

Sande Hendricks was vice president of the Greensburg Chapter of the American Association of University Women in 1995 and went to Beijing as a national delegate of that organization by invitation from the Citizen Ambassador Program of People to People International, who cosponsored her conference with the China Women's Association for Science and Technology. She attended the session on women in management. She was secretary of the Greensburg Art Club for two years and is the owner of the Creative Eye, where she creates innovative stone and wood sculpture on commission. Her work is in private collections from California to New York City.

Dorothy Hill, a graduate of Wellesley College, with a master's degree in education from Bank Street College in New York City, is the mother of three and grandmother of six. She has been a longtime peace activist, serving as president, and vice president of communications for Pennsylvania Peace Links. She is an elder at the Fox Chapel Presbyterian Church, where she does mission and peace work. She also serves on the board of trustees for the Chautauqua Institution. She is married to retired Alcoa executive William F. Hill II.

Elizabeth Vann Hobbs received a bachelor's degree from Hollins College in 1958. She worked for Harmarville Rehabilitation Center as a medical social worker from 1977 until her retirement in 1989. She has served on seven community boards and currently serves on the Children's Home Board and the Episcopal Church Women's Diocesan Board. She has lived in many different states and in the country of Suriname, South America. She attended the NGO forum as a part of the Anglican Women's Network.

Susan Homer is a 1996 graduate of Chatham College with a major in global policy studies. Through the Barbara Stone Hollander Leadership Fund at Chatham, she traveled to the conference with students from several women's colleges and Chatham president Esther Barazzone as representatives of PLEN (Public Leadership Education Network), a consortium of women's colleges that sponsors leadership seminars, internships, and other learning experiences focusing on women and public policy. Currently employed by the Center for Development and Population Activities in Washington, D.C., she interned at Global Links, a Pittsburgh nonprofit organization that distributes surplus medical supplies to developing countries.

Linda Hunt is an activist, actor, and playwright. She is the mother of three sons and is also a grandmother. A graduate of the Chatham College Gateway Program, she works as a family counselor with the Holy Family Institute. She attended the UN Fourth World Conference on Women NGO forum with help from a scholarship from Pittsburgh/Beijing '95 and Beyond. She hopes to write a play about her experiences at the forum.

Dorothy Jacko is a member of the Sisters of Charity and chair of the Religious Studies–Theology Department at Seton Hill College in Greensburg, Pennsylvania. Her interests include theologies from the Third World, women's theologies and spiritualities, and ecological theology. She also has a long-standing interest in dialogue with Asian religions, especially Hinduism and Buddhism.

Florence L. Johnson, who holds a master's of education degree from the University of Pittsburgh, taught school for twenty-three years in the Chicago and Pittsburgh public school systems. She attended the NGO forum as a member of Pennsylvania Peace Links. She is active in the Presbyterian Church and served as the 1996 commissioner to the general assembly. In 1997, she was elected moderator of the synod of the Trinity of the Presbyterian Church, USA, the first African-American female to be elected to this position. She is cochair of a special committee to raise funds for the work of the Pittsburgh YWCA and is on the board of Women's Space East, a shelter for abused women.

Brenda J. Kagle, a retired research engineer for Westinghouse Science and Technology Center, is the founder of the Pittsburgh chapter of UNIFEM. She became active in UN work through Zonta International and now serves on the board of the United Nations Association of Pittsburgh. She also does volunteer work for Domestic Violence Services in Butler County.

Valerie Lawrence, Pittsburgh poet, playwright, fiction writer, editor and educator, is the driving force behind the Children's Window to Africa, a program that connects children to their cultural origins. She has published poems and plays and has edited an anthology *Crossing Limits: African American Poets and American Jewish Poets*. She has received many awards for her work including the Java Sonata Music and Poetry Competition first-place poetry award; she is a visiting poet with the International Poetry Forum's Poet-in-Person project.

Tanya Kotys Ozor, as director of marketing communications and Womancare International for Magee-Women's Hospital, was instrumental in establishing the Magee-Savior's Family Planning Clinic in Moscow. She participated in Pittsburgh/Beijing '95 and Beyond and is a member of UNIFEM and the Women's Leadership Assembly. Since returning from Beijing, she has been working to promote breast cancer awareness within the Russian-speaking community of Pittsburgh.

Judy Palkovitz, chair of the National Hadassah Delegation to the UN Fourth World Conference on Women, is a national vice president of Hadassah, the largest women's volunteer organization in the United States. She is also extremely active locally. She is an officer of the United Jewish Federation, Riverview Center for Jewish Seniors, and the Jewish Healthcare Foundation. She is a full-time volunteer and represents Pittsburgh in many national and international venues.

Leone P. Paradise is a trial attorney practicing labor law with the National Labor Relations Board. Her community activities include serving as a member of the Urban Affairs Committee and as secretary of the North American Board of the Institute of Progressive Halakhah. She is a member of Pennsylvania Peace Links and the Pittsburgh AIDS Task Force Legal Committee. She says she has been a feminist since she was five years old. She is married, has a bunch of children and grandchildren, and bakes chocolate chip cookies for them.

Suzanne Polen has postgraduate training in biochemistry and micro-biology and worked for twenty-five years in research, most of the time at the University of Pittsburgh. She worked an additional five years with the Thomas Merton Center, doing organizing for justice in Central America and some work on the nuclear issues. She is one of the founders of the Three Rivers Community Fund, which gave a beginning grant to Pitts-burgh/Beijing '95 and Beyond.

Miki Rakay has traveled extensively in Europe and Asia. A retired teacher, she serves on the boards of Pennsylvania Peace Links and the World Federalist Association of Pittsburgh. She is the founder of the an-nual James Wright Poetry Festival in Martins Ferry, Ohio. While living in Ohio, she served as chair of the Mental Health Board of the Tri-County Women's Center and Children's Services. She was one of five Peace Links women invited by CPAPD to visit China in 1997.

Roseann P. Rife is executive director of the World Federalist Associa-tion (WFA) of Pittsburgh. A graduate of the University of Pennsylvania, she has also studied in France and China and holds a master's degree in international affairs from George Washington University. During her graduate studies, she interned at WFA and published a monograph on the United Nations financial crisis. From 1991 to 1992 she was a profes-sor at the Xian Foreign Language Institute in Xian, China. She attended the UN Fourth World Conference on Women as a representative with observer status from the WFA.

Mother of six and grandmother of six, Molly Rush is cofounder of the Thomas Merton Center, Pittsburgh Ministry for Justice and Peace and has been on the staff since 1973, currently as an organizer. She is west-ern Pennsylvania coordinator of the Citizens Budget Campaign. In 1980 she was one of the Plowshares Eight, a group of peace activists, including Daniel and Philip Berrigan, who were arrested after they entered a General Electric plant in King of Prussia, Pennsylvania, to protest against the first strike nuclear weapons being assembled there. That story is told in Liane Ellison Norman's book *Hammer of Justice: Molly Rush and the Plowshares Eight* published by the Pittsburgh Peace Institute. She traveled on the WILPF Peace Train.

Mary Rusinow traveled on the WILPF Peace Train from Helsinki to Beijing to attend the forum and conference as an observer for Pittsburgh/Beijing '95 and Beyond. She had lived for twenty-two years in Eastern Europe and Vienna before moving to Pittsburgh when her husband accepted a position as research professor at the University of Pittsburgh; she was particularly interested in the problems of the women of the former Communist countries. She worked for the UN Branch for the Advancement of Women in Vienna at the time of the Third Women's Conference in 1985 but did not attend. She was eager to attend the Beijing conference.

Edith Scheiner says her "life's interest and expertise has been to bring together people, groups, or projects that have the potential to change values or to create new ways of doing things." Professionally she has enjoyed many "firsts" as a woman. She was one of the first women to enter the University of Pittsburgh's midcareer graduate program for women in public administration (1964); first woman appointed to the board of the Public Housing Authority in McKeesport, Pennsylvania (1968); first woman director within Pennsylvania–Twin Rivers Council of Governments, a voluntary federation of eleven municipalities in the Mon-Valley of Allegheny County (1974). Along the way she was wife, mother, grandmother, widow. Today, at seventy-two, her favorite role is that of mentor.

Sohini Sinha describes herself as "a citizen of the world." Born in Britain of Indian parents, she grew up in Zambia and Zimbabwe, then moved to the United States to attend college. She has an undergraduate degree in business administration and economics from Edinboro University of Pennsylvania and a graduate degree in public and international affairs from the University of Pittsburgh. Employed by the World Federalist Association of Pittsburgh as program manager, she served as forum committee convener for Pittsburgh/Beijing '95 and Beyond and was a Peace Train scholarship recipient.

Adelaide Smith, a passenger on the Peace Train, is a past president of Pennsylvania Peace Links and has also served on the board as treasurer and vice president of development. In May 1993 she retired as the codirector of the Allegheny County Bar Association Secretarial and Paralegal Placement Service. A founder and former president of Work Time Options, an organization that promoted alternative work patterns, she now serves on the Board of ACTION-Housing and is president of AHI-Development Corporation, a subsidiary board of ACTION-Housing. She and her husband, Henry, who have six children and eleven grandchildren, were a part of the Pennsylvania Peace Links group that returned to China in 1997.

Bebb Wheeler Stone is associate minister of Third Presbyterian Church. She is pursuing doctoral studies in the cooperative Ph.D. program between Pittsburgh Theological Seminary and the University of Pittsburgh. She was named a Merrill Fellow by Harvard Divinity School for the fall semester of 1996. She serves on the executive board of the Interfaith Alliance of Southwestern Pennsylvania and is an active advocate for women.

Clarke Thomas has long been influential in the international activities of Pittsburgh. He has served on the boards of the United Nations Association of Pittsburgh and the Pittsburgh International Initiatives and was a member of the original steering committee for Pittsburgh/Beijing '95 and Beyond. Retired from his position as senior editor of the *Pittsburgh Post-Gazette*, he continues to travel and to write about intercultural and international issues.

Mary Leigh Touvell has been active for peace and justice since the 1970s through the Presbyterian Church (U.S.A.) and Church Women

United organizations. A great-grandmother and retired nurse, she is interested in the justice and peace of future generations of the world. She traveled on the WILPF Peace Train.

Vail E. Weller grew up in Pittsburgh, where her family still lives. She attended graduate school at the Pacific School of Religion in Berkeley, California, to prepare for the Unitarian Universalist ministry. She traveled to the conference with an interfaith delegation from the Center for Women and Religion of the Graduate Theological Union. She is interested in economic justice issues as well as environmental concerns and how the consumer vote can affect positive change.

Louise Wilde is an educator who has traveled extensively and studied the role of women in many cultures, particularly China, Egypt, the Philippines, and the former Soviet Union. She was a member of a Peace Links delegation invited to China in 1991 to study the changing role of women in Chinese society. As Asian studies outreach coordinator at the University of Pittsburgh, she organized a program of workshops and other resources to aid western Pennsylvania educators in teaching about Asia. She is international relations chair for the North Hills–McKnight branch of the American Association of University Women and leader of the annual Great Decisions Foreign Policy Discussion Series.

Adelle M. Williams holds a master's degree in business administration from Robert Morris College and a master's in education and a Ph.D. in rehabilitation counseling from the University of Pittsburgh. She is a professor in the Department of Allied Health at Slippery Rock University, director of the Health Services Administration Program there, and is faculty liaison to Queen Margaret College in Edinburgh, Scotland. She has made presentations at a number of local, national, and international conferences on a variety of subjects including geriatrics, minority health concerns, cultural diversity, women's health issues, mentoring, rehabilitation counseling, and physician-prescribing practices.

John M. Wilson (1931–96) was president of Wilson Associates, an insurance and investment firm. He was the husband of Teresa Wilson and the father of three grown children. Jack was active in community work, an avid traveler, and through his business in providing security for friends and their families, was described by many people as "my best friend." He died in March 1996, in a bus accident in India, while traveling with the Semester at Sea program of the University of Pittsburgh.

Patricia D. Wilson launched a three-year term as president of the Episcopal Church Women of the Diocese of Pittsburgh with Project Home Again, a project to help the homeless, sponsored by World Vision. In this capacity she proudly represented the women of seventy-four churches in this area at the NGO forum as a part of the worldwide Greater Anglican Network. An educator, mother of three, and grandmother of four, she helped found a school for GED classes in Greensburg, Pennsylvania, and taught GED courses in the local prison in the evenings. In addition she serves her own church as a lay reader and eucharistic lay minister (taking Communion to shut-ins), using the International-Interdenominational Order of St. Luke the Physician as a guide for health of body, soul, and spirit.

Teresa Wilson, a founding member of Pennsylvania Peace Links and co-convenor of Pittsburgh/Beijing '95 and Beyond, has a master's degree in cross-cultural education, with particular concerns about racism. Describing herself as "spiritually grounded in the Grail—an international women's organization," she has been a peace activist for fifteen years. She is the mother of three grown children and has two grandchildren. She was the wife of John M. "Jack" Wilson. She and Jack were passengers on the Peace Train.

Index

Violence, 137, 184; increase in, 67, 70, 137; as issue at Beijing conference, 219, 226; against women, 108, 176
Visas, 131, 148
Voronezh, Russia, 55

Wasserman, Hannah, 198
Wilde, Louise, 35
Wilson, Teresa, 33, 196–97
"With Cup in Hand We Talk About Women Meeting in Beijing" (poem), 173–74
Wollenstonecraft, Mary, 24
"Woman's Question, A" (poem), 203
Women: contributions of, 17, 108; in leadership, 3, 15–16; status of, 15, 67, 92–93, 131–32, 175–76
Women in Black, 66, 184; reports to Peace Train about, 49, 71; and Thursdays in Black, 141, 200
Women's conferences, 43–45. *See also* United Nations women's conferences
Women's Convention. *See* Convention on the Elimination of All Forms of Discrimination Against Women
Women's Development Agenda for the Twenty-first Century (document), 185
Women's International Democratic Federation, 8
Women's International League for Peace and Freedom (WILPF), 14, 41, 43–45; and Peace Train, 48–49, 63
Women's movement, 20, 118–19; antiwar work by, 43–45; history of, 12, 24–25; participants in, 129–30, 224; reports to Peace Train on, 49–50; seriousness of, 107–08, 111

Women's organizations, 48–50, 64
Women's rights: demands for, 16–18, 226; as theme of NGO forum, 98–100, 139; and UN women's conferences, 7–10; violations of, 165–66. *See also* Convention on the Elimination of All Forms of Discrimination Against Women
Women's roles, 14, 18, 112–13, 220
"Working Women Count" honor roll, 179–80
Workshops, 8; at NGO forum, 115, 126, 159; and Peace Train, 53, 56, 64; on women's health, 131–32, 156
World Conference of International Women's Year (Mexico City), 7–8, 21
World Council of Churches, 216
World Federalist Association delegation, 145–52
World Health Organization (WHO), 13, 19–20
World Plan of Action for the Implementation of the Objectives of IWY, 7
Wu, Harry, 92

Xie Zhiqiong, Deputy Secretary-General, 197

Young women, 62, 64, 151; acceptance of, 73, 105; targeted as audience, 34, 128–30
Youth: as focus of Beijing conference, 193; tent at NGO forum, 129

Zahniser, Melissa, 156
Zhang Jian, 123
Zionism, 153